It's About You!
A Trilogy

Know Your Self, Free Your Self,
Live Your Purpose

BOOK I: KNOW YOUR SELF

It's About You!
A Trilogy

Know Your Self, Free Your Self,
Live Your Purpose

BOOK I: KNOW YOUR SELF

C.W.E. Johnson

BOOKS

Winchester, UK
Washington, USA

First published by O-Books, 2013
O-Books is an imprint of John Hunt Publishing Ltd., Laurel House, Station Approach,
Alresford, Hants, SO24 9JH, UK
office1@jhpbooks.net
www.johnhuntpublishing.com

For distributor details and how to order please visit the 'Ordering' section on our website.

Text copyright and illustrations: C.W.E. Johnson 2012

ISBN: 978 1 78099 111 5

A CIP catalogue record for this book is available from the British Library.

Design: Stuart Davies

Printed in the USA by Edwards Brothers Malloy

We operate a distinctive and ethical publishing philosophy in all
areas of our business, from our global network of authors to
production and worldwide distribution.

CONTENTS

Preface   1

Acknowledgements   10

Introduction   12

First a book, then a trilogy...   16

Introduction to intent...   17

A neglected source of knowledge...   21

We have consciousness because we have Consciousness...   25

Say That Again (1) Consciousness...   27

Why not God or Source for capital "C" Consciousness?...   27

The emerging new worldview – a shifty business...   30

Say That Again (2) Worldviews...   31

You have some work to do...   32

PART I: CONSCIOUSNESS AND THE
     NON-PHYSICAL YOU   37

Chapter 1: Reawakening to intent   38

The Source is always with you...   38

Intent and Purpose – aren't they the same thing?...   39

Say That Again (3) Intent and Purpose...   40

Consciousness getting to know Itself...   40

Say That Again (4) The Individuation of Consciousness...   43

If you're getting nervous – don't worry –
     we actually live in a safe universe...   44

While we're on the subject of our consciousness again...   46

Say That Again (5) Areas within Consciousness...   48

Consciousness comes in packages – Energy too!....   49

Say That Again (6) CUs and EEs...   51

Chapter 2: Formation of the non-physical you   **53**

Identifying your identity...   53

Your Identity...   56

Your Essence...   57

Your inner self...   57

Your Subconscious...   58

Figure 1. The fundamental elements of your
     non-physical self...   59

Feeling the Identity of your Essence...   60

Exercise 1. The Tone of your Vibrational Signature...   61

Chapter 3: Natural Principles and your Inner Senses   **63**

Natural Principles...   63

Consciousness creates the natural principles...   65

Say That Again (7) The Natural Principles...   68

Your inner senses – in tandem with natural principles...   68

Empathic inner senses...   72

Conceptual inner senses...   74

Time-based inner senses...   75

Say That Again (8) The inner senses...   76

Chapter 4: Your Natural Powers and the vital ethical code   **80**

Your Natural Powers...   80

The Natural Power of Divine Love...   81

Say That Again (9) The Natural Power of Divine Love...   84

The Natural Power of Attraction...   84

Say That Again (10) The Natural Power of Attraction...   87

The moral sense that offers a vital ethical code...   87

Do not violate...   88

Natural guilt and unnatural guilt...   90

**Chapter 5: The genera of the intent of human
     consciousness**   **93**

Intent expressed through you...   94

Say That Again (11) Nine basic expressions of
    human intent...   95

Belonging to and aligning with...   95

The nine families of human intent...   97

A purposeful intentional path...   99

Choosing your own expressions of intent...   100

Colorful characters...   102

A contemporary coincidence...   104

Exercise 2. Finding your alignment...   106

Ten things about the nine families of human intent...   110

PART II: CONSCIOUSNESS AND THE PHYSICAL YOU 117

Chapter 6: Who am I after I'm born?   **118**

Let's get physical...   118

Say That Again (12) Your outer self...   121

You do need an ego...   121

Manipulating the personality...   123

Say That Again (13) Your ego/ego-self...   126

Your ego needs a Mind...   126

How do I get a personality?...   129

Why do I need a personality?...   130

Say That Again (14) Mind, Conscious-mind,
    and Personality...   133

Chapter 7: Your mind's subconscious "area"   **135**

Subconscious, not unconscious...   135

Inside the subconscious library...   136

The ego's folly...   139

A graphical representation of your Self – the iceberg
    analogy...   142

Figure 2. A depiction of the totality of your Self...   143

Jungian theory parallels...   144

**PART III: YOUR CREATIONAL KEYS TO YOUR
PHYSICAL EXPERIENCE**   149

Chapter 8: Being thoughtful   150

Here's a thought…   151

Electric fields of action…   152

I've just had a thought…   153

Your inner self's dilemma…   154

Independent thought…   156

Thought's contribution to the creation process…   158

Problems with being too reliant on thought…   160

A final thought…   162

Say That Again (15) Thought as a mechanism…   163

Exercise 3. Using your thoughts to feel good…   164

Chapter 9: Four information processing routes   166

Crown Chakra…   167

Throat Chakra…   168

Solar Plexus Chakra…   169

Base Chakra…   170

Exercise 4. Which type of processor are you?…   172

Chapter 10: Believing is perceiving   176

So what exactly are beliefs?…   178

Figure 3. Your personality's tonal frequency…   180

The Theory of Evolution, a confusion of beliefs…   181

Your beliefs don't just grow from your thoughts…   184

Chapter 11: Truths   186

Degrees of truth…   187

Say That Again (16) Truths…   189

The truth of your reality…   189

How can I better establish my own truths?…   191

Chapter 12: Systems of beliefs   **193**

Ten core topics of thought that we have developed
   into belief systems...   194

Spirituality...   194

Truth...   195

Emotions...   196

Sexuality...   196

Relationships...   197

Perception...   198

Sensing...   198

Science...   199

Physical creation of the Universe...   200

Duplicity...   200

Ten things about your beliefs you won't believe...   201

Chapter 13: Feelings are not the same as emotions   **206**

Feeling inspired...   208

A particular type of feeling...   209

Say That Again (17) Feelings...   211

The feeling comes first...   212

Your "vibrational signature" revisited...   213

Catch the emotional-signal early...   215

Chapter 14: Feelings ebb and flow   **218**

In a bit of a mood...   219

Seeds of thought offered by others...   221

Your conscious-mind seduced...   223

A truly conscious conscious-mind...   228

Feeling or emotion?...   231

Chapter 15: Clearly defining emotions   **233**

Separating feelings from emotions...   234

The communication of an emotion...   235

Say That Again (18) Emotions...   237

The origin of emotions...   238
Translating emotional language...   240
The independence of emotions...   242
The function of emotions...   243
With no emotional content, communication suffers...   245
Emotions play with time...   245

Chapter 16: Getting all emotional   **247**
Dissolving anxiety...   248
The sequence of thoughts, feelings, emotions and beliefs...   252
Figure 4. The sequence of mental machinations...   254
Emotions in relation to beliefs...   255
Emotions denied, rejected and repressed...   256
Please Say That Again (19) The ego's attempts to rebuff
    an emotion...   259
Emotions and expectations...   259

Chapter 17: You're either in love or in fear   **264**
Let's talk of love...   265
A will free to disregard Divine Love...   267
Human love...   270
Human love and sexuality...   271
A loving relationship...   272
Love your self...   275
Science on love...   277

Chapter 18: So what of fear?   **281**
Fear and lack of trust...   281
Our greatest fear...   283
Fear of loving...   284
Your greatest limitation...   285
Eliminating fear...   287
Ten principles for conscious living...   289

Epilogue   **299**
A message from Elias...   303

Appendix I: Catalog of *Say That Again* boxes...   305
Appendix II: A basic "shortcut" version of EFT...   307
Appendix III: The nine genera of the intent of human
    consciousness...   312
Appendix IV: Feelings, Emotional-signals and Emotions   320

Endnotes and References...   **342**

Bibliography...   **363**

Glossary of Terms...   **372**

Index   **392**

In the forecourt to the 6th Century BCE temple of Apollo at Delphi an inscription reads:

Know Thyself
It became the guiding principle of Socrates and many scholars over the centuries.

Knowe thy selfe: that is to saye, learne to knowe what thou arte able, fitte and apt vnto, and folowe that. (1545. R. Ascham *Toxophilus* ii. 36)

Dedicated to the lifetime of Harold Edward Johnson
(1923—2012), aka Hari Jansingh. One personality of an Essence
committed to the evolution of human consciousness.
Harry was the editor-in-chief of *It's About You! Know Your Self.*

PREFACE

It was the beginning of January 1988.

Following yet another heated debate with my wife on the futility of our marriage, and with a view to move out of the marital home, I picked up the phone and rang a friend of mine who lived close by.

He was a work colleague I especially liked because when we played tennis together I would invariably beat him. His accommodating tennis game, I thought, might transfer to an offer of accommodation for me whilst I searched for somewhere more permanent to live. His initial reaction to my request for temporary shelter was, "I'd rather not get involved... sorry."

"Shit," I thought, "I wish I had more friends."

He rang me back twenty minutes later after his wife had reminded him that we *were indeed* friends and that it would only be for a few weeks—and, who knows? I might be able to improve his game! So, for six weeks I gratefully took advantage of our friendship.

In that time I started to read a book given to me by my father on the suggestion that its content may help me come to terms with my life crisis. The book was *Seth Speaks* by Jane Roberts. I knew that my father had had his own marital problems, as was apparent when he divorced my mother; but he was now happily married to *the love of his life* and lived in a manner approaching the bliss I envied. I concluded that I would take his advice and began to read *Seth Speaks* in earnest anticipation of finding the answers to my woes.

I stopped reading it after the first paragraph of the introduction:

This book was written by a personality called Seth, who speaks of himself as an "energy personality essence" no longer focused in physical form. He has been speaking through me for over seven years now, in twice weekly trance sessions.[1]

I rang the old man. I told him that although I could respect any pearls of wisdom that came from him or from learned philosophers who had demonstrated a very *definite* physical form, I wasn't too happy about being lectured to by a dead guy talking through one of those dodgy psychic medium types he was hanging around with. (Dad was always frequenting spiritualist churches and suchlike!)

"Read it," he said, "and keep reading it, despite any statements that trigger beliefs and attitudes you hold that will attempt to get you to stop reading it. Simply recognize that you have a *belief* that doesn't agree with what you're reading. Acknowledge that to be the case, turn a page or two, and continue reading." ...It proved to be sound advice.

I completed the book whilst at my friend's place, and over the next eighteen months, I worked my way through several more tomes of enlightenment produced by Seth, Jane Roberts, and her husband Rob Butts. The knowledge I absorbed certainly lifted my mood and helped steer me through a time fraught with emotion.

In 1989, I attended my first conference dedicated to exploring the Seth works. I ventured all the way into America's Wild West – the Rocky Mountains next to Denver, Colorado – along with my new partner in life and the old man and his. By 1992, I had read quite a bit of what became known as *The Seth Material* and was probably one of the most enlightened people in all of Chris–tendom. Alas, by the end of 1992 my "enlightenment" had turned to depression.

The cause was elusive. I went to see several eminent psychologists and psychiatrists who were very sympathetic to my plight – a regular consumption of antidepressant drugs ensued. In the May of 1993, after lengthy periods off work, my employers dismissed me – which, like the drugs, did little to alleviate my depression.

Then it dawned on me! Seth's guidance throughout the time of my marital morass had provided me with not only a better understanding of myself, but had also helped me, through some simple exercises, to lighten my mood. I returned to my Seth studies and found that on the second or perhaps third reading, it was clear that I was not quite as enlightened as I had previously imagined. Further study, though, along with renewed practice of various exercises, finally did the trick in getting rid of my depressive interludes, which freed me to consider my next course of action in life.

Discussions with my father ensued. We bounced our under-standings of the Seth Material off each other and then decided upon a way forward for me that took into consideration the aspects of the Material that held me in fascination.

Seth's portrayal of the psyche in *The Nature of the Psyche* was an aspect that enthralled me; I wanted to study the psyche and know more of the nature of our minds. Since Seth often repeated, quite categorically, that the reality we perceive we create first in our minds, *before* it manifests in the physical world, I wanted to understand the mechanics of *how* that might be true.

I concluded that the first step on my path of fascination would be to learn more about how conventional institutes of learning approach the subject of the psyche. As Beattie from the old British Telecom adverts would say by way of encouragement to her son, "...'ologies are good"; in my case, it was to be *psych*–ology, the study of the psyche. I resolved to gain a degree in the subject.

Supported by my partner, in 1994 I returned to full-time education and became an undergraduate at the University of London. I subsequently began to study the psyche from two disparate perspectives – one backed by objective empirical research over the past century, the other supported by subjective personal experiences.

Perhaps mesmerized by the empirical approach and the success it brought the classical sciences during the 20th Century; psychology appeared to me to have taken its eye off the ball. The physical expressions of the psyche that are conducive to experimental testing too often distracted it from the key non-physical expressions of the psyche.

Psychology expected brains, physical senses, behaviors and blatantly observable by-products of animal experimentations to reveal the workings of the psyche and its non-physical associates – not least, the ever-elusive phenomenon of consciousness. My academic education, in comparison with my alternative education, brought me an awareness of the timid and consequently limited perspective psychology had acquired over the most part of a century.

Academia may have had its attention elsewhere, but my broader knowledge of *channeled* information provided me with a clearer path to my goal of understanding the true nature of our minds. In the 1990s, with Seth's Material as my benchmark, I began to expand my examination of channeled information to include other sources.

Lazaris, through Jach Pursel; Abraham, through Esther Hicks; and Elias, through Mary Ennis were but a few of a burgeoning number of metaphysical scribes whose messages I began to compare and contrast for consistency and similarity. I also took a Master's Degree in Occupational and Organizational Psychology after graduating. I'm not quite sure why. In retrospect, it was probably a subconscious drive to enhance my credibility as a scholar. A degree in an '-ology' is good to have, but a Master of Science qualification would provide me with an educational background better suited to the personal intent I was yet to discover.

By the new millennium, metaphysical tuition had led me to investigate the links between the Mind and the Body – how bodily symptoms, or "dis-ease" (as the channeled sources would have it), within the physical or psychological frameworks of our Selves, point to the non-physical elements within our minds (thoughts, belief systems and emotions) as the instigators of such manifestations. I am indebted to the works of Gary Craig, Louise Hay, Debbie Shapiro, and Donna Eden and David Feinstein—again, to name but a few—who have contributed pioneering work in establishing a clearer, more holistic depiction of the structure of our Selves. Much of their work confirmed the assertions made by our channeled friends on the complex, multi-faceted nature of our Selves.

The emerging discipline of *Energy Psychology (EP)* became the next focus of my studies. As its title suggests, EP addresses both our minds and our energy systems. Our energy systems are those subtle forces within our bodies that Eastern medicinal practices promote and manage, and have done so for centuries. In the West it is only recently that we have begun observing and mapping these energies through instrumentation.

After two years of training and research in EP, then marrying its healing approaches with recommendations on healing from channeled sources, I began a complementary health practice in 2000. I found that the various treatment methods of EP were indeed as powerful as its promotional literature suggested. I soon began to regard myself as "the complete physician," a term used by Seth to describe the doctor of the future – a healer with a genuinely holistic approach.

My health practice trundled along for the next six years with an excruciatingly small client base that tended to get smaller as the clients got better. Things then took a dramatic change on the day before my fifty-third birthday.

Following a week of feeling very weak, I took to my bed. After a couple of days in bed, occasionally hallucinating erotic images taking shape in the floral patterned curtains, I was rushed to the intensive care unit of the nearby hospital. For the next six days I lay in a drug-induced coma as the medical staff took charge of fighting a virulent form of the streptococcus bacterium that was freely expressing itself in my body through the symptoms of pneumonia, septicemia and pleurisy.

On awakening, my family informed me that the medical staff had not really expected me to do so. I had had my very own near death experience. In addition, the bedroom curtains no longer excited me.

While convalescing and ruminating over this reality I had created for myself, my thoughts turned to the clients I had that showed a limited response to treatment. Although repeated sessions were reassuring to my income, their loyalty to their condition and me was perplexing. Until I realized that perhaps their loyalty was more to do with a persistent residual energy being "held" within them by an elusive subconscious element. I began to surmise that the causal event anchoring this held energy in place might be unrelated to the experiences of their current lifetime; perhaps a far deeper layer within their Selves required attention.

In 2007, thanks to financial backing from my father and my now long-suffering partner, I travelled to the Omega Institute in New York State to train under Dr. Brian Weiss in Past Life Regression Therapy (PLRT). On graduation, I hastened home and included the technique in my practice. I was surely now the most complete of any complete physician and the world would flock to see me and be healed!

Apparently not.

Despite continued success with EP clients and further success with PLRT cases, my client base remained precariously low. If it had been up to me to bring home the bacon (or win bread for that matter), I would have had to abandon things for a more conventional means of income. I was beginning to get depressed – again. Aha!

Depression means it's time to do some more research on the

metaphysical teachings – I had learnt that much. So that I did, and I quickly found what my underlying problem was.

Seth had touched upon it, more in passing than with any great importance; however, it was what Elias had to say about it, and the way each individual expresses it that astounded me. My problem was to do with my ignorance of the concept of *intent*. Intent is the force that drives all action; a force that governs the direction behind any reality we create for ourselves – the spiritual element within us that steers our path through life. Discovery of the nuances of intent as expressed through our Selves reveals what we should be *doing* with our lives – it uncovers our "forgotten" sense of purpose.

In 2008 I discovered my own intent and purpose in a session with another channeled guide – Rose, through Joanne Helfrich. Rose revealed my purpose to me; I was not to focus solely on *healing* others on a one-to-one basis, but to concentrate on artfully *teaching* others.

"O–k–a–y," my brain clunked slowly in reply. "Thanks for that." End of session.

Teach? Teach what? A moment's contemplation helped me realize and appreciate an edict put forward by virtually all channeled sources: *all experiences have meaning*. Experiences perceived by us to be "negative" in nature (as I perceived my success as a "healer" to be, and my near death experience) are in fact our souls' way of communicating to our conscious minds that we have strayed from our intentional path. To get back on this road to fulfillment, we need to examine what we are *doing*.

Is what I am doing in alignment with my current life's purpose and intent?

Disappointment, depression and negativity tell you it isn't.

I was encouraged by Rose to look at a different path forward, one of teaching. Nevertheless, *what would I teach?* Well, you can only teach what you know. All that I knew had taken me more than twenty years to construct. Although, I admit, its architectural plans came from characters of questionable credibility, it was nonetheless an extensive library of knowledge. It is, though, as most readers will find, a library containing a fascinating collection of ideas that allow us to understand our Selves from a far broader perspective than the narrow conventional worldview.

My studies had taught me that we each have the ability and the knowhow to create the reality of our desires. We achieve our desires by understanding our personal intent and adhering as much as possible to the purposeful actions that our intent prescribes. By *doing* this, we can feel the bliss of fulfillment and live a life well lived. It is my desire that this book will begin to teach you this.

Since learning of and fully engaging with my own purpose, I have attained, both in my personal and work life, new heights in clarity of communication and empathic understanding. *Applying* the knowledge I have accrued has freed me from the grip of my ego's superficial needs and fearful reactions. Life has become delightfully mellow. Challenges still arise of course, but I am now far more adept at clearing them with relative ease, and indeed, *appreciating* them for the messages they contain. I get to be grateful, appreciative of my life, and compassionate towards those around me. Moreover, I enjoy communing with my inner self on a far more regular basis. You can't beat your inner self for a friend!

This trilogy of books will take you through much of the process I went through – hopefully minus the depressing interludes and the near death experience!

Sure, you have to put in some work to get the most out of these books. The work involved revolves around practicing various exercises and living a certain lifestyle. The exercises are highly efficient at producing an awareness of the breadth of your Self beyond just your ego's estimation – to genuinely and comprehensively *Know Your Self* (Book I). They are renowned for clearing one's baggage – so that you can *Free Your Self* (Book II).

In addition, they instill a routine that hones your mental and emotional faculties for a clearer overall picture of what you are about and what you are here to do – *Live Your Purpose* (Book III).

A light-hearted approach to all of this self-discovery stuff runs through the books as much as possible. You will be able to tell when I am serious about a point of knowledge, as I will repeat it in an aside box entitled, *Say That Again*.

Don't get bogged down with any particular point that may be tricky to understand. Do as my father suggested to me and move onto the next section; make a note to reread that section later. This is particularly relevant to when you find a topic that makes you angry or cranky – this just means that part of the material challenges your current beliefs. So make a note if you want to, but move on. Such uncomfortable or challenging moments, I can assure you, will be minimal compared to the many moments of delight and reassurance you will experience.

Above all, enjoy your Self.

C.W.E.J.

Acknowledgements

I am grateful to many people who have contributed to this book and the two that follow it. Quite a few of them have no idea that they contributed simply by being part of my life over the last 25 years or so, reflecting back to me evidence validating the knowledge contained within this trilogy.

Since setting off on an educational journey that has brought me a profound sense of Self and a broad base of knowledge that best describes the nature of our existence, there are four people who deserve my deepest gratitude – without whom the journey would never have started, or have come to a premature end.

They are, my extraordinarily patient partner over this period, Judy Johnson, who has afforded me the time and space to work things through without me needing to concern myself with "earning a living" in some conventional sense. My father, Harry Johnson, who's Self I know has always been collaborating with my Self on more than just the physical plane to bring this project to paper or whatever newfangled electronic medium of expression is on offer. And my dear friends Joanne and Paul Helfrich, for keeping me on this particular path of intent, as well as help edit my thoughts into a legible form.

I'm grateful to my friends and family members for bearing with me over the last eighteen months as I learnt how to write proper English, without chiding me too often with, "When are you going to get a proper job?" I'm grateful to my granddaughter Georgia for allowing me the time to write when I really should have been creating paintings with her to stick on the fridge.

Others that deserve my heartfelt thanks for a variety of reasons connected or otherwise to this project are Darryl Anka, Alan Aspinall, Bronwen Astor, Anne Baring, Andreas Bauer, Dana Beardshear, Teresa de Bertodano, Mark Bukator, Laurel Butts, Tilda Cameron, Andrew Cohen, Jim Colvard, Jude

Currivan, Lynda Dahl, Mary Dillman, Andy Dooley, Larry Dossey, Tim Dungan-Levant, Wayne Dyer, Tina Fiorda, Paul Ekman, Mary Ennis, Lloyd Fell, Jim and Carol Funk, Sarah Gerrard, Jim and Loretta Gilbert, Paul Gilbert, Neil Gilson, George Goodenow, Amit Goswami, Serge Grandbois, Arthur Hastings, Esther and Jerry Hicks and the Abraham-Hicks team, John Hunt, Christine Hunter, Anodea Judith, Jon Klimo, Joyce Kovelman, Bruce Lipton, David Lorimer, Alison Marks, Joanna Martin, Julia McCutchen, Dawn and Morgan McKay, Richard Merrick, Florence Meyer, Wendy Millgate, Anita and Danny Moorjani, Tony Neate, Claire Norsworthy, John L. Payne, Leanne Rhodes, Elisabet Sahtouris, Rick Stack, Helen Stewart, Victoria Stibal, David Tate, Jennie Turner, Robert Waggoner, Nancy and Helen Walker, Brian, Carole and Amy Weiss.

If I've missed anyone, let me know for Book II!

INTRODUCTION

How well do you know yourself? Do you think you know what your "Self" is?

Assuming you are confident with answering these questions, are you living a blissful life? Of course, it's impossible for anyone's life to be blissful the whole time, but when things go somewhat awry, are you satisfied by how quickly you can sort things out, get back to well-being, and get back on track with your life?

If you are confident that you can at least answer this question in the affirmative, then put this book down, you have no need for it. Its content may actually disturb your equilibrium.

It's About You! is a trilogy of books, the first (*Know Your Self*) written to help you truly *appreciate* your Self – the totality of who you are, and the nature of your existence at this time – physically, non-physically, and imaginatively.

Book II (*Free Your Self*) offers help on maintaining well-being – to help you overcome your fears and challenges so that you can liberate your Self from any psychological, emotional, and perhaps even physical restraints.

Book III (*Live Your Purpose*) looks to guide you on how to live a mostly healthy, mostly joyous (it is indeed unlikely to be completely plain sailing) life, with an invigorated sense of *purpose*.

The work is a fusion of thoughts, beliefs, ideas, and theories about the structure of our Selves and how the reality we call the physical realm comes into being. Over more than twenty years of study, I have taken a dual track approach in accumulating and examining such knowledge. One line of enquiry focuses upon metaphysical literature, specifically the information communicated by characters from the non-physical or "spiritual" realm – now termed *channeled information*. The other has been the study of learned contributions from scientists, philosophers, psychologists, and spiritual leaders who we all acknowledge to be solidly situated in the physical dimension – either now or at some time in the past.

In order for you to assimilate this knowledge, we need to speak the same language.

The nature of the subject matter can of course be very complex, with some ideas and notions almost impossible to describe within the vocabulary of the English language. Because of this, and in order to get the most from these books, it is necessary that we expand the vocabulary, tweak the grammar, and redefine some normally familiar terms.

For example, in the first sentence of two paragraphs above I have split and capitalized the "s" of "ourselves." You should become used to my separating out "self" occasionally and capitalizing the "s." Self with a capital "S" denotes the entirety of the Self or *Whole Self*. Self with a small "s" denotes a *part* of the Self, as in your "inner self," your "outer self" and your "ego-self." Another example is the term "mind." It will come with a capital "M" when I refer to it as a collection of psychological constructs and with a small "m" when I'm talking about the various minds within the collective Mind.

A *Glossary of Terms* containing much of this new language and different ways of defining the old is at the back of this book. You may find it helpful to familiarize yourself with the glossary before embarking on the main content. A brief knowledge of it should ease the flow of your reading.

To accompany this glossary I am also providing a series of "aside" boxes throughout the books entitled *Say That Again*. These explain new, fundamental, and complex ideas as succinctly as possible. I have made every attempt to confine what is essentially the jargon of the language of metaphysics to a minimum, and settle upon conventional terms that come closest to the broader meaning of the unconventional concepts found in channeled literature. *Say That Again* boxes are numbered and listed in *Appendix I* with a note on their subject matter for easy reference.

My accumulation of this knowledge on the Self did not begin until I had reached the grand old age of thirty-four. Before this, I knew nothing other than the fact that I was a high-earning heterosexual who found the materialism of the physical realm to be most enjoyable – especially its fleshy forms. It was at this age that I experienced my first significant *life crisis*.

To help me overcome this crisis, my father gave me the first of many books dictated by Seth – a "personality essence" no longer focused in physical reality. Seth's wisdom was "channeled" through the writer Jane Roberts when she entered into an altered state of consciousness – a type of trance. From the outset, I was both astounded and affronted by the Seth Material. I was also intrigued by its perspicacity and began to study it in earnest, along with a whole bunch of other works by "dead guys" and "live gurus."

After lengthy study of material that pertains to the nature of our reality, who we are and what we are here for, I have finally learnt (primarily from the dead guys) that you cannot know it all. As Socrates lamented, what I know will always be inconsequential in comparison to what I don't know. Because such knowledge is constantly unfurling in accordance with our evolving state of consciousness, you can never catch up.

True education is all about drawing out the innate knowledge contained within our Selves—and there is an awful lot to draw out—it's not about cramming our brains with more and more information. When you consider the channeled claim that your inner self has access to a subconscious library of information so vast that all of our world's libraries would pale into insignificance; then no, you cannot know it all.

This trilogy builds upon the bedrock of wisdom provided by

The Seth Material – now archived at Yale University's Sterling Memorial Library in New Haven, Connecticut.[2]

Consisting of thirty books produced from recorded sessions between 1963 and 1984, there is considerable recognition and praise (albeit whispered) within the scientific community for its clarity of insight. Many transpersonal scholars regard it as *the* leading metaphysical information source.

Despite the Seth Material remaining mostly ignored by the modern world, I am convinced that the current emergence of a postmodern worldview will revitalize its contribution to our societal mores.

Seth advocates a pro-active approach to self-development, exploration, and healing. His works therefore include many exercises designed to promote learning through experience and encourage the development of our latent *extra-sensory* abilities. His foundational exercises furnish us with the opportunity to commune with our *inner self* (soul) and to begin utilizing those extra senses we rarely engage. Rudolph Steiner referred to these as our "organs of supersensory perception" – whereas Seth simply calls them our *"inner senses."*

It's About You! follows this pro-active pattern by presenting a variety of exercises that are reformulated from suggestions by several channeled guides as well as proven practices taken from more conventional schools of learning.

These exercises are important to initiate an educational process that encourages you to *apply and experience* the perennial wisdom voiced by many inspirational characters – wherever their voices come from! Their design is to help you take the next step forward from just an intellectual *understanding* of what you and the world are all about, to a confidence boosting *assimilation* of that knowledge. They are chosen for their ability to bring you in contact with your inner self and your inner senses – with the greater part of your Self that holds all knowledge of who you are, why you chose to participate in this world at the present time, and most importantly, what may have blocked you from participating more joyfully.

The practices will clarify any psychological or emotional blocks that create challenges in your life – and provide the means to remove them. Collectively, their intention is to nurture self-development, self-healing, and self-love.

Mindful of common scientific opinion regarding the validity of channeled information I have attempted to substantiate its ideas and concepts by drawing parallels with conventionally acquired philosophical knowledge. In doing this, you will hopefully become aware of how our *acknowledged* truth seekers over the centuries have come to similar conclusions on aspects of our reality that the mostly *unacknowledged* metaphysical guides put forward.

You will become aware of several profound but fundamental premises that appear in the channeled literature but remain undiscovered or undetermined by orthodox study. I begin familiarizing you with such new ideas later in this introduction. First, though, let's look at the trilogy's structure.

First a book, then a trilogy

When I started writing, *It's About You!* was to be one book divided into three *Parts* entitled Know Your Self, Free Your Self, and Live Your Purpose. After two years of hard labor, drafting these parts into very lengthy chapters, it became apparent that the book's size was untenable. Reading, after all, has become in this technological era a thing of snatched moments, with our attention span reduced to an hour or two at most. The organizers behind TED[3] might even argue that twenty minutes is as long as we are able to maintain focus. With such thoughts in mind, I didn't want to produce an unwieldy tome that no one would bother pulling off the shelf, let alone read in its entirety.

My father was the first to suggest that I split the book into three separate ones, each devoted to the topic of the Parts. This first book of the trilogy is concerned with providing you with the broadest possible view of the structure and nature of your Self and the psychological elements – thoughts, beliefs, feelings and emotions – that affect your Self-expression. Its content will radically augment your Self-knowledge.

The second book focuses on the current state of your outer self[4] – the parts of your Self that engages with the physical realm. The book deals with the healing and balancing of the psychological and emotional energies that shape your personality. It's concerned with clearing your baggage, or the decks, or whatever else you need to clear in order to bring your reality under greater conscious control. This is an essential cathartic process required for true Self-expression, which will free up your creative abilities and help keep you on your path of personal intent.

The final part, now book, intends to outline as precisely as possible practical guidelines for living your life in due deference to your Self's evolutionary intent and your outer self's purpose for being in the physical world. This book will expand your awareness of how you fit into the world and how you can best operate within it. It suggests methods for living a purposeful life, and for becoming, as Seth would say, a "practicing idealist" – someone who seeks to make the world a better place.

In order to become a practicing idealist, you do need to realize that it is indeed about you! To get from the perhaps not so ideal you to the practicing idealist, you do need to first *Know Your Self*, so that you can *Free Your Self*, to *Live Your Purpose*.

This first book, *Know Your Self*, divides into three *Parts* of its own.

Part I: Consciousness and the non-physical you, covers the nature of Consciousness (what many refer to as God, or the term's equivalent) and how it goes about expressing itself, through *you*, for one example, in the physical realm.

We examine the *natural principles* that drive the myriad expressions of Consciousness. These principles underpin the laws of physics, thus explaining more fully how the physical realm actually operates. We survey the structures of your Self that do not have their attention solely focused upon the physical realm, and the *natural powers* and *inner senses* that you use to maintain your existence in physical reality – and quite a few other realities besides.

We look at the metaphysical concept of "purposeful intent," inherent within all creatures of Consciousness, and the way in which you and I interpret and explore this intent in the physical playground.

Part II: Consciousness and the physical you, includes a definitive guide to the psychological "layers" that form your *outer self*. We look into your *conscious-mind*; take several trips to the subconscious area within your *collective Mind*; and begin to explore your personality's *garden of beliefs*.

Part II concludes with a graphical representation of the structure of the entirety of your Self, a further embellishment upon the iceberg analogy first depicted by Sigmund Freud, and later modified by Carl Jung.

Part III: Your creational keys to your physical experience, carefully examines and redefines the psychological elements that contribute to the expression of your Self in the physical realm. Here we get into the nitty-gritty of the very real, independent, unprejudiced by space-time, electromagnetic energy configurations, that bridge the gap between other realities and our physical one in order to inform our minds and govern our behaviors – I like to refer to them as thoughts, feelings and emotions.

They make up the weather systems of your mind; the rain, wind and shine that your personality has to deal with in its efforts to cultivate its garden of beliefs. We speak of love – *Divine Love* – in the penultimate chapter, a subject that we have great difficulty in understanding, and clear up a few misconceptions.

Introduction to intent

Let's now begin to get acquainted with a couple of fundamental principles that underpin a new way of thinking about your Self and the primal forces that shape your existence.

We begin with a central concept that appears constantly throughout this book and the ones that follow – a concept that may be new or even surprising to you. Metaphysical literature suggests that this fundamental premise governs all forms of existence – it's called *intent*. Here is the fuller metaphysical meaning of this seemingly bland term:

> *Intent is an acutely focused mental concentration that directs all actions.*
>
> *Intent–ion means to act with purpose, to have an aim in mind. It is a more immediate expression of intent, more in line with physically focused desires than your lifetime's overall intent.*
>
> *Personal intent is the potential each person holds to fulfill his or her own spiritual ambitions within the pool of probabilities chosen for this lifetime.*

It's About You! incorporates a learning process designed to bring you an awareness of your own *personal intent* – the psychic "thing" driving your actions and behaviors. With this learning, it is possible to deduce your life's *purpose*. To know and follow your life's purpose gives you the confidence and freedom to express yourself fully in the world – which leads to a consistent enjoyment of life.

Awareness of your intent and purpose results in personal growth that reverberates throughout the totality of your Self.

You can view your personal intent as a *relatively fixed* set of life filters that attract to you experiences associated with your chosen path of growth and learning. We're not talking "fate" here; we're simply saying your personal inten your actions and behaviors along certain paths of learning. As it does so, congruent "probable realities"[5] naturally gravitate toward you. Deviation from or resistance to your natural path of learning occurs when beliefs are formed that contradict these chosen preferences.

Thoughts, dreams, beliefs, feelings and emotions are all involved in the creation of your reality. Together they form your "perception" – which is but one familiar term that undergoes a profound overhaul of meaning during the course of this trilogy. We will explore dreams and a broader perception of perception in *Book II: Free Your Self*. Book II centers upon what you can *do* with the information learnt from Book I. It contains the bulk of the exercises recommended for self-healing and maintaining well-being.

This book introduces you to some simple exercises and pursuits in preparation for the more concentrated actions of Book II – the practical work you need to do to have any chance of making lasting changes to your personal circumstances. Not that any of the recommendations are particularly strenuous; it's more to do with changing habits of behavior through consistent, committed actions – practices that will eventually become your new, healthier, habits of behavior.

As this book presents you with a deeper understanding of your feelings and emotions, you might like to prepare yourself for conscious self-management of your emotions by familiarizing yourself with a recently developed method for doing this, known as EFT (Emotional Freedom Techniques).

EFT is one of the most efficient and safe methods for dissipating static emotional energy; as such, it stands as a highly useful lifelong tool for helping you in the creation of your preferred reality. Practicing this basic procedure will hold you in good stead for when you decide to tackle your innermost challenges.

Appendix II **describes a basic "shortcut" routine of EFT**. You may find it particularly useful if any frustration or anger arises from reading this book!

EFT is easy to learn and apply to your Self. As with anything new, practice and self-discipline is required, especially when doing things on your own. If you are unsuccessful in its use, or feel nervous about releasing emotional energy whilst alone, then seek out a reputable practitioner close by for an introductory session or two. There are now many practitioners worldwide. A good practitioner would make nervousness regarding your release of emotional energy a priority!

A neglected source of knowledge

Integral to this book's purpose is to make you aware of a treasure-trove of knowledge provided by sources that have for many decades been dismissed as untenable by prejudicial belief systems.

Such knowledge confines itself to a Pandora's Box labeled "metaphysics" – the philosophical study of the nature of being – a box that the prevailing worldview (currently led by scientific doctrine) considers full of speculative and unexamined assumptions.

The term *metaphysics* can also mean abstract and theoretical, without material form – which, in view of our prevailing worldview, is exactly why metaphysical information remains largely unexamined. We also accredit metaphysical information as "originating not in the physical world, but somewhere outside it." Well yes… we got that bit right!

This book chiefly confines its metaphysical information sources to those that come under the umbrella term of "channeled information" – the literature produced by individuals able to channel[6] (act as a conduit) information from outside the physical world into it – *in-tu-it* being the operative term.

The essential thing to know about channeled information is that it is not the same category of information commonly relayed by stage mediums or clairvoyants – supposedly via a deceased party or an undefined field of intelligence. Such psychics tend to relay *information* of comfort or use to the inquirer, whereas a channel will relay *knowledge* imbued with education and learning for a far broader reception – the goal being human growth and evolution.

When you read or listen to a channeled source, it's important to trust in your *feeling of validity* whilst you absorb the material. Trust of your feelings is not something currently promoted by our contemporary worldview, but it is an intrinsic part of our incubating new worldview. Many of you will find some concepts simply *ring true* or you may say to yourself, "*I've always known that to be the case.*" The question to keep in mind is, "*What does my heart say?*"

Because channeled knowledge claims to be from a yet unproven dimension of reality is, of course, the primary reason for doubting its integrity.

To overcome this all too hastily erected mental hurdle keep in mind that this "unproven" factor simply challenges your *beliefs* on validity – beliefs, which in all probability, conform to and are thus steered by scientific and materialist dogma. Any apprehension or *fear* in pursuing this alternative path to knowledge would suggest that religious dogma of some kind is influencing your beliefs on the matter.

We are all subject to psychological laziness. It's easier to dismiss than to examine; easier to assume something outside of common consent is not worthy of attention. It is easy to ridicule, safe in the knowledge that general opinion will back us up.

However, whenever you narrow your *ways of knowing* by being quick to judge an alternative viewpoint, you also narrow your chances of discovering more precisely who you are, and why you chose this physical experience.

As "Gaia" (a channeled entity through Pepper Lewis)[7] has said, to ignore any path to knowledge is to remain in "ignorance." All you need to do mentally when absorbing the information in this book is keep an open mind regardless of the dictates of other belief systems and *let your Self be your guide* to its validity.

It may surprise you to learn that the teachings of channeled sources influence the work of many well-known names within the Mind/Body/Spirit movement and some could claim to be channels themselves – Eckhart Tolle, for example. Many other influential authors play down exactly how much such wisdom has inspired their thinking – due in part to fears of ridicule or loss of credibility if they are engaged in mainstream scientific endeavors. In the main, however, the majority of these individuals have come to embrace at least some part of this knowledge and incorporate its worth in their own work.

Over the last twenty years, there has been a plethora of channels appearing – evidence to suggest channeling may be another form of intelligence most of us are yet to exploit, and that *we are all capable of channeling*.[8]

As with any form of tutoring, the styles of delivery of channeled information varies considerably, as do the depth and complexity of concepts put forward. This book will introduce you to a variety of channeled sources that I consider worthy of mention. By way of a reminder, from here on the channeling author's name will occasionally appear in parentheses immediately after the name of the source.

Again, Seth (Jane Roberts) provides the bedrock of wisdom upon which a new understanding of our Selves is constructed. Elias (Mary Ennis) makes a considerable contribution to the metaphysical message as Elias' teachings expand upon concepts mentioned by Seth relating to crucial qualities forming our personalities.

Abraham (Esther Hicks) is probably the only channeled

source you may have heard of, as Esther and her husband Jerry[9] provide one of the most popular sources of channeled knowledge in the USA. Their early work acknowledges the profound influence the Seth material had upon their own experiences with channeling.

Many gems of wisdom can be gleaned from the Abraham archives; not least Abraham's take on *the natural power of attraction* (discussed in *Chapter 4*), more commonly referred to as the "Law of Attraction" as championed by Rhonda Byrne in her bestselling book of 2006 – *The Secret*.

If at this point you still regard such sources to be unsound, then you may not be able to fully appreciate or engage with what is put forward in *It's About You!* If this is the case, I suggest you first read something from the Seth library, for example *Seth Speaks* or *The Nature of Personal Reality*.

If you find these books a little too heavy going, then two books, which do an excellent job of encapsulating the primary teachings from the non-physical realm, are *Omni Reveals the Four Principles of Creation* by John L. Payne, and *A Book of Insight: Wisdom from the Other Side* by Tilde Cameron and Tina Fiorda.

Alternatively, there are plenty of works within the Abraham-Hicks library that can encourage a deeper awareness of the totality of your Self to come through – *Ask and it is Given* and *The Amazing Power of Deliberate Intent*, for example. Short-extract video clips of Esther Hicks/Abraham are also available on the internet if you prefer a quick and easily accessible sampling.

Experiencing the messages directly from "the horse's mouth" may set alight that feeling of validity that can be trusted enough at least to suspend judgment on how such knowledge came to be here.

If you are someone who places more value on a scientific approach to the investigation of paranormal phenomena (such as channeling), then I recommend Lawrence LeShan's book, *A New Science of the Paranormal: The Promise of Psychical Research*.

If you're still with me, let's now begin to unravel some of the complex ideas that appear in the metaphysical literature. In order that you may approach this book with your eyes wide open to the many unusual ideas on the nature of your Self and why you are here, I need first to present you with one such alternate but critical concept.

It is a fundamental issue that evades scientific description to this day—*consciousness*.

Here is how I now understand the term, devised through lengthy study of the metaphysical literature. If from the outset, you too can grasp this alternate viewpoint on consciousness it will speed your digestion of the other seemingly odd notions presented.

We have consciousness because we have Consciousness

We conventionally understand consciousness to mean *an ability to be aware of one's surroundings and oneself*; the possession of a conscious mind (*conscious-ness*).

We generally restrict consciousness defined in this way to be an asset of humankind, with some arguing that other animals, such as dolphins and whales, also possess consciousness. The prevailing worldview of the West sees consciousness as a secondary by-product of brain function; that is, the material comes first – the brain – which gives rise to consciousness.

This belief drives neuropsychology's preoccupation with brain mapping techniques such as fMRI (functional magnetic resonance imaging) in the hope they may provide clues on where and how consciousness emerges from the material of the brain.

Metaphysical sources categorically state, however, that consciousness is primary.

It is something that exists *before* anything material, such as a brain. Furthermore, consciousness is *the* causal factor in any *thing* created either in the non-physical (spiritual) realm –

including our own psychological structures – or in the physical dimension.

We each have a conscious mind, but this part of our Selves is purely a facet of an individuated, personalized expression of the consciousness of our species, which is in turn an expression of the consciousness of "All That Is" (aka God).

Confused? I'm not surprised if you are.

Already we can see the term "consciousness" being used to convey more than one phenomenon. Psychological science uses it to describe a mental phenomenon that allows us to be aware of ourselves and the world around us, whereas metaphysics uses the term not only in reference to the human mind, but also when describing the features of our collective psyche *and* the nature of All That Is or God.

To prevent possible confusion, from this point on, this book will use a capital 'C' for Consciousness when referring to the *primal cause of all creation*, the religious equivalent of God, that metaphysics also calls *All That Is* or *Source*. When you come across the word "consciousness" with a small "c," it refers to **an expression** of Consciousness (*with a capital "C"*) – as evidenced in our own psychological make-up and, as will be explained, by *all forms of creation*.

Your consciousness *is a pure stream of energy imbued with intent that emanates from Consciousness.*

The American philosopher and psychologist, William James, remarked in his *Principles of Psychology* that the stream of consciousness our brains experience should simply be called "sciousness," and do without the prefix, "con," which infers a degree of separation. A separation, I take his inference to mean, from our originating Consciousness. The characters producing metaphysical transcripts concur, as they constantly remind us that our personal consciousness, contrary to what we may believe, *is not separable* from Consciousness.

SAY THAT AGAIN (1) Consciousness.

The simplest way to understand consciousness from our point of view in the physical realm is to recognize it in three forms:

(1) Consciousness (with a capital "C") is **the** non-physical force that patterns energy into representations of *Itself*, which can take non-physical and physical forms.

(2) *Your* consciousness (small "c") is a non-physical expression of Consciousness – called a *psyche* – which utilizes a *Mind* for playing with thoughts, ideas and imagination. There is *only a correlation* between this form of Consciousness and brain activity.

(3) The third form of Consciousness is *physical matter* – individuated, "solidified," patterns of energy that fall within the electromagnetic spectrum of light.

Why not God or Source for capital "C" Consciousness?

I use such alternative names whenever confusion may arise, but the reason for keeping a capital "C" and a small "c" consciousness whenever possible is to familiarize you with the fuller meaning of the word in its metaphysical sense and to highlight the limited way we normally use the term in our culture.

It's also time for us to move away from the term *God*. ("*No way!*" I hear some of you cry.) What I mean by this is the word God, to those of you with a particular faith, immediately associates your mind to your faith, which sets up a mental stance that separates you from others; it separates your "sciousness" from other people's "sciousnesses!" It is also, for many, an expression ingrained within the mind that associates with emotions such as fear, and feelings such as separation and isolation.

Metaphysical literature constantly reminds us that Consciousness/God is not about separation; it's all about the Oneness of being. Therefore, using a neutral term such as Consciousness to refer to our God(s) – to All That Is or Source – seems appropriate to our spiritual evolution.

To comprehend fully that *your consciousness* is born from *the* Consciousness, and all physical creations express Consciousness in their own way – have their own consciousness – is an important factor in appreciating that we actually live in a *safe universe* (discussed in *Chapter 1*).

Assurance that the universe is a safe one is provided by the knowledge that Consciousness is imbued with *intent* (discussed further in *Chapter 1*) – the force directing all actions and creations. Consciousness' intent is essentially to evolve through *action*[10] and experience.

In order that Consciousness can pursue its own intent, a *natural principle* comes into being. This principle – referred to as a *natural power* from hereon, is one of **Divine Love** – an innate quality of Consciousness that promotes, encourages, and nurtures the maximum development of every individuated expression of Itself (discussed in *Chapter 4*). Because we are expressions of Consciousness imbued with intent, our personal consciousness rests within the arms of Divine Love – or simply *Love*, with a capital "L," as other metaphysical sources refer to it.

A broader understanding of the meaning of the term consciousness, to include more than just our ability to be aware of our surroundings, has actually been with us for some time.

An interpretation of capital "C" Consciousness dates back centuries in some Eastern philosophies and religions, but this elevated, more encompassing, meaning has also crept stealthily into the minds of leading philosophers, scientists and psychologists in the West – particularly since the end of the 19th Century and more so with the emergence of quantum physics.

For example, Sir James Jeans, a physicist of the early 20th Century, declared that the universe in which we live is the creation, from thought, of a great universal mind (Consciousness) that underlies and coordinates all individual minds (consciousnesses).

William James, the American philosopher and psychologist, suggested that *our* consciousness (the conventional understanding of the term), "… is but one special type of [capital C] consciousness, whilst all about it, parted from it by the filmiest of screens, there lie potential forms of [capital C] consciousness entirely different."[11]

More recently, the quantum physicist and philosopher, Amit Goswami, stated:

> In our efforts, we miss the simple thing—the simple truth that it is all God, which is the mystic's way of saying that it is all consciousness. Physics explains phenomena, but consciousness is not a phenomenon; instead, all else are phenomena in consciousness. I had vainly been seeking a description of consciousness within science; instead, what I and others have to look for is a description of science within consciousness.[12]

There is a fundamental characteristic that pervades most of our broader attempts to understand Consciousness, which places these estimations under the doctrine of *panpsychism*.[13] The characteristic, is that Consciousness is *a force that patterns energy;* that is, It is a universal force that sculpts energy into coherent mental or physical forms.

If we are able to acknowledge this fundamental characteristic, we might then come to accept that every *thing*, however limited in physical complexity (such as protons, electrons, atoms and molecules), is *conscious* in the sense that it is an expression of Consciousness. Consciousness shapes energy into simple patterns and very complex patterns, such as living organisms and, of course, our Selves. It is independent of our Selves, as well as being implicit to our psychological and physical being. It is integral to our brains' functioning, but is not simply a phenomenon born of its functioning.

The emerging new worldview – a shifty business

You exist in a time of significant change. Throughout *It's About You!* there are many references to the expression *"shift in consciousness."* This *"Shift"* (the most popular abbreviated term) refers to both your own individualized consciousness and the consciousness of our species.

On a personal level, the Shift involves a radical change to the psychological energies that constitute your worldview. On a societal level, it is a necessary change in humanity's psyche, a deeply profound shift in our collective perception of the physical dimension and its creation. Our shift in consciousness is a very real psychological process, often mentioned in the metaphysical archives, that heralds a more evolved level of consciousness for humankind.

The Shift affects our worldviews. We form our personal and collective worldviews by gathering and nurturing beliefs and values from approved authorities on *truth* – a subject examined in *Chapter 11*. Included within your own worldview are the truths of your parents, those you trust, and the truths of your experiences.

SAY THAT AGAIN (2) Worldviews.

Worldviews are the entire collection of an individual's or a society's beliefs and values held about the world and how we interact with it. You can regard worldviews as the frameworks on which we build our realities. Your own worldview is a unique interpretation of reality, a dynamic phenomenon that interacts and combines with other worldviews.

Worldviews are always in development. They take on new thoughts, grow them into beliefs, and eventually turn these into values and truths. Our current global worldview primarily promotes beliefs taken from two trees of wisdom contained within our garden of beliefs – two sets of beliefs that vie for the accolade of knowing *the* truth on what life is all about.

These are, *traditional* sources of knowledge (religious doctrine and subjective experience) which state that the purpose of life is to serve and commit to others (primarily God); and *modern* sources based on reason (science and objective experience) which state we have no purpose or intent as life has come about through chance.

The Shift though, is growing a third tree in our garden. The tree is a fabulous hybrid that integrates both ways of knowing – objective and subjective. We nurture this tree with the energies of our imagination – ideas and thoughts concerning who we are, the meaning and purpose of our existence, and what constitutes "reality." The contemporary philosopher Ken Wilber suggests our shift in consciousness may see us move quite rapidly along from the pluralistic worldview that currently branches from our postmodern tree. He proposes an *Integral Systems Worldview* existing alongside an *Integral Holistic Worldview* as a likely outcome of the Shift.[14]

Seth confirms we are going through a period of "Change" (Seth's term for the Shift), that will culminate around the year 2075.[15] Many other channeled sources confirm the current era to be one of change on various levels of consciousness that began around the start of the 20th century, and is due to end around the same time mentioned by Seth.

The Elias (Mary Ennis) teachings expand upon how this shift in consciousness might affect us personally – information given due consideration throughout this book.[16]

Many people intrinsically believe change must involve some form of destruction – which invariably entails trauma – before we can usher in the new. This book will show you, on the contrary, that although we are all susceptible to fears associated with change we need not incur great distress. If we choose to shift our consciousness with ease, then with ease it shall be.

You have some work to do

This trilogy of books will help you discover the direction of your intent and help bring you into alignment with it in order that you fulfill your life's purpose. The books will assist you with any psychological adjustments needed for a smoother ride through the Shift.

As mentioned, channeled sources see the completion of the Shift to be around the year 2075. If you are already approaching your hundredth birthday, please don't toss this book aside thinking that your possible contribution to collective changes is an impossibility. It matters not how old you are at present. What matters, is that you make the effort to understand as fully as possible the way you currently think and behave and where appropriate, shift your patterns of thinking so that your children and future generations benefit from the work you do now for your Self.

A change in your personal beliefs, which trigger your thoughts and behaviors, reverberates through the *entirety of your*

Self and on into *our* collective consciousness – the collective consciousness inherited by future generations. For most of you, some preliminary work is likely to be necessary before you can strap your Self in for the ride through the Shift. All of us will need to work at remaining strapped in. *It's About You!* serves as your seatbelt, your guide, and your driver's manual.

These books will provide you with an awareness of how we create the realities we do – individually and *en masse*. With this reawakened awareness, you will begin to fathom the underlying "hidden" messages of your personal experiences. You may also gain a better grasp of the underlying communications from our collective psyche that explain our co-created mass events. In essence, you will begin to exercise your psychic abilities – your Self "channeling" valuable information from the subjective realm to your objective, conscious-mind.

Our collective psyche informs us of the meaning of shared events, just as our inner selves inform us of the meaning of personal events. Mass events are a reflection of the workings of our collective psyche, physical realities that reflect back to us the affects the Shift is having upon the thoughts and beliefs of our prevailing worldview.

The shifts in our consciousness therefore produce the various events we estimate to be part of a fundamental cultural upheaval. The word "fundamental," since the early 17th Century, we define as relating to "primary principles or rules." The latter part of the word – mental – suggests where these principles and rules reside.

The foundations of our thinking are shifting. Religious fundamentalism, a feature of mass events since the beginning of the millennium, naturally arises from the Shift's affects upon our mental world.

Other mass events highlight other changes needing to occur in the way we think and what we believe to be true. The foundations – a word etymologically linked to "fundamental" – of our financial systems are trembling for example, as too are the under-pinnings of antiquated systems of government such as dictator-ships. Certainly, our actions relating to our quest for energy resources require new ways of thinking.

The Shift is set to continue over the next few decades and for those of us not willing to review our personal set of beliefs it may be an anxious time. It's possible, however, for you to ride the change relatively unscathed if you are prepared to put in some work on identifying how much your personal worldview aligns with the developing postmodern one.

In other words, if you're feeling anxious about the Shift, look to your current thoughts and beliefs and become aware of those that may require adjustment. These books can help you adjust.

Changing your beliefs and your habits of thought isn't as straightforward as simply trashing the inappropriate and replacing them with "affirmations" of the newly preferred. Subtle energies are involved which need to be addressed for a permanent change to occur. You need to open a clear path of communication between your *outer self* and your *inner self* – the part of you that knows which of your beliefs are problematic and what energies supporting them need dissolving.

The trickiest element in addressing your beliefs is to become *consciously* aware of them in the first place! Often there are core beliefs within your mind cunningly concealed within a subcon-scious security vault as they surreptitiously go about governing a large number of your undesired behaviors.

These books supply you with a variety of keys and combina-tions for accessing your personal vault and methods for dissi-pating the energy held behind the belief systems that inhibit you. I'm sorry to have to bring you back to the fact that some work is involved, but it is important work that leads to personal transfor-mation.

It's equally important to maintain a light-hearted attitude to the work involved – so that new habits of thought can be formed, rather than resisted, by a suspicious ego. *It's About You!* adheres to the metaphysical rule of keeping things fun throughout the learning process.

The exercises and practices in the books, particularly Books II and III, will bring you to a point of enthusiasm for life you may not have reached before. They help you draw out and permanently deal with any beliefs that have hindered you from expressing your true personality. You will awaken a trust of your Self that will guide you through a life of ultimate fulfillment; and by the end of the books, if not absolute clarity, you will certainly have a deeply felt awareness as to *the purpose of your life.*

I advise you to get yourself a "work journal" to keep track of your progression through the exercises. It is important to do the exercises, usually more than once, and write down what comes up for you. You should include in your work journal any revelations that may occur during or after an exercise; and any moments of insight that may appear during your day or during your night – recalled dreams for example.

The next few decades will herald a momentous change in the psychological fabric of human consciousness. We are apparently all the more aware of it right now as the process, according to one metaphysical guide, is now in fast-forward. The Shift has been going on for most of the 20th century, the birth of Quantum Theory being a "mass event" reflecting its instigation – ideology that challenges the worldview of classical physics.

Early pioneers that recognized the need for psychological and sociological change were scholars such as Carl Jung, F.W.H. Myers, William James, Rudolph Steiner, Pierre Teilhard de Chardin and Arthur Koestler at the end of the 19th and early 20th Centuries. We also witnessed at this time, in the suffragette movement, a mass event reflecting the need for the feminine aspect of our collective psyche to break free of suppression.

A century mostly filled with brutal wars to illustrate our ignorance of the subtle complexion of beliefs, and the futility of treating them as truths, has brought us to a crisis point.

A century ago, the aforementioned truth seekers needed to stand apart from "religion's dictates and dogmas."[17] Today, it is similarly difficult to challenge the dictates and dogmas of the new religion of science, or *Church Scientific*, as T.H. Huxley called it. However, the Shift now dictates we take notice of our beliefs and do the personal and collective work required for our consciousness to stand any chance of evolving.

Quantum physics has fairly recently begun to realize its capacity for explaining the reality of the non-physical realms of probabilities and potentials – what religious doctrine describes as the spiritual realm and the channeled literature regards as the myriad expressions of Consciousness. Wolfgang Pauli, a pioneer of quantum physics, urged us to seek ways of marrying Eastern mysticism with Western science, a spiritual/scientific divide that Consciousness also seeks to resolve through the intentional forces of the Shift. Indeed, part of the Shift's design is to draw us closer to Rudolph Steiner's desire for the conception of a "spiritual science."

It's About You! will lead you through the maze of knowledge found in both metaphysical literature and classical fields of study and identify similarities in their core messages. It seeks to clarify exactly what the Shift entails, how this relates to you, the individual, and what you can do for your Self, and thereby others, to ease your passage through this era of transition.

PART I:

CONSCIOUSNESS AND THE

NON-PHYSICAL YOU

CHAPTER I

REAWAKENING TO INTENT

If like me, you are not one for introductions, particularly where books are concerned, and have decided to jump right in at this "real start" of the book, think again. Trust me when I say that you need to read the introduction if you are to stand a decent chance of understanding what this book is talking about. You really do need to start at the beginning – which is the introduction.

The Source is always with you

You came forth into this physical environment with enormous, excited intention. You are pure positive energy expressed from Source Energy.[18]

There are few absolutes in our reality. The idea that intent – the directional force behind all actions – is an absolute property of reality has been systematically denigrated by the modern, scientific worldview because it implies that everything in our reality (be it in the objective physical realm or the subjective non-physical mind) has a meaning and purpose for its existence. The channeled literature[19], on the other hand, categorically informs us that intent impregnates all of our realities. If we are to believe this, it means that *through identifying our own intent we can identify the purpose of our being.*

> *The primary aim of this book, and those that follow, is to awaken you to your personal intent in order to clarify your purpose in this lifetime.*

Your intent and purpose are the steering forces behind a life of joy and fulfillment. As you will discover, *your* intent drives personal psychological change, the intent of human consciousness drives the Shift, changes in our collective psyche; and the intent of Consciousness drives all such changes in the subjective realm. In deference to the biblical notion that a little piece of God (Consciousness) resides in each of us, you can equate your own personal intent with that very portion of God. This implies that your purest personal intent is an outworking of God's intent. Such intent relates to expansion, creation and growth and leads to the evolution of your own consciousness.

Intent and purpose – aren't they the same thing?

They are not quite the same thing:

> *Intent is a directional force powering learning and growth within Consciousness and ALL its forms of expression.*
> *Your purpose is your own unique goal that you plan to attain in this lifetime whilst utilizing the Natural Power of Divine Love.*

Contrary to the modern scientific worldview, you have a reason for being and there is meaning to your existence. The reason you exist is to expand and evolve Consciousness. For you, this begins with the consciousness of your current personality. Growth and expansion of your current personality in the physical realm simultaneously involves the evolution of the entirety of your Self in the non-physical realm. *Your* evolution adds to the evolution of the collective consciousness of our species, which in turn expands and evolves Consciousness Itself.[20] "Intent" is the term given by the metaphysical guides to this compulsion to expand and evolve.

SAY THAT AGAIN (3) Intent and purpose.

Intent is the directional driving force behind all actions that expand and grow Consciousness and all individuated expressions of Itself – *including you.*

Your *Purpose* is a set of actions, a directional path of intent you desire to pursue for the expansion, growth and evolution of your own consciousness – a unique individual expression of Consciousness.

Consciousness getting to know Itself

Consciousness chose to explore the possibilities of *Its* expansion and growth by creating dimensions of existence – playgrounds of experience. Our beloved physical reality is one such dimension. Apparently there are others; some "more" physical and some "less" physical than ours. Let's stick with the one we know for the moment…

Consciousness creates our physical dimension in order to know Itself more thoroughly through a process of *individuation*. That is, It "separates out" (as our ego's understand it) distinct portions of Itself to focus upon particular aspects of learning and growth within the medium of physicality. Consciousness infuses all of these portions with a sense of self-awareness (they are *"aware-ized"*) and independence; they also have an identity that can utilize the power of intent for exploring the physical dimension. These individuated portions are *all* forms of matter – sub-atomic particles, atoms, chemical elements, compounds of them, life forms, plants, animals – *you.*

Consciousness created life forms as a way to develop Its exploratory process. An inorganic portion of Consciousness has an awareness of Self, is aware-ized, but it is very limited in the expression of its individuated self on the physical stage. Compounds of the elements (coming together under the natural principle of cooperation, discussed in *Chapter 3*) expand the repertoire of expression for matter; but life forms add a new level of expression for individualized portions of Consciousness. *Life forms bring **freedom of expression** to such individuated portions.*[21]

Compared to inorganic matter, living organisms have a more sophisticated form of consciousness, a greater sense of Self-awareness. Consciousness took an evolutionary step in knowing and expanding Itself. That step was to allow inorganic matter to take cooperation a step further in complexity – to become alive, organic, and "natural" – become part of all that is Nature as expressed in physical form.

Individuated expressions of Consciousness moved up a gear from cooperative inorganic compounds to highly cooperative, interdependent cellular complexities able to interact with the environment. And briefly consider how Nature has run with this freedom of expression under its intentional belt!

At this point, we need to bear in mind that all expressions of Consciousness in the physical domain are subject to *natural principles* – primarily the *Natural Power of Divine Love* mentioned in the introduction. This means no one organism or species, given the freedom of life, can ever run away with itself and dominate the physical environment to the detriment of other representations of Consciousness.

To prevent this from happening, Consciousness can end participation in the physical realm for such individualized portions – death, or even extinction, eventually ensues.

Alternatively, when a consciousness as complex as our own is running amok, a change in the psychological structure may work to bring the wayward species back into compliance with this natural power directing intent. Shifts in the complex consciousnesses created by Consciousness do occur as the fossil records show!

In other words, if humankind does not address the core psychological aspects within its collective psyche that run in contradiction to the natural power of Divine Love; if *we* do not *allow* the individuated consciousness of humanity to evolve – then yes, our alternative is extinction.

Concerning our own representation of Consciousness, we are organic and therefore have freedom of expression. We have an awareness of Self and a desire for Self-expression.

Our awareness of Self – integrated within our personality – has though been married with another psychological structure as part of Consciousness' evolutionary drive for experiential knowledge. Our individuated portion of Consciousness comes with an ego! Our ego/personality psychological combo is an attempt to ratchet up the individuation experiment, to take our consciousness from awareness of Self in relation to physical expression, to *conscious* awareness of the totality of the Self operating in realities other than just the physical dimension.

We have until recently though been far too preoccupied by our ego-self's insistence that *it* represents the entirety of our Self and that the only reality is the physical one. With conscious awareness of Self comes the ability to Self-reflect. The ego's vanity has meant that its form of self-reflection has narrowed to its own concerns, its own preoccupation with physical expression, and no longer encompasses the totality of the Self.

For many centuries, our ego-selves have usurped the right to navigate our Selves through the perilous seas of the physical world. The *shift in consciousness* humanity is currently experiencing is aimed at readjusting our Self-reflective settings. It is correcting the psychological bias on Self-reflection created by the ego.

The ego-self is not to be abandoned, or made extinct, (it is after all extremely adept at reasoning, logic, and planning – which we require of our physically focused outer selves) but simply brought back into harmony with the other aspects of our Selves.

Our troublesome times suggest Consciousness has it in mind to see humanity's consciousness regain the full scope of conscious awareness. Our shift in consciousness moves us from the limited ego-self evaluation of who we are to the big Self potentials that will expand who we are.

SAY THAT AGAIN (4) The Individuation of Consciousness.

If you equate Consciousness with being pure energy, this quote by Seth from *The Nature of the Psyche: Its Human Expression* may help clarify the individuation process:

"Pure energy, or any 'portion' of it, contains within itself the creative propensity toward individuation, so that within any given portion all individually conscious life is implied, created, sustained."[22]

Consciousness uses individuation as a method to know itself through experience. Individuation of our species gave us freedom of expression in the physical realm – a self-aware (note the small "s") organic form. Another evolutionary step, under the intent of Consciousness, gave us the power to consciously create the events we wish to see in physical reality – *conscious* self-awareness (still a small "s") made possible through the psychological addition of an ego-self.

Conscious Self-awareness (capital "S") is the next step in the evolution of our species encapsulated by the Shift. A readjustment and broadening of our ability to Self-reflect.

The work of Chilean biologist and philosopher Humberto Maturana and his student Francisco Varela (1946–2001), notably the theory of "autopoiesis,"[23] presents an alternative yet intuitively perceptive take on the process of individuation – the production of "selves," in relation to evolution, in the physical domain. The theory suggests that new selves (biological cell production, for example) emerge through an autonomous process from an external flow of molecules and energy. We might consider the "energy" supplied in the process as originating from "Source Energy" as Consciousness goes about Its own automated process of replicating Itself in the physical domain.

If you're getting nervous – don't worry – we actually live in a safe universe

If you have absorbed the introduction, with its talk of radical cultural change, forces that drive your actions, your consciousness being an expression of God Consciousness, and your life having a purpose after all, you are probably getting palpitations... Then take a deep breath... and know that, contrary to what it looks like on the surface, the universe, in which all this happens, is a safe one.

The media provides us with our "on the surface" view of reality; it reflects back at us the beliefs we currently hold to be true. Its reporting focus is to seek out events that capture our fears – fears generated by our core beliefs. As you may have gathered from the media, the prevailing worldview suggests we live in an *unsafe* universe – echoing a primary fear within our collective psyche. The beliefs of both science and religion predominantly support this view.

For centuries, distorted religious doctrine has led to the undermining of our self-worth and a "victim mentality"[24] now thrives. You can expect your life to be one of struggle and suffering – something you supposedly need to get through as undamaged and untainted as possible if you are to receive redemption and enjoy yourself after death. Generally speaking, religious views at present do not nurture our personalities whilst we are in the physical domain. To add to our existential anguish, we also have to contend with science's promotion of notions such as:

- Every *"thing,"* which includes our Selves, has come about through chance.
- To maintain our existence, we are constantly embroiled in a competition for finite resources.
- We are the subject of *"selfish genes"* that follow the "survival of the fittest" axiom (a Darwinian distortion). And,
- Our primal drive – our vitality – rises uncontrolled from a psychological cesspit (a Freudian distortion).

These are all scientific views that further weaken, rather than encourage, our indomitable quest for the meaning of life. The fundamental core beliefs of science and religion contained within our worldview engender fear. It is a primal fear that originates from the belief that underlies all such core beliefs (*the belief at the very core of core beliefs!*) – that we are *"separated from our Source"* – of spiritual guidance.

For those of you who feel the insecure child within stirring into panic mode because of talk of radical change, take heart in the knowledge that this debilitating belief (that we live in an unsafe world) is under serious review. This book espouses a new worldview, one that re-establishes a truth that has been suppressed for many centuries; the truth that we do indeed live in a safe universe – one imbued with meaning – a universe designed to nurture all forms of consciousness – whether you believe it or not!

The sooner we embrace this truth, the better our ability to ride the rollercoaster of change harmoniously and remain relatively unscathed by personal trauma. Once we accept that our beliefs form our reality, and that we are free to choose the beliefs that work for us (rather than acquiesce to dictatorial beliefs) we are better able to adopt a new, postmodern worldview. This would be a postmodern worldview that nurtures both groups and individuals while exploring the meaning of life unimpeded; a worldview that expects change to be invigorating rather than traumatic; a worldview that appreciates change as an on-going expansion and evolution of our consciousness.

While we're on the subject of our consciousness again

Without wishing to overload your mind with yet more to contemplate on the subject of consciousness, the concepts below expand a little on the metaphysical mechanics of creation. They are an aid to understanding *how* we create our realities and how the physical *you* is produced from its non-physical beginnings. They are important concepts to grasp on how your individualized identity forms "before" the construction of your non-physical self – the subject of the next chapter.

You should have gathered by now that *your consciousness is an expression of Consciousness* operating in the dimension of physicality. The question arises as to what and where is Consciousness outside of the physical realm? If It resides in a non-physical dimension, what's that like? And are the non-physical aspects of my Self in the same place?

To help answer these questions, we need to introduce you to... *Areas within Consciousness.* Seth uses the term "Frameworks" and other channeled sources use terms such as "Regional Areas" or "Planes of Existence"[25] in order that we might better understand the notion of places of existence outside the physical dimension.

As you take your awareness into these non-physical areas – in order to understand – do be aware that in actuality there are no divisions, no "places" within a "space" as we are used to, no levels, no hierarchy; just areas within Consciousness where the attention of *your* consciousness can be focused. Moreover, we do need to accept and allow for the reality of such "places," such Areas, if we are ever to understand the complexity of our Selves. For the purposes of this book, and for you to begin to comprehend the enormity of your Self, we can confine ourselves to four such Areas within Consciousness.

The three Areas we are most directly concerned with are:

- **The Objective Area** – an area within Consciousness where It expresses Itself in a manner confined to *natural principles* and their physical interpretation. We call this area *the physical dimension* and summarize its description as the "space-time continuum."

  The Laws of Physics are the interpretations of the natural principles established by Consciousness for this area of expression. Your individualized consciousness is an integral part of the expression of Consciousness in this dimension and as such, its own expression conforms to the natural principles and their interpretations.

  You perceive this dimension of your existence through your five physical senses (and any enhancing instrumentation). Importantly, your thoughts, your beliefs, your dreams, and your emotions all influence your perception of the Objective Area.

  We assume "cause and effect" to be a physical law within this area because we usually perceive "time" as a linear construct. We can interpret the Quantum Fields postulated under Quantum Theory to be an area of interface between the Objective Area and the Subjective Area within Consciousness.

- **The Subjective Area** is the area within Consciousness that is closest to and aligned with the Objective Area. We commonly regard this area as the "spiritual realm" or *the non-physical dimension*. It is a *subtle field* within Consciousness containing many "layers" and properties, not least properties of an alternate electromagnetic nature.

  Our concept of time does not operate in this area, yet it is within this area that "things" destined to manifest in the Objective Area "begin" their construction. This area acts as

a communication bridge between all Areas within
Consciousness – it is the dimension from which *"Source
Energy"* originates.

You can perceive the nuances of your own existence in
this Area through "altered states" of your "waking state"
of consciousness – through dreams, meditation, prayer and
other manipulations of your inner senses.

- **The Subconscious Area** (explored in *Chapter 7*) is an area
within Consciousness concerned with projecting the
vitality of Consciousness into the physical plane of
existence. You can access this area through investigative
psychological techniques such as hypnosis, meditation,
and the various mental exercises presented in the
metaphysical literature. The portal to this domain is within
your *Mind*.

There is mention later in this book, but more in Books II and III,
of a fourth Area within Consciousness, the *Transitional Area*,
which relates to the act of physical death.

SAY THAT AGAIN (5) Areas within Consciousness.

The *Objective Area* – the *physical dimension* (admirably
defined by Newtonian physics and the work of Albert
Einstein[26]), that our everyday selves find all around us and
take to be the one and only reality.

The *Subjective Area* – a *non-physical dimension of
probabilities* that we commonly interpret to be the
"spiritual" dimension.

The *Subconscious Area* – an Area bridging the
Subjective Area and the Objective Area for Consciousness
to transfigure non-physical energy into physical energy

forms.

The *Transitional Area* – an Area within Consciousness where your Self creates certain psychological structures in order that your outer self can operate within the Objective Area. It is this Area where your ego-self and personality come to re-orientate and acclimatize to existence outside of the Objective Area. It is here that your outer self's personality invariably "positions itself" after physical death. You can imagine this area to be within the Subconscious Area.

Consciousness comes in packages – Energy too!

Well… actually they don't! However, it may just help you to understand fully the broader concept of Consciousness and how your personal consciousness individuates from It, if we indulge ourselves with a bit of over-simplification.

Seth was very much aware that science likes to comprehend things by breaking them down into their constituent parts. Pandering to this naïve and narrow form of investigation, he uses a metaphor to help us appreciate how everything in the physical domain comes into existence through Consciousness.

Seth's metaphor breaks Consciousness down into units, which he calls "Consciousness Units" (CUs), and their progeny, "Electromagnetic Energy Units"[27] (EEs), in an attempt to explain the mechanics of physical creation.

My own attempt to explain what's happening when your non-physical self is created within the Subjective Area within Consciousness begins with a small visualization:

Imagine taking your awareness away from the physical realm for a moment and into a realm of nothingness. Imagine, if you will … no-thing.

(Okay, this might be easier if we put some background things

into this area of no physical thing.)

As a backdrop… all around you is a deep, deep blueness… an ocean of Prussian blue – within which you appear to be suspended. Your awareness is placed somewhere in this deep ocean of blueness… within the *Subjective Area* where nothing is physical.

As your awareness drifts casually about this ethereal location, you begin to sense certain things within the no-thing-ness. You sense a rush of energy around you… You can feel an invisible breeze; indeed, it would appear that your awareness is included within, yet is separate from, this movement of energy.

You can sense that this energy in motion is *aware of itself…* as you become conscious that *your awareness* is part of this vast sea of e-motional *vibrational signatures.*

What you were aware of in this ocean of nothingness was the very breath of Consciousness – Electromagnetic Energy Units (EEs). These Units move faster than light[28], are "just beneath the range of physical matter"[29] and consequently remain undetected by our physical senses. EEs gain their substantial presence within the Subjective Area by the action of Consciousness forming energy into patterns of aware-ized units of identity – Consciousness Units (CUs). CUs become EEs in order that they may transmute into physicality – emerging as physical matter by condensing energy into a *perceivable* form – within the velocity of light – within the physical dimension's electromagnetic spectrum of light.[30]

In other words, to get energy from the non-physical to the physical dimension, Consciousness needs to organize Itself and slow up a bit. More precisely, Consciousness patterns energy, *Itself*, into more succinct packages for physical realm explo-ration. CUs – the "smallest" indivisible Units of Consciousness that have their own inviolate identity, their own prototype self, are aware-ized – come together to form an autonomous parcel of Consciousness that too will have its own identity created by the cooperative mass of CUs that form it.

The identity of each CU within the whole is not lost in this process. They agree to come together to form a more complex expression of Consciousness that builds its own overseeing identity (along with its own awareness of self) in order to maintain cohesion and durability for the "new" entity. Once energy patterns into a cohesive mass of CUs, they then need to "slow down" their vibrational signature if they wish to enter the physical dimension's restricted vibrational frequencies.

Slowing down their frequency turns CUs into an Electromagnetic Energy form – EEs. EEs then slow the vibrational frequency further in order to enter the physical dimension via the *Quantum Field* – a "place" postulated by Quantum Field Theory where the non-physical and physical domains come together.

SAY THAT AGAIN (6) CUs and EEs.

Consciousness Units (CUs) are part of the metaphor Seth employs to convey how the physical realm comes into being. Consciousness is an omnipresent force – existing in all areas, universes and dimensions of being. Within the Subjective Area, Units of Consciousness – indivisible, aware-ized kernels of energy – coalesce to form more complex cooperative entities that are a result of Consciousness' intent to express Itself continually through limitless creations.

Consciousness Units are not *particles* as they are not physical and they possess and retain their own identity despite their propensity to combine with other Units. Combinations of CUs begin to "slow down" their energy

---

> frequency in order to become Electromagnetic Energy Units.
>
> **Electromagnetic Energy Units (EEs)** develop from Consciousness Units and remain within the Subjective Area until their energy frequency is further "slowed" to within physical frequencies.[31]

Okay… take a deep breath (or a slurp of Merlot) and vow to come back to the above if you need to when working through the book. Go to *Appendix I* to locate a specific topic summarized in the *Say That Again* boxes should you need to remind yourself of any key concepts you may be struggling with. Do persevere, for to understand fully the magnificent entirety of who you are and what you are all about rests on these key concepts.

CHAPTER 2

FORMATION OF THE NON-PHYSICAL YOU

When studying a creation or construct, such as our Selves, we are so used to breaking things down into their constituent parts (the reductionist approach) that we lose sight of the *wholeness* that is intrinsic. The approach ostracizes the invisible and essentially indivisible component that is *Consciousness*; yet it is intrinsic to all creations and is the crucial element that turns any creation into a *gestalt*[32] – something that you cannot understand completely by analyzing its parts. Seth reminds us that although there may appear to be various layers to the Self there are no definitive lines between them. Furthermore, as Seth also reminds us, because Consciousness is ubiquitous – it can be everywhere at the same time – there are in fact no definitive boundaries "... between what is self and not self."[33]

With this said, we shall now examine the non-physical aspects to your Self by using... reductionism! Why? Simply because this methodology is the one we are most used to and therefore find most conducive to understanding. Do remember though, that your ego-self's favored method for understanding its environment sets up divisions and boundaries that are not really there; all partitions presented are in actuality blurred, overlapping and highly flexible.

Identifying your identity

Just previously, you were asked to imagine a place of "no-thing-ness" – the non-physical reality of the Subjective Area within Consciousness – conventionally referred to as the spiritual realm, and occasionally by metaphysical guides as the "Electric Universe" or "Electric Field"[34] – suggesting that the only

53

tangible form within it is of an electromagnetic nature. Briefly remind yourself of this place once more...

All you can perceive is the occasional breath of "air" in a deep blue sea of nothingness – the movement of Electromagnetic Energy Units (EEs) going about their business of slowing down the energy of Consciousness Units (CUs)... getting ready to manifest in physical reality.

You are aware that the EEs are self-aware... having their own sense of identity.

Imagine yourself surrounded by this deep ocean of aware-ized electromagnetic units... this energy in motion (EE-motion)... each unit exuding its own unique tone of being.

Now that you are reminded of your Subjective Area within Consciousness, let's start with building the non-physical "you" that resides there. We begin with your *identity*.

Within the Subjective Area, wavelets of energy formed by CUs begin to come together to produce a more complex identity – the beginnings of your Self, the beginnings of a "you." This is not to do with EEs yet. This is the coalescing of CUs to form a co-operative gestalt – Units of Consciousness prepared to broaden their experience and augment their own expression through a *shared* intent, safe in the knowledge that each Unit within the complex maintains its own identity and individuality.

To conceptualize this *unit identity* maintained within a *gestalt identity*, a useful analogy would be the cellular structure of a living organism. Cellular biologists, in particular those involved in the burgeoning field of epigenetics (the science that studies "the molecular mechanisms by which environment controls gene activity"[35]); teach us that cells maintain their own identity and purpose within the body.

The cell membrane, far from being the point where it separates from the whole, is actually the surface of transformation; an electro-chemical interface that keeps the cell and the whole body informed of the intentional state of play. Cells are aware of their environment and are conscious of their importance to the living whole. Each individual cell is conscious of the collective cooperation required to maintain the organism.[36] Similarly, Consciousness Units come together by instinct, with a collective ambition, to form the *Identity* of your *Essence*.

To further your understanding of how and why CUs come together, you are asked momentarily to place yourself in the position of Consciousness (or God, if you can't yet relinquish the term). Imagine *your* mind is the mind of Consciousness/God. As it is difficult to imagine being everywhere at the same time, let me suggest you place your Self on a bench in a vast "causal field" of ripened grain nodding gently in the soft summer breeze.

As Consciousness, you are aware that you are a limitless source of energy. You are in a constant state of becoming – of self-actualizing – and you exploit this growth and development of your Self through endless acts of creation. Whilst in this exalted position on your comfy bench, consider now the individuated portion of your Self that you are about to create (*that would be you, the reader, by the way!*) with your marvelous little individuated Units of your Self. –You, Consciousness, have decided upon a *human expression* of your Self. As such, you want it to be able to explore various dimensions of experience – with a particular focus upon the physical dimension – that Objective Area you created earlier that everyone's talking about.

To do this, you (as Consciousness) first construct the non-physical "capsule"[37] required to maintain the integrity of your creation's existence – the *Essence* body (*which is explained below*). As you form the Essence body, you incorporate psychical characteristics that will reflect the nuances of intent you wish for it to explore. From this foundation, you can begin to create the necessary conditions for this part of you to enter your Objective

Area – the physical dimension.

One psychical condition you have concocted for this imminent person-to-be is adherence to the concept of *time*.[38] Time is a very clever twist to your own principle of learning through experience. In order to contrast the all-at-once simultaneous conditions in the causal field where you are currently situated, you have integrated a "dimension" (time) to the reality of your human expression that *you* can examine within *its* portion of *your* psyche. In the Objective Area that you have created, intentional actions are "drawn out" in their manifestation because of this psychical property you have installed.

Our physical dimension of existence becomes a medium for Consciousness to explore, where everything – all action, any experience, any progression of an idea – is more readily distinguished, more open to examination, and more observable by the incorporation of the elasticizing property of time.

Returning to your own mind now… CUs then, as representatives of Consciousness from the causal field, begin patterning energy in the Subjective Area into your psychological gestalt – your Essence. We can condense the highly complex body of CUs that make up all of the non-physical aspects to your Self into four core elements:

- **Your Identity** – The coming together of CUs to form your Essence creates a *psychic gestalt* that has its own unique Identity. This "greater" or broader Identity exists independently of the physical domain and is, from your viewpoint within the physical domain, immortal.

  Your Identity, which you occasionally sense as being the "I" of "who I am," is a constantly adjusting artifact of your subconscious (see below) that takes into account your development and experiences within the physical realm. The identity your ego-self uses to describe who you are is usually a narrowly confined list of physical attributes and achievements relating to your experiences within the physical realm.

Your non-physical Identity is inviolate – meaning that nothing can extinguish it once it has formed. Attachments to other such Identities do not occur without the approval of your Essence.

Remember that your Essence is a collective organization of CUs, each with their own inviolate identities coming together in cooperation to form a more complex expression of Consciousness than their own. The integrity of a CU's identity exists for your own Identity, and for any other psychic alliances you may form when CUs come together – *cooperation for mutual benefit of expression.*

Your *inner self* (see below) takes care of your Identity's cohesion via the *inner senses* (see *Chapter 3*). This entails maintaining the integrity of your Identity along with the identities of the cells, molecules, atoms, EEs and CUs that are all cooperating to make up the entirety of your individuality.

Your Identity comprises a psychic bank of intentional plans, abilities and purposes that your physical self can draw upon at any time.

- **Your Essence** – The total configuration of energy relating to your Self in the Subjective Area within Consciousness. More commonly termed "soul," metaphysical literature suggests various other names for your non-physical self; for example, *Source* (Abraham), *Source Energy, Entity* (used by Seth), *Essence/Essence self* (most frequently used), *Oversoul,* and *Higher Self* (Omni).

- **Your inner self** – This aspect of your non-physical self is referred to in channeled literature as *source self, inner ego, inner being,* or even *Entity* or *Essence.* We shall keep to the term *inner self* as much as possible throughout this book to provide consistency.

Your inner self employs the *inner senses* to translate essential data on the integrity and condition of your overall Self for your *outer self* (ego, conscious-mind[39], and personality) to assimilate. Its main concerns are to do with maintaining the foundations and overall stability of your Self.

You can regard your inner self as the emissary of your Essence, a soul from your Oversoul, an agent of Essence whose mission is to maintain communication with the outer self on matters pertaining to your Essence and the Subjective Area within Consciousness.

Your inner self maintains a focus upon how your consciousness expresses itself in the physical dimension.

- **Your subconscious** – *The* Subconscious is an *Area within Consciousness,* as mentioned in *Chapter 1. Your* subconscious is your mental gateway to this Subconscious Area within Consciousness.

  Your subconscious is an area within the "psychic gestalt" of your Mind, a "place" where your inner self is able to communicate and interact with your outer self. You can think of it as a mental place where your inner self's psychic operations mix with the psychological structures of your outer self – the structures that focus their attention on the physical playground.

  Your subconscious utilizes both your inner senses and your outer physical senses and is easier to understand as an *area within your portion of the psyche or Mind,* rather than a *level* or *layer* of the Self. Within your subconscious area, various zones handle the complexities involved in maintaining and supporting your outer self.

  Your subconscious maintains a vast library of

knowledge and information pertaining to the entirety of your Self – not least your greater Identity. It also provides an access to far deeper wells of knowledge relating to our species, and even to the workings of Consciousness Itself.

You might visualize the subconscious area as a university campus – a set of buildings, the library of knowledge being one, nestled in landscaped parklands.

Figure 1 presents a graphical representation of these non-physical aspects to your Self. Remember that there are no boundaries or sizes involved with this structure; all elements blend seamlessly together in this psychic gestalt of your Self. The spheres with a 'P' at the center of the structure represent the individualized person-alities of other lifetimes. The personality and its continuance within Essence is a subject covered in *Chapter 6*.

Figure 1. The fundamental elements of your non-physical self

Feeling the Identity of your Essence

Your Essence maintains a unique vibrational signature at its core – your Identity. To better conceptualize the rareness of your vibrational signature, you might compare it to the matchless quality of light emitted by a star. Chemistry and astronomy have shown us that not only does each of the ninety-two naturally occurring elements emit a signature color under combustion, but also each star in the night's sky emits its *own unique spectrum of light,* a distinct "color" made from countless hues and tones produced by a precise combination of elements burnt within it. Just imagine how many stars there are in the Universe, each, like you, with their own vibrational signature!

An exercise intended to put you in touch with your Essence and its core vibrational signature follows. Your vibrational signature has a unique tonal quality. Seth and other channeled guides call this your "feeling-tone"[40] To resonate *consciously* with your vibrational tone encourages a deeper awareness of the broader aspects to your Self and helps rekindle a line of communication between your conscious-mind and your Essence.

While emotions and feelings come and go, the unique tone of your Essence remains with you during your physical experience. Your vibrational signature's tone transmits to your conscious-mind the overall tonal quality of your Self's greater Identity.

This vibrational tone surfaces on a rhythmical basis and although most of us are unaware of it or ignore it, this does not make it disappear. Your vibrational tone constantly shapes a channel through which an unabated flow of "Source Energy" (an Abraham term) comes to you; and it also provides you with information on the vibrational tones of other physical creations that are part of your immediate experience.

Getting in touch with your vibrational signature's tone helps acquaint you with the primal reason behind your participation in the physical realm – your directional path of intent – which will lead you to your life's purpose. Practice of Exercise 1 will bring you a feel for the part of you that knows all about your intentional leanings for this lifetime – your Essence.

Take no longer than fifteen minutes on this exercise. *Read through it first before closing your eyes!*

EXERCISE 1: THE TONE OF YOUR VIBRATIONAL SIGNATURE

Sit as comfortably as you possibly can without crossing your legs. Close your eyes. Take a couple of deep breaths, breathing in through the nose and out through the mouth. Quickly scan through your body, relax any muscles that appear cramped and allow your jaw to open slightly. Set an intention to experience your own deep vibrational tone within you—no matter how briefly.

Begin to quiet your thoughts and tell yourself that you will deal with any invasive thoughts later.

Similarly, if any emotions come to your awareness, put these aside; they are not what you are wishing to sense at the moment.

Imagine your awareness to be drifting in clear, transparent space. There is nothing above you, below you, or around you. Simply feel the tone of your being. Ask your inner self to allow you to experience this deep rhythm of your Essence.

Maintain a mental stance of gratitude and appreciation for your uniqueness.

There is no right or wrong way of doing this. It is not a meditation; it is simply giving yourself the time to allow the tone of your vibrational signature to appear so that you may familiarize yourself with its feeling. Know that it exists; you just want to be able to sense it in some conscious way.

> Keep things light-hearted; everyone experiences their unique tone in their own unique way. You are not concerned at all about *how* it should feel. However, you will *know* it's *your* vibrational tone when it appears within your senses.
>
> Now allow yourself to experience the tone of your vibrational signature.

You should realize that this exercise is not some sort of test; you get what you get. Initially, that might not be very much. So be persistent and practice the exercise as often as possible. Do know that once you can sense your vibrational tone quite easily, you can put yourself in touch with it at will – allowing yourself to feel confident and secure in moments of distress.

If you are unable to get past any feelings or emotions that come to the fore while practicing, then you might consider using the EFT[41] exercise *(Appendix II)* to dissipate any emotional energy getting in the way. Make the specific feeling or emotion "the problem" when using the EFT Exercise. Be persistent and run through the protocol at least twice. Remember to keep this exercise and EFT work as light-hearted as possible. Treat it as *first conscious contact* with your Essence – the non-physical part of your Self that exists before you are born. I promise you, it won't bite.

The next chapter introduces you to some of the natural principles from channeled literature that underpin the laws of physics. You also get acquainted with your *inner senses* – the facilities utilized by your inner self and subconscious in helping you see the fuller picture of your reality.

CHAPTER 3

NATURAL PRINCIPLES AND YOUR INNER SENSES

You may have noticed that the construction of your non-physical self comes with a set of *inner senses*. The inner senses are the means by which you create your reality. Your outer physical senses are simply reporting to you what you have already created; your inner senses are the agencies that put it there. This means, does it not, that to have conscious control over your inner senses would be tremendously advantageous to you.

Before you rush into egoistic fantasies on the possibilities available to you; be aware that precisely because your inner senses have the power of creation, they must conform to a set of *natural principles* that govern the way in which you create and sustain something. You would therefore do well to apprise your *outer self* of these rules or "laws" of creation, before attempting to engage fully with your inner senses.

Natural Principles

We know the Objective Area within Consciousness conforms to the laws of Physics. What we don't know, according to metaphysical teachers, is that there are natural universal laws that underpin our physical laws. These laws transcend our usual understanding of the word "law." They are not a set of mandates handed down from on high; they are simply *how things work* within our physical and non-physical worlds – as Sir Arthur Eddington may have sensed more than eighty years ago:

I believe that the mind has the power to affect groups of atoms and even tamper with the odds of atomic behaviour, and that even the course of the world is not predetermined by physical laws but may be altered by the uncaused volition of human beings.[42]

Seth refers to these natural laws as "the basic laws of the inner universe,"[43] naming ten such laws between sessions 44 and 59 in *The Early Sessions: Book 2 of The Seth Material* by Jane Roberts. "Creation" is one example of his inner universal laws, the principle by which "idea constructions" become manifest in the physical realm; and the law of "energy transformation" is another, which is a principle that supersedes the empirical law of physics that declares that energy can neither be created nor destroyed. This particular inner law allows for energy to *transform* from one state (non-physical reality) to another (physical reality).[44]

In order to quash any associations your thoughts may have with the word "law" being an unquestionable dictate, rather than, in this case, a set of values by which Consciousness adheres; the expression *natural principles* is adopted as much as possible from hereon. As Omni (John L. Payne) points out, "A principle tells of the nature of things, an action or a flowing of energy, more of a state of being."[45] A description, and thus term, far better suited to the concepts about to be unveiled.

These principles do not therefore *govern* us. Consciousness does not decide that we must adhere to them; they are *universal* principles that describe the *nature* of the universe and how *Consciousness* works. The free will of *our consciousness* allows us to follow these principles or not. Not following these principles though, creates problems for our individual selves and humanity's collective self. A deeper understanding of these principles will aid in our understanding of how our Selves work and how the universe works as a medium for the expansion of Consciousness.

By way of introducing you to some of the most important natural principles that shape your existence, the following story on the individuation process of Consciousness as It went about getting to know Itself through experience is presented. If you need to remind yourself of the individuation process, refer to *Consciousness getting to know Itself* and *Say That Again (4)* in *Chapter 1*.

Consciousness creates the natural principles

The first principle that we must realize is the existence of Consciousness Itself. Consciousness is an ever-present property of any dimension or plane of existence. Consciousness instills Itself within *all* creations, giving each creation *self-awareness* to some degree. As Seth remarks in *The Early Sessions: Book 2 of The Seth Material*, "There is no case where this is not so."[46]

Because Consciousness has the intent to expand and evolve Itself through experience, it uses *creation*, another natural principle, to do so. It creates an infinitesimal number of theaters or playgrounds, some "physical" (as we might perceive them) like our own world, some "non-physical" or, "other dimensional," to our way of thinking. Creativity is a natural principle for going about knowing your Self, it is a first step in the individuation process.

To help Consciousness explore the complexities of this principle of creation It devised the natural principle of *Divine Love*. The influence of this natural principle upon all expressions of Consciousness, particularly organic matter, is so powerful that it seems appropriate to reclassify this principle as a *natural power* (discussed in *Chapter 4*). In short, Divine Love is a principle through which all creations can reach fulfillment of their individual expressions whilst also aiding other creations in their own potentials for expression.

For Divine Love to work efficiently Consciousness requires another natural principle in Its creative endeavors – *cooperation*. This natural principle gives rise to the myriad structures observed within the physical world. The less complex structures formed by Consciousness, such as atoms and molecules, apply this principle in order to form more complex, multifaceted structures – gestalts – which range from inorganic matter to living organisms, such as you and I.

These cooperative structures form their own identities, without the identities of the less complex structures losing theirs. By cooperating, the composite structures (the atoms and molecules) gain in their ability to express themselves through mutual regard and joint endeavor acting within the natural power of Divine Love. Cooperative structures are an expression of the natural principle of creativity couched in the natural power of Divine Love.

When Consciousness creates physical realities as opposed to non-physical realities, it requires a further natural principle by which to transform Its energy. We are yet to realize that energy (*Source Energy,* the equivalent of Consciousness Itself) transforms from non-physical states into physical states such as our physical dimension. In doing so, we may think energy has created itself from nowhere – thus breaking the empirical law of Physics – but the natural principle of energy transformation supersedes this law. The following "path of transformation" derived from channeled information on how energy moves from non-physical expression to physical expression may intrigue the physicist reader:

Consciousness ≡ Energy > CUs > EEs > QFs (Quantum Fields) > space-time continuum.

This transforming sequence is essentially about slowing the vibrational frequencies of energy to within those of the electromagnetic spectrum we call "light." Consciousness is the originating force that patterns energy (sorts out the vibrational frequency) for whatever dimension it is using to express Itself. Energy *transforms* itself across all dimensions of Consciousness and this natural principle is continuously occurring.

In transforming energy into the medium of physicality,

Consciousness has introduced the concept of *time*. You can view this "dimension" within our own particular physical realm as a way in which experiences can be more thoroughly examined. Time "draws out" an experience into all of the nuances of its expression – just as each frame on a film reel captures the detail of an action.

Time is an invention. It is only of importance to us because our form of consciousness is utilizing this invention to explore the minutiae of physical experience.

From the point of view of Consciousness, time is an interesting (and probably amusing) psychical construct. From where Consciousness is, there is only one "moment" and that moment encapsulates how Consciousness expresses Itself outside as well as inside the concept of time. Seth refers to this moment point as the "spacious present." The spacious present, the one moment of Consciousness, exemplifies another natural principle – that of *spontaneity*.[47] Consciousness behaves in a spontaneous fashion – when time is not a factor, it cannot be otherwise.

If you are following this hugely difficult premise of "no time" but for a moment point for Consciousness operating in the Subjective Area of existence, then you may be thinking about how anything might "last" – what happens to a "thing's" continuity in the Subjective Area?

Continuity is our interpretation of a final natural principle in this introduction to them. Because we view things through the spectacles of time, we assume that physical things continue to exist because of it. They don't.

Time is not something that controls the continuity of existence – this is under the management of the natural principle of *durability*. The length of *duration* of a physical construction is in direct proportion to the construct's embodiment of the natural power of Divine Love and its ability to sustain the natural principle of energy transformation.

Death occurs – cessation of focus upon the physical

dimension – when the principle of durability ceases to operate for the physical construct.

SAY THAT AGAIN (7) The Natural Principles

The natural principles underpinning all existence are notoriously difficult even to begin to understand. Seth's "laws of the inner universe" found in *The Early Sessions: Book 2 of the Seth Material*, provide further understanding and Omni's "four principles of creation" in John L. Payne's book *Omni Reveals the Four Principles of Creation* simplify matters to a considerable degree. The above story on individuation and Consciousness getting to know Itself should provide you with an outline of the most important natural principles that affect the use of your inner senses. If you encounter difficulties when you come to exercise your inner senses, you are likely to be acting against one or more of these important principles.

Which of the above would be the essential ones to embrace? If you can get to grips with *creation, cooperation* and the power of *Divine Love* you'll be well on your way.

Conscious creation is a difficult thing to master if you are unpracticed in the use of your inner senses and are not conversant with the natural principles that underpin their use and describe *how "things" really work*. Let's now take a look at the tools by which you form your personal reality.

Your inner senses – in tandem with natural principles

We are reliant upon our five physical senses and their extensions (scientific instrumentation) to provide us with information about our physical reality. On occasion though, and as adults it is likely to have happened at least once, we become aware of information that cannot be attributed to the five-senses. We usually assign such occasions to a mysterious *sixth sense*—a moment of intuition (tuition from within) all too often dismissed as inconsequential by our ego-self's fixation with its physical senses.

Your inner self uses a variety of ways to grab your outer self's attention. Feelings, intuition, inspirations, and even coincidences are a few of the ways it uses to make you aware of information, often important, gathered by your inner senses. Your inner senses are picking up subconscious information that is highly relevant to your perception of reality.

Just as your outer senses determine the nuances of information relayed by physical objects (size, color, smell, etcetera), your inner senses determine the nuances of information pertaining to the object (or event) found only in the Subjective Area within Consciousness. Your inner self relays this *inner information* to the conscious-mind to augment the information of the outer senses – providing you with the *subtler* details. Essentially, your inner senses – if your ego-self allows – are simply trying to bring you a fuller picture of the reality you perceive. They take you deeper into the exchange of information between *what you have just created in the physical realm* and how it relates to your Self.

Seth describes nine inner senses in Chapter 19 of *The Seth Material* by Jane Roberts and you can find further elaboration in *The Early Sessions: (Books 2 and 3) of The Seth Material*. It is recommended that you explore Seth's depictions of these highly important extra-sensory perceptions presented in these works. Understanding "Inner Vibrational Touch" (instant comprehension of the "being-ness" of another living expression of Consciousness beyond simple empathy) and "The Conceptual Sense" (a direct "knowing" of the broadest expression of a concept beyond intellectual terms), for example, will stand you in good stead for any future exercising of your inner senses.

Whilst your outer self has the capacity to receive and include most information supplied by your inner senses, there are some inner senses that reach into areas of knowledge that at present your ego-self would have difficulty handling. This difficulty arises through lack of use. We only rarely acknowledge our inner self's counsel, let alone consciously employ our inner senses.

This general dismissal of the value of communing with our inner selves and exercising our *extra-sensory* perceptions creates within us a psychological condition not unlike schizophrenia.[48] We have a schism that separates our inner self (thereby Essence self) from our ego-self (that controls the conscious-mind) – a condition that necessitates caution as we seek to begin to heal the divide and allow *conscious* manipulation of our inner resources.[49]

Your inner self and subconscious constantly organize inner sense information about the probable realities available to you for manifestation. Your ego-self *filters* these probabilities through the act of perception.[50] Due to our schizophrenic condition, and that we don't *believe* we have anything to do with the creation of physical things and events, we create our realities *un-intent-ionally*, or, *un-consciously* – with very little conscious steering from our ego.

Right now, this may not be such a bad thing, as our ego-selves would not be able to manage the abilities that fully utilized inner senses would afford them. We therefore need to take things slowly, involving and practicing just a few of our inner senses to begin with. Re-establishing the connection to our inner selves and mastering our inner senses may be a lengthy business for some, hard work for most, and not lacking in anguish or even trauma for a good few. Our intransigent egos will need to be persuaded that the inner senses are a valuable aid for gaining knowledge of the outer world and are thus worth pursuing.

However, on a brighter note and before you lose heart, as mentioned in the introduction there is a change, a shift in our consciousness happening. Vital to this Shift is each individual's growing awareness of and ability to exercise his or her inner senses – a reconnection is underway. Several channeled guides inform us of this collective shift, what it means for the individual and their personal reality, and how to participate in it more fully and more positively – swimming with the current and not against it.

The burgeoning phenomenon of channeling in recent years may well be one form of persuasion that Consciousness is using to awaken us to the breadth of personal and collective reality.[51] It will take time and practice to reconstruct a conscious connection with our inner self; but, for each of us to do so at our own pace and in good heart is quintessential to the ease by which we navigate our shift in consciousness.

We should remember though that due to our detachment from these senses over many generations, to jump right in and fully activate them all would be a shock to your outer self as well as your nervous system. You are unlikely to be able to handle the considerably increased stimuli and should approach re-engagement of these senses carefully and with guidance. With this in mind, a general overview of your inner senses is presented below.

Primarily, trust that your inner self will guide you in this re-engagement process. This book can complement your inner self's guidance as you reawaken your inner resources. Begin by employing the exercises and suggestions presented within this book slowly and carefully. They will prepare you for the more challenging work presented in Books II and III. If you become frustrated at your progress or lack of "getting something," know that your inner self knows what your outer self is capable of handling and when. Use the EFT routine (*Appendix II*) for any frustration that may surface and perhaps block your progress.

Frustration is a feeling that signals to you that you are beginning to criticize yourself in some way. Many of us regard frustration to be a normal, natural expression of feeling; however, in actuality the feeling comes from your inner self to warn you that you are discounting yourself. It may be that you perceive yourself to be "not good enough" or lacking the necessary skills. You do not lack the necessary skills; you just need to practice them. Frustration demotivates you, so make sure you address this feeling, using EFT, whenever it arises.

Although Seth outlined nine inner senses, the more recent information from Elias (Mary Ennis)[52] suggests they have three generalizing qualities that we can assign to them for ease of understanding. The inner senses are all working together and overlap in their actions, but we can loosely categorize them according to these three essential qualities:

1 Relating to empathy – **empathic** (your ability to sense, understand and merge with the 'being-ness' of things);
2 Relating to conceptualization – **conceptual** (your ability to fully connect to concepts and ideas); and
3 Relating to your perception of the psychological construct of time – **time-based**.

Remember that there is no hierarchical structure to the inner senses, as they are all equally important to you.

Empathic inner senses:

The empathic senses are an instant "knowing" of the "being-ness" of any structure within your field of perception. Without losing a sense of your own identity, these inner senses give you the ability to expand your conscious awareness to incorporate and perceive the identities of Consciousness expressed through the other structure. Employing these inner senses in the perception of another organic structure, such as an animal or another individual, brings you an understanding and compassion for the other that "empathy" can barely describe. You are able to "merge" with their vibrational signature.

Where another person is concerned, empathic inner senses bring an instant knowing of various elements pertaining to another individual's Essence self, including the feelings and emotions affecting their psychological climate.

This does not imply any form of take-over of another's Essence. Our Essence selves possess *energy retaining capsules* for reasons of integrity; however, they are still able to connect with each other under certain circumstances managed by these empathic inner senses, without compromising the inviolate identities involved.

Utilizing these empathetic-like inner senses stimulates a far greater understanding and compassion for another living thing. We call those who regularly engage these inner senses "empaths" *(would you believe!)* – people who can "read" the being-ness of another person or animal. An accomplished empath might use these senses to feel the being-ness of a tree, a butterfly, or even a pebble from the beach.

At present, our outer selves are incapable of utilizing fully these inner senses. Our inner selves, on the other hand, regularly employ them in the understanding of others. They are inner senses that invariably act subliminally, with very little of the information gathered being made available to the subconscious area of your mind – let alone your ego-self.

As mentioned earlier, an energy retaining capsule encapsulates your Essence self in the non-physical domain to prevent the energy forming it from dissipating. Seth refers to such energy boundaries as "tissue capsules." Terms that you might be familiar with that are also attempting to describe this containment field, or protective sheath, are your "Astral Body," or "Subtle Body."

The skin of your Astral Body can contract and expand to enable exploration of other realities associated with our physical reality. It enables us to experience projections of consciousness, as in lucid dreaming or out of body experiences (OBEs).

Conceptual inner senses:

The conceptual inner senses also offer a type of mergence, but rather than merging with the "being-ness" of physical structures, where you experience the qualities of their inner identity, these inner senses bring you a direct "knowing" of the broadest expression of a concept or idea.

Concepts have very real electromagnetic energy patterning properties that exist outside of the physical dimension. Utilizing this set of inner senses provides you with an understanding of an idea far beyond that achieved by intellectual analysis alone. *Impulses* and moments of *inspiration* are signals to your conscious-mind from your inner self that it is actively engaging the conceptual inner senses.

When engaging the conceptual inner senses, it is possible for you to play guitar like Eric Clapton, or paint a picture like Picasso. The Brazilian medium Luiz Antonio Gasparetto may be the finest living example of an individual able to tune into one or more of the conceptual inner senses as he produces works of art in the style of a number of artists – Pablo Picasso being one.[53] Albert Einstein would be another obvious example of someone highly attuned to the use of his conceptual inner senses.

These inner senses are not solely an artifact of human consciousness; all living organisms are capable of exercising one or more of the conceptual senses in order to enhance their physical experience. They provide the deepest awareness of the basic *natural principles* that power the vitality of the universe – *creativity*, for example. Through these senses, organisms can access packages of inner universal knowledge for their own use, in a manner that is pertinent to that organism's ability to manipulate energy within their own area of expression.

For example, for a spider to exercise its creative abilities, manipulating energy to create its web, its consciousness utilizes a conceptual inner sense to access inner knowledge on the subject – downloading, if you will, a package of data from the inherent inner knowledge on web building held in the archives of the Subconscious Area within Consciousness.[54]

Recent scientific research into dolphin communication may also be revealing this animal's ability to engage the conceptual inner senses. One symbol used in the signing of researchers to communicate with the dolphins means, "be creative" – essentially asking the creature to come up with its own behavioral display rather that any specifically learnt one. A suggestion readily accepted and carried out by the enthusiastic cetaceans![55]

Time-based inner senses:

By experimenting with their use, our time-based inner senses offer us the opportunity to understand better the psychological construct of time and how it relates to other dimensions of reality. These senses can reveal to us the *natural principle of spontaneity* and its importance to our enjoyment of our physical experiences. They can put us in touch with *"natural time"* (how the natural rhythms and cycles of Consciousness actually control the sequencing of events in the physical world) so that we can develop the virtue of patience; and they open the gates to other time frameworks and dimensions.

Playing with these particular inner senses facilitates an ability to switch between the two psychological environments – our inner realm and its expressions "outside" of time, and our outer physical realm's expressions "within" linear time. Exercising these inner senses brings a greater appreciation of the totality of your Self and can act as a gentle introduction to the other inner senses.

Time-based inner senses can combine with empathic and conceptual inner senses to allow you to enhance your perception of the "being-ness" of a structure (living or otherwise), pattern or concept – bringing it into the *spacious present* where time barriers do not exist in the perception of past and future expressions of that structure, pattern or concept.

Utilizing these inner senses frees your perception from the confines of beliefs that stem from our accepted understanding of time being linear in nature. The notion of "cause and effect" becomes a moot point, with realization that both cause *and* effect are codependent in the initiation of an action.

The time-based inner senses are a prominent feature of the dream state. Many of us, after pressing the snooze button on the alarm clock, can recall seemingly lengthy, perhaps hour-long, sequences of events in a dream taking just the five or so minutes set as snooze time. Such occasions remind us of our time-based inner senses in action.

"Precognition" and *"past life recall"* are phenomena that point to the existence of the time-based inner senses. If you factor in the concept of a *spacious present* at the heart of all things to do with time, it isn't difficult to imagine that we should be saying "other life recall," or perhaps "probable self accessing," when experimenting with exploring the depths of our Selves. With practice, engagement of our inner senses may allow us to experience the richness of a long life, whether "past" or "future" in a relatively short period of linear time.

SAY THAT AGAIN (8) The inner senses

Your inner self manages your inner senses in conjunction with subconscious considerations within your Mind. Our outer selves have some awareness of these inner senses, but for most of us, our current belief systems do not encourage their involvement. At present, there are a number of inner senses that we have no conscious awareness of at all. We have therefore not even begun to utilize them consciously.

Non-use is partly due to the ignorance of our dictatorial ego-selves and partly due to safeguards constructed by our

---

inner selves. These safeguards are in place because our inner senses are the means by which we create our realities; and for us to take on the responsibility of *conscious* reality creation while our minds pander to shallow egocentric considerations would be... well, rash at the very least!

This is precisely why we are currently undergoing a shift in our consciousness. A change in our psychological constructs is an evolutionary requirement necessary for us to utilize consciously the inner senses without making our present *unconsciously* created reality any worse. Each individual that learns to use them in accordance with the natural principles will contribute to the ease of transition of the Shift and thus enrich their personal life and our collective reality.

When you come to exercise your inner senses in pursuit of creating a preferred reality and you meet with little success; rest assured it is not because your inner senses don't work properly. In contrast to your outer senses, the keenness of your inner senses does not rely upon a physical system of information relay. Your inner senses don't falter like your hearing or eyesight. You will find the solution to any problem with your creativity by examining the beliefs you hold.

Your beliefs can act as dams to the natural flow of creativity that courses through you, and your actions can be in contradiction to the natural principles that govern creation. Your inner self though, is always there to enlighten you with information gathered by your inner senses on errant beliefs or dubious actions that interfere with your creativity.

Meditation is a conventional way of activating the inner senses when we are not exploring our dream realities. *Exercise 2,* in *Chapter 5*, gently introduces you to the process of activating your inner senses through meditation. This is how Lynda Dahl sums up the inner senses in her book *Ten Thousand Whispers: A Guide to Conscious Creation*:

> When we consciously use the inner senses, we transcend physical reality and play in the universe unfettered by restrictive beliefs. We can enter other realities, clearly communicate with our inner selves, develop telepathic, precognitive and clairvoyant abilities and sense the workings of the universe. We become aware of our multidimensionality, aware that physical reality is a very small portion of our existence, and aware that we have at our disposal an incredible tool to use in everyday life to consciously manipulate physical reality to our liking.[56]

As explained in *Chapter 1*, physical reality (the Objective Area within Consciousness) is essentially a patterning of energy that your outer self focuses upon. It is a particular set of energy configuration patterns– *the* reality – that has captured your perception. The inner senses are your means for accessing a far broader perception of this dominating reality *and* the highly informative non-physical realities that are associated with it. Their employment builds a stronger platform upon which you can create the reality you desire for your Self.

Remember that your inner senses comply with the natural principles. They do not, and cannot, act outside of these principles. The summary of the natural principles presented earlier in this chapter does not include two that we might consider primary. That is, even though they are all equally important in understanding how things work, two can appear more important than the rest. This may be that we find ourselves more directly able to relate to these two because their existence is more easily verifiable – they *show* us how things work.

In order to reinforce the premise that natural principles are not laws in the conventional sense, but are in fact describing the way in which the physical world and everything in it ultimately works, we are calling these two special natural principles – *Natural Powers*.

CHAPTER 4

YOUR NATURAL POWERS AND THE VITAL ETHICAL CODE

In this chapter, we investigate the two primary forces that guide your creations – your *natural powers*. We also examine the one basic ethical code that originates from the use of these powers and your compliance with the natural principles.

Your Natural Powers

The two natural powers feature in many channeled teachings. The first is that of *Divine Love*, referred to by Seth as "value fulfillment" – a "law of the inner universe." The second – the *Power of Attraction*[57] – is one you may be familiar with, now commonly referred to as the *Law of Attraction (LOA)*. Seth does not include the LOA in his list of ten laws of the inner universe, but elsewhere in his legacy he does mention "… certain laws of attraction… "[58] – unfortunately, he does not elaborate upon them, and instead simply reminds us repeatedly that when it comes to reality creation "you get what you concentrate upon."[59]

This phrase sums up what the power of Attraction is all about when we consider the various explanations given by other channeled sources. However, the Power of Attraction is far more complex than is suggested by this motto, or by media bandwagons that place knowledge of this natural power at the pinnacle of reality creation. The mechanics of manifesting what you perceive to be "real" is not as simple as concentrating upon what you want and applying some positive thinking. The Power of Attraction is, though, a crucial factor for you to understand when creating your preferred reality.

To understand the workings of the Power of Attraction more fully, together with developing a deep appreciation for Divine

Love – the natural power that monitors your actions in accordance with the grand scheme of Consciousness – will provide you with the basic and most essential knowledge required in your quest for *conscious creation*.

The Natural Power of Divine Love

Divine Love transcends human love as we interpret it, for it is not simply an action, it is a state of being – an innate quality of Consciousness Itself – of which you are a part. Divine Love is a natural principle that promotes the maximum development for each of us within the myriad expressions of Consciousness. It provides the impetus toward all creative action in physical and non-physical terms. Because of this universal power, every aspect of Consciousness inherently nurtures your growth, creativity and happiness in a *cooperative* lifelong endeavor – for the maximum benefit of every *one* and every *thing*.

Our attempts to interpret Divine Love through our rationalizing minds results in an understanding confined to such terms as "growth,"[60] or "evolution."[61] These are superficial interpretations of the power of Divine Love made by minds held in trance by the dimension of time. Some metaphysical attempts to define Divine Love's all-pervasive quality of existence range from the acutely succinct "allowing" to the seemingly apathetic "complete acceptance of what is."

Such brief definitions though have us ask ourselves, how can lovingly allowing and accepting what is an abhorrent reality make any sense?

To answer this question, and help us further understand the nature of Divine Love we need to realize its importance to how Consciousness goes about its own Self-expression. From our perspective, in order for Consciousness to "grow" and "evolve," it needs to gain *experience of Itself*. To do this, as described in *Chapter 1*, it individualizes Itself into smaller units. *You* are a highly complex smaller unit of Consciousness consisting of an orchestra of still smaller units!

Divine Love *must* be a part of this individualizing-in-order-to-experience process so that all experiences are *allowed (the succinct metaphysical description for Divine Love)* expression. Divine Love is the oil in the individualizing machine.

For Consciousness, and you for that matter, to experience what you are, you need to include what you are not. This comparison, or "contrast," as Abraham (Esther Hicks) refers to it, in our world of experiences, drives *creation* (another natural principle) through *desire* – and existence cannot exist without it as Consciousness "vibrates with desire."[62]

The actual design and purpose of contrasting experiences is to move you past creating what your ego-self *wants*, to creating what your inner self *desires* for full Self-expression.[63] To know what you want to experience, you must include experiences that you do not want. To create the reality you desire, you must be clear on what is undesirable. Sadly, some of us spend our entire lives making clear to our ego-selves what is undesirable but not learning from it.

Physical things are expressions of Consciousness – individualized portions. They only persist in time—*that is, stay in the physical dimension*—for as long as the expression is required to be there by Consciousness, and Divine Love is sustainable. In other words, death in the physical realm is to do with the realization that Divine Love in relation to the organism is unsustainable – evolvement of the particular individualized portion of Consciousness has lost its *durability* – another overlapping natural principle within the expression of Divine Love.

There is a huge gulf in our understanding of the sustainability of a living physical form and its actual durability under Divine Love. We interpret the natural principle of durability as "growth" and "evolution" because our minds are fixated with linear time. As part of our *shift in consciousness* however, our inner selves are developing our ability to express *fully* our personalities in the physical realm through use of the inner senses. It is only when we are better aware of the natural principles by which Consciousness operates – particularly Divine Love – and practiced in our use of the inner senses, will we be able to begin to create and manipulate physical forms *consciously* – and sustain them in time.

We have known for a long time that physical matter is essentially energy being "held" in a particular vibrational frequency. We perceive different frequencies to be different "things." What we don't realize is that this holding of energy is sustained on a moment by moment basis, and managed by the various individualized forms of Consciousness under the natural principles and natural powers. Things do not "grow," they change form; they change their vibrational frequency. Moreover, time does not govern the rate of change in vibrational frequency, that rate is managed by the physical expression's *embodiment* of the power of Divine Love. This is why cancerous cells that take "time" to "grow," can take relatively no time to change back into healthy form.[64]

Seth makes the assertion that "Matter does not grow."[65] There are obvious hints to the validity of this statement found in examination of the matter of any "growing" organism. Your body, for example, completely replaces its cells – the entirety of its matter – in around seven years. In other words, the crucial physical matter that constituted the physical structure of your Self seven years ago has "disappeared" to be replaced by completely new cells that observe the natural power of Divine Love.

Another example, would be the transformation (that is, energy-pattern transformation under the natural principle of *energy transformation*) of a caterpillar into a butterfly – a rather obvious demonstration of the more complex issues involved in physical change and development of an expression of

Consciousness than can be described by "growth." We imagine that children *grow* into adults, that plants *grow* from seeds, and that life forms *evolve* by random mutations of the gene pool. These beliefs persist despite the physical evidence before our scientific eyes that suggests subtler forces are at work.

SAY THAT AGAIN (9) The natural power of Divine Love

Divine Love is a primary measure of all existence; "... all things exist within this law and are created out of it."[66] It is a natural principle pertaining to an innate quality of Consciousness that promotes the maximum development of every expression of Itself. Divine Love provides the impetus toward all creative action in physical and non-physical terms. It is behind the reasons *why* creations occur. Consciousness inherently nurtures every aspect of our evolvement, creativity and happiness through Divine Love in a *cooperative* lifelong endeavor – for the maximum benefit of everyone and everything.

Incidentally, when we consider the "lifelong" (unrestricted by time) endeavor of your Essence self, Divine Love operates as a tool for its expansion, evolution and development. *Reincarnation*[67] is one way in which your Essence self exploits the natural power of Divine Love.

The Natural Power of Attraction

We can think of Divine Love as a feature of Consciousness that can help us fathom the reasons behind *why* we create our physical reality. Without it, there would be no *form* of physical existence for us to perceive through our senses – either inner or outer senses. The natural power of Attraction, on the other hand, helps us to understand *how* we create our reality.

The power of Attraction and that of Divine Love feature in most channeled literature. Over the last decade, under the title of "Law of Attraction (LOA)," the natural power of Attraction has gained notoriety as *the* mysterious rule or law governing the creation of your reality. Many in the Mind/Body/Spirit movement have highlighted it as such since it came to prominence with the release of *The Secret* in 2006.[68] The book you are currently reading will have you realize that reality creation isn't quite as simple as understanding and adhering to one metaphysical ruling alone.

The power of Attraction is most definitely an important natural principle involved with the mechanics of how you form your reality. However, as Alexandra Bruce helps to point out in her book *Beyond the Secret*, when taken out of context, extracted from the other interweaving natural principles, and without due deference given to Divine Love, which explains the why of creation, knowledge of the LOA is unlikely to provide you with *the* answer to your creational woes.

The metaphysical descriptions of this natural principle underpinning how we create our reality are generally succinct but non-too enlightening, "… all that is like unto itself will be drawn to it."[69] and, "You are the attractor of everything that comes into your experience."[70] being examples.

The general idea is that we each incorporate a psychological force that behaves in a similar fashion to a magnetic field.[71] You are essentially a "magnet," drawing to yourself not iron filings but the *probable realities*[72] that best express a reflection of the complexion of your personality!

Let me explain. Energy has electro-*magnetic* properties. Thoughts are an electromagnetic energy form and they, along with everything else in physical and non-physical realities, attract other forms of energy of a similar "vibrational signature." The natural power of Attraction allows all forms of

Consciousness (including you) the ability to experience their Selves. The reality you perceive to be "out there" is actually a reflection of the accumulated electromagnetic energies you build through your thoughts, beliefs and emotions. In other words, what you perceive to be real—the reality you draw to you is a reflection of your Mind, a mirror of the state of your psychological Self.

Here is how Bashar (Darryl Anka), makes this point:

What you put out is what you get back. The energy you give off based on your beliefs – your emotions, your behavior – the [tonal frequency] you give off is what determines the kind of reality experience you have. Because physical reality doesn't exist except as a reflection of what you most strongly believe is true for you. That is all physical reality is – it is literally like a mirror.

If you are looking in a mirror and you see your face with a frown on it, you know that you don't go over to the mirror and try to force the reflection to smile – you must smile first. There is no way to change the reflection without you smiling first.

But, you can also conversely understand that when you decide to smile the reflection has no choice but to return the smile, because it doesn't have a mind of its own.

So the idea to understand is that physical reality very much is really like a mirror – it will not change until you do first. But if you do, it has no choice but to follow suit because it is only a reflection of what you have put out.[73]

The power of Attraction describes how you attract to yourself one of innumerable probable realities available to you in the moment point of now – the *spacious present*. The message that comes with this natural power is how important it is to monitor the thoughts you entertain, as they will attract similar thoughts, which gain energy in their assembly and thus become more *real*. If your

accumulated thoughts run contrary to the natural power of
Divine Love, then you will eventually encounter challenges
within your life. If they are in accordance with Divine Love, you
are on a roll!

SAY THAT AGAIN (10) The Natural Power of Attraction.

Otherwise known as the Law of Attraction (LOA), it is one
of an important set of "natural principles" that relates to
how you create your reality. This particular principle
pertains to the electromagnetic properties of your
thoughts, beliefs and emotions and how these psychological elements combine to form the "tonal frequency" of
your personality – which, in accordance with this law,
attracts to you energy forms, and "probable realities," of a
similar resonating frequency.

The moral sense that offers a vital ethical code

When you come to understand fully the existential qualities of
Divine Love, you will find that its power exudes a primary moral
sensibility by which all life operates. Precisely because Divine
Love is at the forefront of the operating system Consciousness
uses to get to know Itself – thus underpinning *all* existence –
there arises from it a vital ethical code that dictates how all
sentient life should behave in order to sustain their own
existence. We can interpret this vital ethical code as, *"do not
violate."*

It is not a question of whether following this code is right or
wrong – again, like all of the inner, natural principles – it's
simply how things are. Your free will allows you to live by it or
not to live by it. What your inner self will remind you of
constantly throughout your life though, is that to not live by it

compromises your own existence in the physical realm.

In the non-physical realm, your Essence self adheres to this code, as it knows that ultimately, that's how things work for the best outcomes. Your inner self, emissary to your Essence self, uses various means to make your outer self aware of when attunement to this vital code of being is lost or wavering. Apart from compromising your existence, when you are not in harness with Divine Love from which it emanates, you are not being natural to whom you are.

If we split the word "natural" into "nature" and "all," it becomes more obvious where we can find Divine Love and its vital ethical code expressed – throughout all of nature. Divine Love and non-violation are principles intrinsic to the world of nature, defined by the *Collins English Dictionary* as, "the whole system of the existence, forces and events of the physical world that are not controlled by human beings." If you would like to include yourself as part of nature, they are thus intrinsic to your Self as well.

Systems that human beings do control, the realities we create together, also need to be in tune with this natural power and vital code. In this, we need to develop a postmodern worldview that incorporates ecological awareness (awareness of these intrinsic principles) as well as recognize that there are no actual boundaries between our Selves and reality – as every "nature-all" *thing* is both a projection of human consciousness, and ***ultimately** a projection of Consciousness Itself.*

Do not violate

Metaphysical literature defines a violation as a deliberate act to end, harm or undermine the physical or psychological freedom of another expression of Consciousness.

The code of non-violation is relatively easy to adopt and comply with in relation to living things – do not indulge in physical or psychological acts of violence towards yourself or other selves, be they human, animal or any other life form. However, on reading the definition again, you will find non-violation also applies to inorganic compounds – we need to appreciate and respect *all forms of matter* as expressions of Consciousness cooperating in the creation of our reality.

With this fullest meaning in mind, we can better understand that we violate the Earth's body (the physical manifestation of the consciousness of "Gaia") by our constant manipulation and extraction of her resources without paying due consideration to her existence and the effects of such actions on the existence of other expressions of Consciousness on our planet. To comply with the vital code of non-violation requires nurturing a real appreciation and love of the natural world. Nature, which includes your Self, constantly reminds us of the beauty of the natural principle of creation, the means by which Consciousness expresses Itself. So don't forget to ask permission of a pebble to take it from its beach!

Okay, I can see that we can manage the forests and plant life by replacing trees and growing afresh; but if we can't kill anything to eat, are we all to become vegetarians? And what will befall me if I swat a fly or tread on an ant? Surely we can kill nasty viruses and bacteria?

The Seth Material and several other channeled teachings, notably Omni (John L. Payne) in *Omni Reveals the Four Principles of Creation*, present answers to these sorts of questions that stem from consideration of the broader aspects of non-violation. Suffice to say here that Divine Love and the natural principles infuse the natural world with a much deeper appreciation of the act of killing than we currently hold. The natural world *always* achieves this transition from the physical to the non-physical with due mutual regard for its necessity (one animal killing another for food, for example) and the integrity of the event.[74]

Our current understanding of death, the transition from the

physical realm to the non-physical plane, engenders fear – which, according to Elias (Mary Ennis), is an emotion that indicates we have a deep lack of understanding! Fear always indicates an absence of understanding. When we come to understand our death to be *a transitional phase of our existence*, we shall be in a better position to understand and appreciate all life as a joyous, creative, self-aware expression of Consciousness.

Non-violation is the most vital code you need to follow when living your life as it emanates from the natural power of Divine Love. It should therefore be at the forefront of all of your thinking and doing.

Following on from this base standard for maintaining your existence, you do of course need to take heed of the physical laws we currently place our faith in. The law of Gravity, for example, will operate for you on the vast majority of occasions – so don't go jumping off a cliff expecting to fly gracefully to the bottom – such feats are not yet achievable within our current set of belief systems!

Natural guilt and unnatural guilt

Your inner self, in association with the energies of feelings (explored in the final chapters of this book), issues instant notices to your conscious-mind whenever your actions transgress the code of non-violation. Your inner self alerts your outer self to this because not only have you breached the vital code, but you are also, in doing so, placing your outer self *outside* the natural power of Divine Love. Remember, you have the will to live either within it or outside of it. To continue such actions will eventually compromise your enjoyment of life and ultimately, your very existence.

The "instant notice" (to some it will be during the act, to others immediately afterwards) you will experience when committing a violation is the *feeling* of *"natural guilt."*

Natural guilt results from transgressing the code of non-violation. The feeling of guilt is essentially a message from your inner self telling you to stop acting in this way – *for your own good*. This is essentially what the feeling of natural guilt is all about.

There is though, another feeling that we confuse with natural guilt, which is unnatural in origin. Seth refers to this feeling as "artificial guilt."

Artificial guilt stems from the transgression of laws and ethical codes constructed *as part of a particular belief system.* You may be experiencing a sense of guilt, but you need to ask yourself whether your actions are a violation against your being or another being, or they are contrary to a system of beliefs you hold.

For example, feeling guilty about performing a sexual act because you believe it to be wrong or sinful can produce artificial guilt. It is not the same feeling of guilt as natural guilt because in such a case you are simply transgressing the ethical codes laid down by a belief system of some kind. Provided the act is consensual if involving others, and enjoyed, it is not a violation. The beliefs in question could be to do with your beliefs on sexuality and its expression or your religious beliefs that dictate approved methods of sexual expression.

Natural guilt will occur if the act has violated your Self or another Self. Rape is therefore a violation producing natural guilt. If the natural feeling, which demands the cessation of such actions, does not occur, or the individual represses it, a psychotic disorder either exists or can develop.

The *natural principles* and the *natural powers* form a platform from which to understand better what is going on with your inner and outer worlds of expression. These forces are intimately involved in the construction of your physical environment. For you to absorb the principles behind why and how we create our realities, you need to experience their presence for yourself. That is, you can only achieve a thorough comprehension and appreci-ation of the validity of these principles and powers by directly applying them to your own mental actions and physical behaviors. To do this, you must become familiar with, and begin exercising, the inner senses that your Essence self holds in readiness.

The *inner senses* provide a gateway into a much broader understanding of your Self and how you create your reality. You can utilize them in uncovering psychological and emotional restraints that not only impede the full expression of your personality, but also prevent you from engaging fully with your life's intent and purpose. They also allow you to understand your connection, or otherwise, to family members and other individuals of importance in your life.

From a societal point of view, learning to use our inner senses will re-energize our communication with others as the inner senses cannot but work within the natural principles – *cooperation* in particular. The inner senses take us beyond empathy for others into a mutually deep understanding of the differences we choose to express in our world – an understanding that *allows* for differ-ences rather than judging them.

Re-awakening to the natural principles by exercising your inner senses is a primary message conveyed by many channeled sources. By doing so, you are able to ease your transition through the momentous period we are calling the *Shift*.

CHAPTER 5

THE GENERA OF THE INTENT OF HUMAN CONSCIOUSNESS

At the end of *Chapter 2* we had put together the basic elements that make up your non-physical self – aspects of your *Essence self* (soul if you wish). Your Essence has its own unique inviolate *Identity* as well as an *inner self*, dedicated to maintaining your physical self's well-being. You also have a *subconscious* area within your Mind that acts as a vast library of knowledge as well as the meeting ground between your inner and outer psychological structures.

From *Chapter 3* you will be aware that the inner self has at its disposal a set of *inner senses* that are far more adept at providing an in-depth analysis of your mental and physical reality than the five physical senses championed by your ego-self. After all, they can inform you of the "being-ness" (vibrational signature) of another person or thing (empathic inner senses); the being-ness of an idea (conceptual inner senses); and the durability and consistency of such expressions of Consciousness in relation to time (time-based inner senses). You should now also be reasonably conversant with the "rules" (*natural principles and powers*) under which the inner senses function if you are to utilize them *consciously* in playing the game of life.

Before you rush back onto the playing field armed with this new found awareness, it would be prudent to first avail yourself of the skills you bring to the game – the unique behavioral actions you can contribute, what it is you are naturally good at doing. Most of us have no idea as to the innate skills and abilities we bring to the world, or we have spent most of our lives denying their expression for one reason or another. This book and the ones that follow will help you reveal to your conscious-mind your inherent talents so that when you get back into the game you can effortlessly display those talents and enjoy yourself!

Intent expressed through you

How does your Essence self choose to express itself in the physical domain? According to several channeled sources, your outer self's physical expression conforms to a special configuration of intent – intent being *the way energy (from Source/Consciousness) directs your actions*. There are distinct, discernible patterns to the way you, as an individual, can express the omnipresent force of intent. Your actions – your *behaviors* – are primarily governed by these patterns of expression. Your personality conforms to a discrete and distinguishable blend of intentional drives in order to voice itself in the physical world. Moreover, your Essence self chooses – **before it individuates itself for entry into the physical domain** – which way it will express intent through the physical you, through your personality.

Seth made an important contribution to our understanding of the different expressions of intent within human consciousness. Because we understand a "family" to mean a distinguishable primary bloodline produced by unique individual variations, Seth exploited this meaning for the word "family" in a metaphor to help us comprehend the differing ways in which we express intent through our actions. By calling the different intentional leanings the *"families* of consciousness" – which are described in *The Unknown Reality, Volume II* – he provides a sense of idiosyncratic variations within a themed unity of focus – a family.

He focused upon nine such "families" of intent, with emphasis drawn to his so-called "Sumari" family's intentional leanings as he, Jane Roberts and her husband Robert Butts all belonged to this particular "psychic grouping." In *The Unknown Reality, Volume II*, Robert Butts summarises the function of Sumari intent as providing "the cultural, spiritual, and artistic heritage for the species."[75]

In the main, other channeled sources agree on "psychical groupings" describing humanity's display of intent.[76] The metaphysical literature suggests then that as with the differing physical races within humans, we have differing *"psychical races"* – psychological frameworks that display their own distinct abilities and characteristics. These psychical leanings are similar to the classification of personality *types* used in psychology, although they are far more complex because of their interdependency. For ease of understanding, you should be aware that there are nine loosely delineated ways in which human intent expresses itself. As a human, all of your behaviors fall within these distinguishable subtleties of expression.

SAY THAT AGAIN (11) Nine basic expressions of human intent

The human articulation of intent loosely conforms to nine distinguishable types of expression – first referred to by Seth as the *families of consciousness*. Essentially, they are differing developmental paths of activity peculiar to humankind, involved with the growth, learning and evolution of each individual and humanity itself. Although your personality encapsulates all types of intentional drives, it chooses to experience the physical dimension with particular expressions of intent to the fore.

Belonging to and aligning with

The Elias (Mary Ennis), Kris (Serge Grandbois), and Rose (Joanne Helfrich) teachings add complexity to the concept of human intent as they tell us that whilst your Essence self *belongs to* a particular family of intent (in relative perpetuity), your personality also *aligns* itself with a family for your current lifetime.[77]

The alignment family is "chosen" by your Essence to support your overall Self's growth and development. Remember that the force of intent encompasses expansion and evolvement through creation and experience – which leads to the evolution of your consciousness, the evolution of humankind's collective consciousness – and ultimately, the evolution of Consciousness Itself.

We can translate the subtle nuances of human intent, our psychical leanings, into dominant interests, roles and physical pursuits. With the help of several channeled teachings on this subject, it is possible to come up with simplified and succinct generic names for the nine types of human intent. Below is a minimal guide to this typology. You can find a fuller description of how these "genera" or families of intent transfer to the personality characteristics that drive human activity in *Appendix III*.

Your current personality's family of *alignment* may become vaguely apparent to you if you compare descriptions with the concerns and interests that are at the forefront of your mind. In addition, gauge which of the actions described by a family resonates with what you *like* to do, what activity brings you the greatest pleasure.

Alternatively, which of the described actions would you like to do most given the right circumstances, the time and the resources? Does any one of your passions appear within the listing?

Don't worry if more than one family seems to resonate with you. You can have more than one family in alignment, they are constantly merging with one another, and *all* have expression to some degree through your personality. Just have some fun at this stage seeing what comes up for you as you read through the descriptions.

The nine families of human intent

- **TEACHERS** – an intent to keep and convey knowledge in its purest form. A focus upon accuracy and detail. An aim to encourage originality through teaching.
- **SPIRITUALISTS** – explorers of the spiritual and mystical. A great connection with nature.
- **INNOVATORS** – vital, inventive, innovative and creatively aggressive. Inclined towards forming social systems and organizations.
- **REFORMERS** – restless and passionate about reformation. A focus upon examining, challenging and changing the status-quo.
- **EXCHANGERS**– an intent to spread ideas and information amongst all cultures. Enjoy traveling in order to trade religious, social and political concepts.
- **ARTISTS** – non-conformist *doers*. Artistically inclined. Apt to speak out for change and the expression of creativity through the arts. A playful sense of humor. Prone to be impatient.
- **HEALERS** – an ability to "read" the distortions or "disease" of energy flow within physical and non-physical structures. A primary focus upon the healing of physical, spiritual, and psychological structures within cultures and individuals.
- **IMAGERS** –a focus upon the aesthetics of design and appearance of physical forms. An intent to bring the fullest expression of physical forms, particularly the human body, into manifestation.
- **NURTURERS** –possessing the qualities of patience, affection and understanding. An intent focused upon the nurturing of individuals, particularly children in relation to a balanced, healthy upbringing.

The channeled literature that supports this arrangement of the types of human intent is quick to point out that this separation is solely to do with ease of understanding. Elias adds that we should not consider them as absolutes – personality characteristics that we unerringly adhere to under all circumstances. Instead, they mean to convey *the key elements of a distinct line of human intent*. As the Rose (Joanne Helfrich)[78] character chides "... do not make the mistake of thinking of these types as groups or tribes that exclude others. This will not be a healthy expression of your Divine Source." In other words, don't imagine that any one family of characteristics, *your* alignment family, is superior to or more desirable than another.

Furthermore, as your personality contains all of these expressions of intent to some degree, the varying extents to which your personality exercises any one of a family's characteristics can increase or decrease within you in relation to an experience. For example, the Healers intent aspect of your personality would come to the fore (ordinarily) when confronted with someone in obvious need, especially a loved one.

The crucial point for us to understand about these intricacies of intent expression is that your personality *usually* (this is not an exact science) adheres to the characteristics displayed by one of these genera (families) listed above. This "alignment" is your *primary intent*, your preferred area of activity – what you like to do, the roles you prefer to adopt, what truly "floats your boat." Your family of alignment is a fundamental statement of character that your personality has chosen to explore in your current lifetime.

With this understood, you can then add to this the complexity of your Essence self's intentional leanings. Your Essence comes with its own "psychic grouping" – a family of intent to which it *belongs*.

Your Essence self, more specifically its family of belonging, continuously influences your personality, and in so doing *brings subtlety and definition* to your alignment family's characteristics. *Discovering your own combination of both of these intentional directors can have you realize the general purpose of your current life.* One of the functions of your inner self is to ensure that your outer self does not stray too far off this purposeful intentional path.

Here is an example of how this complexity of intent translates to the real world:

If your personality's family of *alignment* is Artists (artistically inclined), then you may gravitate towards doing something artistic as a main occupation – the *overtly expressed* intent. Let's say you become a painter. Now if your Essence' family of *belonging* is Teachers (teaching, accuracy of information transfer), then this *subtly expressed* underlying intent may draw you to teach art, with a probable penchant for fine art (attention to detail).

This is but one extrapolation drawn from numerous possible activities that remain in accordance with these families of alignment and belonging. This combination of alignment and belonging can just as easily produce a fulfilling path in life for someone involved with educational reform – promoting change (Artists intent) in teaching methods (Teachers intent). In other words, your intentional leanings do not necessarily restrict the fields of activity you can successfully engage with. You can mine life fulfillment from virtually any field of endeavor provided you focus upon those activities that allow you to express your intentional leanings.

A purposeful intentional path

Your *purpose* in life has nothing to do with fate. Imagining that fate governs your actions is actually a distorted interpretation of the subconscious knowledge you hold regarding your life's purpose. You may find it prudent in future to say that, *"my purpose took hold,"* rather than, "fate conspired against me." For most of us, it is extremely unlikely that there is but one particular occupation that we *must* follow. You have though; chosen intentional themes to explore that shape your purpose for this lifetime.

You can think of the genera of human intent as a palette of nine main colors that you use to paint your reality. As with Picasso and his "blue period," you restrict your use of color to the hues and tones of one of these nine genera, apply definition with the hues and tones of another, and occasionally make use of the other seven. Like Picasso, you are exploring and experimenting with your chosen primary color for a time – in your case, your lifetime. The reason you adhere (most of the time) to your family of alignment is to do with the development of the entirety of your Self. Your inner self constantly seeks to remind you of your purpose derived from your intentional leanings. Your purpose is a developmental goal you have set for your Self.

Choosing your own expressions of intent

Seth and Elias make the important point that when it comes to "choosing" your intentional leanings – *your individuality comes first.*

What they mean by this is that when Consciousness Units (CUs) in the Subjective Area coalesce to form your Essence self with its unique Identity, as a matter of course they also begin to define the psychic structure that forms your individuality – the *individualized* you. Your individualized intent becomes your innate intent – which fuels the activities of your Essence self.

The CUs create an independent, individual identity with its own characteristics of expression. These traits of your identity generally imitate those of one of the genera of human intent, or as Seth puts it, "... your individuality *places you* in a particular family or species of consciousness."[79] Elias parallels this statement by saying that your Essence is not "born into" a particular family, it "magnates" (sic) to one, "... the family being the magnet. You within your individual intents are the metals being drawn to the families."[80]

Therefore, your *Essence* doesn't so much *choose* a family of intent, as naturally gravitate toward one that has intentional drives in sympathy with its own individualized character traits. The complexities behind how the CUs elect a family of *belonging* for your Essence Identity relate to the balancing processes of the collective psyche/intent of humankind – a subject beyond the scope of the introductory aim of this book.

Now, when it comes to your current personality's family of *alignment*, again, highly complex issues are involved, but yes, you, the greater You, get to choose this one. Well, sort of! This time, decisions as to your current personality's psychic structure and nuances of intent are inexorably linked to the balancing of your Self's identity and individuality. Your overt personality type is decided upon by your Essence self. It *chooses* from the intentional paths of activity of the nine families which is the most appropriate for your personality to align with, in consideration of your Self's development. Your Essence "usually" chooses one family for alignment, but it may have you align with more than one – again, a complexity that we shall leave for another time. Your Essence carries out this alignment process "before" you are physically born. Elias:

> Each individual manifest [current personality] incorporates an intent, a reason that they have manifest into this physical reality, an intent that they had focused upon before they chose to manifest within this physical reality.[81]

So the choosing of your families of intent is subtle in its action. How subtle is difficult for us to understand as we continue to adhere to the belief that *outside* forces create our reality, rather than the metaphysical fact that it is created first *inside* by our Selves.

Along with the omnipresent force of intent comes choice. If

intent is all about growth and evolution through creation and experience, then choices need to be made on how this is achieved. As we are imbued with intent, *we consequently always have choice*, even when it comes to choosing our families of intent. During our lives, it is possible to change our allegiances to the families, although Elias reminds us that such a choice is an extremely rare event.

Asked as to the importance of knowing our families of affiliation – *belonging* and *alignment* – Elias states that from one aspect we can take it to be important, as its value is in the understanding of our Selves, our personal intent, and the reality we create for ourselves. A serious warning added to this statement was that we should not overplay the importance of this knowledge. This is because we collectively entertain belief systems at present that stimulate a need in some of us to exaggerate important concepts for self-centered (egotistical) reasons, or to foolishly imagine that an "ultimate blueprint" exists to explain all of creation.

The importance should not be exaggerated to be all-consuming; for this creates more belief systems, and you shall create your cults around your belief systems of your families![82]

Colorful characters

In developing our understanding of the genera of human intent, Elias informs us that we can attribute each family or genus with a color.[83] This is possible as each family has a particular "tone" and a resonance in vibrational quality that, from the physical perspective, we can associate with the different wavelengths of light that we perceive as colors. You may perceive a color or colors when you practice *Exercise 1* of *Chapter 2*. If so, this could be an echo of your unique intentional tone – your *vibrational signature*.

We can extend this analogy between color and intent somewhat further. We know that within the seven distinct hues in the color spectrum there are millions of different hues. Similarly, within the nine distinguishing features of the families of intent there are myriad tones – subdivisions of the originating family. You could say that there are families within the genera that express extremely subtle differences within tone (or hue).

Even though certain colors associate with the genera of intent, thus hinting at numerous familial subdivisions, we should not let our Victorian love for categorizing carry us away. While partitioning the structures of the physical domain can aid our understanding of the physical, it is not a method to rely upon when fathoming the features of our consciousness. In the subjective world of shifting vibrational boundaries, we need to dissolve our desire for division.

The defining lines between the different hues of our personalities are very thin. To illustrate this point, think of the subtlety in difference between identical twins within a conventional family. Surface, physical features may well be virtually the same, and preferences within life-style choices may be remarkably similar, but there is no denying that distinctions remain within the subjective area of the expression of their personalities.

Human consciousness is entering a phase of dramatic expansion and further sophistication. Another level of complexity within self-awareness awaits us. *Total Self*-awareness affords us the opportunity to take our individuation to new heights in terms of choice of experience. The choices do have some limitations, although, from our physical point of view, there would appear to be no restrictions whatsoever.

Choices are "confined" to the manner in which intent is explored through the collective psyche of humanity. The ubiquitous force of intent took on distinguishing characteristics as it permeated the psychological bedrock of humankind.

According to the channeled literature, we can associate the types of intent steering humankind's physical activity to nine "families" or "genera." These primordial "psychic races" are not absolute truths (consistent to all dimensions within Consciousness) as they either do not exist or have different characteristics in other dimensions. They are, however, the guiding intent behind all of the choices and decisions we make in creating our individual and en masse realities.

A contemporary coincidence

Many channeled sources refer to the subject of coincidence. Contrary to our scientific worldview's assessment of coincidence being inconsequential – a happening due to nothing more than chance – metaphysical teachers insist there is greater meaning behind such occurrences.

When exploring today's plethora of personality profiling systems in an attempt to discover a contemporary approach that might offer some form of validation for the metaphysical literature's descriptions of the differing characteristics and intentional roles contained within our personalities, a coincidence occurred.

The search for a comparable approach for assessing the shifting shapes of our personalities uncovered a system that is similar in many ways to the genera of human intent typology. This is the *Enneagram* system, which *coincidentally* settles upon nine basic types, assigning numbers to distinguish between them.

Study of the Enneagram system reveals parallels in thinking that indicate an intuitive, deeper understanding of the human intent concept. One example of this is the use of differing colors within explanation, reflecting the earlier analogy of the hues and tones of color used in channeled teachings to illustrate the subtly shifting vibrational boundaries occurring within the expression of our personalities.

The origins of Enneagram theory have become clouded by the mists of time. It is believed to have been part of a program of spiritual enlightenment passed down through several religious doctrines, primarily Sufi mysticism from Islam. Georgei Ivanovitch Gurdjieff (1866–1949), a spiritual teacher around the time of Carl G. Jung (1875—1961), devised a self-development system originally called the *Fourth Way* and later *The Work,* which revived interest in Enneagram theory. Present day proponents of the theory have taken up Jung's ideas on the Self (briefly reviewed at the end of *Chapter 7*) and the psyche in order to explain the idiosyncrasies of its personality profiling system.

Like the genera of human intent concept, your "enneatype" isn't so much defining *who* you are as what it is you are drawn to *do* – your intentional leanings. In other words, it doesn't describe your personality as much as help define the behavioral habits you are moved to explore. Like your family of *alignment,* your enneatype is a life-long psychological patterning. The system even encompasses a secondary influencing feature of the personality, called a "wing," which can be equated with the subtle persuasions of your family of *belonging.*

It may be that Gurdjieff and his forebears when formulating the Enneagram System were "channeling" into a vein of knowledge deep within their subconscious minds. The "families of consciousness" metaphor to explain human intent promoted by Seth and other channeled guides is a more recent interpretation of how the ubiquitous drive of intent forms and affects our individuality.

Channeled guides categorically state that there is no such thing as a coincidence; they clarify this assertion by explaining that a coincidence is an event that emanates from your Essence self. It is a means, a psychological signal, a synchronicity that plays with your time-based inner senses, by which your inner self can get your outer self's attention. There is always a meaning associated with coincidence, although for your conscious-mind to fathom exactly what the meaning is can prove to be formidable. On this occasion, the "coincidence" of *nine* personality types led to an investigation of a methodology that appears to go some way on the lengthy road to understanding our Selves.

Do the roles and personality traits of the nine families mirror the traits assigned to the nine enneatypes?

Some characteristics do in fact transfer across the systems admirably, but by no means is there a complete match of groupings. However, if we bear in mind all that has been said about the myriad combinations involved in the expression of intent, the subtlety of enunciation, the overlapping nature of their hues and the constant fluctuations in the primacy of expression of any particular family through time, it is hardly surprising to find such a looseness of fit.

Again, our desire to delineate and categorize physical things does not decode too well when dealing with the non-physical psyche. Enneagram theory nonetheless remains a valiant attempt to fathom the complexity of intent as expressed through human personality.

The aim of the following exercise is to give you an idea of which family of intent you are most in *alignment* with for this lifetime. When you have repeated this exercise a few times, you should have a reasonable idea of which role you are naturally inclined to adopt and/or what form of activity consistently brings you enjoyment and fulfillment. The notes and doodles you make will offer clues as to your intentional leanings. Read the exercise through a few times before settling down to do it. You will need to have your work journal and pen handy for making notes and sketches.

EXERCISE 2: FINDING YOUR ALIGNMENT

Sit as comfortably as you possibly can with legs uncrossed, feet on the ground.

Take a couple of deep breaths, breathing in through

your nose and out through your mouth.

Mentally scan slowly through your body, starting at your feet, relaxing any muscles that appear cramped, and allow your jaw to open slightly when you get to your head. Quieten your thoughts and instruct yourself that you will deal with any invasive thoughts later. Just relax.

Now read through this exercise a couple of times to the end to remind yourself of what to do.

This exercise is about recording those moments in your life that have brought you a deep sense of fulfillment.

You will call to mind those times when your actions naturally and effortlessly flowed. You are going to identify those times when you felt passionate and energized about doing something – it doesn't matter what it was you were doing, but it made you feel really good about yourself. You will recall the interests and activities that have consistently drawn your attention to them. They could be actions that others may have commented upon as being something not worthy of your energies – **you** though, have a sense that such actions are right for you. You will bring to mind those moments when time just flew by, as you were so absorbed with and enthused by what you were *doing*.

You will bring to mind episodes that made you feel good about *your self*, – doing an activity, or fulfilling a role of some description. These are moments in your life that brought you more than just a feeling of satisfaction – as when eating a favorite ice cream, or simply enjoying sexual activity.

Close your eyes and begin by casting you mind back to your early childhood. Take yourself to a time when you had no beliefs, no hormones running riot, you just **did** things; particularly things that brought you pleasure. Settle upon a time when you were very young and enjoying yourself, doing something you loved to do, either on your own or with others. Recall your favorite way of playing – if told to "go and play," what would you go and do? What was your favorite color when you were a young child?

Take a moment to focus your attention on that time and when you have a bit of detail to record, open your eyes and note down what you recall – or make a quick sketch if you like.

Don't take too long to make notes, then close your eyes again and bring your awareness to another time when you were young, perhaps in your teens, when you were absorbed in what you were doing, a time when doing what you were doing made you feel really good about yourself. Did you love to wear clothes of a particular color?

After you have captured some details of this second moment, open your eyes again and make a note or a little sketch of what you were doing. If others were involved, note this down. Begin to feel *right now* the pleasurable emotions you felt then.

Now close your eyes once again and let your emotions and thoughts take you to another time, it may be a time as an adult, when you experienced similar emotions in doing what you were doing.

This is another past time when you were being totally absorbed by the experience because it was an experience that stimulated positive emotions - your actions flowed naturally and with no mental effort, no resistance, even though physically it may have been demanding. Were you fulfilling a particular role?

Take a few moments to glean some details of this

experience, and when ready, open your eyes and note down the experience. Remember to make a special note of the *doing* aspects of the pleasurable experience and any colors that may have come to mind. Were you engaged in a specific activity? Were you doing something with others or alone? What was the general theme behind what you were doing?

Don't worry if you only have a few sketchy notes or could only recall one or two moments of great fulfillment. Take your time and go over what you have and as you focus upon a particular experience feel free to add anything, however abstract, to your notes. Just add any more details that have now come to mind.

After completing the exercise, focus your thoughts on any predominant theme of activity or consistent role you seem to be playing that appears to link together the different moments of recall. What, if anything, appears to emerge from your notes carrying a banner of significance? If you can figure out a theme to your activities, or spot a role you like to adopt, but have no colors noted down, ask yourself which color would resonate with your predominant theme or role – don't think about it – just note what color first comes to mind.

Armed with your notes, primary theme, and color if any, first go back to the brief synopses of the activities and traits relating to *"the nine families of human intent"* listed earlier in this chapter and see how they compare. Remember that the descriptions of the families are highly generalized and they overlap and inter-relate with each other, so you may find that more than one family appears to connect with your notes. Jot down the family (or two) that most closely aligns with your mental and physical notes about your predominant or significant activity.

When you have done this, go to *Appendix III* where you will find the families defined more clearly along with their assigned colors. Compare your notes on your possible family of alignment with the fuller description and see if the color you have noted marries with the one assigned to it.

If you can easily link the activity to a family of intent, and the color you have confirms the family – intend to pat yourself on your back! Don't worry if nothing quite worked out on your first experience of this exercise; and don't assume that if you *seem* to have a result, then you're done with this exercise. Practice it, do it several times over several weeks and then take an average of your results. Fluctuations in your results from this exercise are to do with the timing of the exercise. A particular family, not necessarily your family of alignment, may be to the fore because of the circumstances affecting your personality at the time of doing the exercise.

You will know when you are done when you *feel* a deep connection to the family of intent that consistently figures in this exercise.

Rather than squeeze all of the vital information about the families of human intent into another *Say That Again* box, below is a synopsis of the important things to know about how the life force of *intent* expresses itself through the medium of humanity, and the individuality of your Self.

Ten things about the nine families of human intent

1 *There are not necessarily nine!* Nine is the number arrived at by casting a *genera*-lizing eye over the vast number of directional paths of intent we can explore in the physical domain. It is important that you understand the families of intent, for you are not simply associated with them, *they*

are very much a part of you. They are the innate driving force behind the consciousness of humanity.

The families are not "levels" of consciousness or part of a spiritual development process that we can aspire to; they are groups of psychical assemblies cooperating in the exploration of the potentials of human consciousness. While working interdependently, each family holds its own focus of intent. The families are groupings of intent within Consciousness especially drawn to our physical dimension and the creation of it.

2 *Their presentation has nothing to do with separation.* The families are not specific to gender or race as they encompass all of humankind. Because of our propensity for categorization, reductionism and division – and then forming judgments on our separations – it is important to remember that *no one family is "better" than another.* Metaphysical literature offers the "families of consciousness" metaphor as an aid for understanding what is essentially *the Source energies that steer our actions and our Selves.*

3 *These Source energies – directional intents – translate within your individual psyche (Mind)* as a predisposition to teach, connect with nature, innovate, reform, exchange ideas, promote change through the arts, holistically heal, design the perfect form, and nurture. Following your personal predisposition, your path of intent, gains you a life of fulfillment.

Humanity's collective consciousness maintains checks and balances on the proportional representations of the genera of human intent in respect of the collective fulfillment and evolution of humanity. Their interdependency engenders – *intends to encourage* – balanced, healthy psychological and physical communities.

4 *Each family of intent holds a vibrational tone* associated

with its direction of intent – as does any individual expression of intent. We each have a *vibrational frequency* within us that describes our individualized intent.

You can liken a family's tone to the varying wavelengths of light within the visible spectrum – certain colors approximate to their vibrational tones. Elias (Mary Ennis) assigns the seven primary colors we see in refracted light – red through to violet (including indigo) to seven of the nine families. Pink (a hue between red and magenta) and black (because of its absorption of all other wavelengths) are "best fit" colors describing the vibrational tones of the Nurturers and Teachers families respectively.

5 *The genera of human intent are not a truth.* A truth is a facet of Consciousness that remains consistent and unchanging across all dimensions, and as such, the genera do not qualify as a truth; they are an artifact of our physical dimension. There are other groupings of intentional direction within other dimensions, with differing numbers of generality. The nine generalities of the genera of human intent are peculiar to our own physical reality.

6 *We each embody the intentional qualities of all nine families of human intent.* We are therefore, on occasion, capable of expressing any one of the nine families' idiosyncrasies of character. Because of this, the timing and/or circumstances of an attempted enquiry into our own predominating affiliations can thwart our efforts.

7 *Our Essence self does not form itself "first" and then join with a particular family* because of similar intentional leanings. Nor is it born into, or spring from within, one of the families.

Because the linearity of time blinkers our perception, and we are unused to the concept of "simultaneous time" in the "spacious present," we create a distorted view of how our individuated Identity, our Essence, forms and becomes part of a family grouping. In actuality, our Essence self configures its characteristics of intent and "becomes" part of a sympathetic family all within the continuing "moment" of the *spacious present*.

8 *Your Essence self "belongs to," and your current person-ality "aligns with," a particular family of human intent.* We rarely overtly express the characteristics of our family of *belonging* during our lifetime; instead, they bring an underlying subtlety to the qualities expressed by our personality's family of *alignment*. You can ascertain the traits of your family of belonging by focusing your attention through deeply reflective exercises that intend to *feel* your "vibrational signature."

Your primary intentional characteristics fall within the spectrum of activities and issues explored by your family of alignment. It is important to acknowledge that there are many different ways of expressing the primary qualities of a family. You can discover the pertinent activities and roles of your current personality's family of alignment by reflecting on your behavioral consistencies (your mannerisms), your passions, the roles you enjoy, and the significant fulfilling events experienced during your life.

From the point of view of your Essence self, your current personality's intent is a pool of particular probabil-ities created under *the natural principle of spontaneity*. It is a pool of potential actions that is constantly revising itself – moment by moment – in accordance with your chosen actions.

9 *Knowledge of your families of belonging and alignment provides a fuller and clearer understanding of the qualities of your own personality, along with clarification of your purpose for this lifetime.*

Getting to know the primary intentional traits of all of the families of intent offers insight on your interactions with others. Knowledge of another's family of alignment enables you to regulate your communications in a clearer, less judgmental fashion.

Your desires are automatically set to manifest in accordance with your personal intent. Your personal intent is a subconscious contract within your Essence that steers the creation of your personal reality. When your reality appears to be contrary to your desires, it is because a belief you are holding is affecting your automatic choice of action and thus hindering the flow of manifestation.

10 *Our "shift in consciousness" includes a widening awareness of how we create our reality.* Part of the *how* will become apparent when we comprehend the link between intent, the pool of potential probabilities for action, and how our choices influence this pool. A conscious awareness of *all* the inner processes involved in reality creation – the natural principles and powers, the inner senses and not least the intents of the differing families – provides greater creativity and freedom of expression for each of us – and thus, *all* humanity.

To understand your Self – your multidimensional Self – you must begin by nurturing a **trust** of your Self. Trust in your Self allows for you to truly **know** your Self and the various psychological elements, such as your personality and ego, that make up your outer self. Familiarity with the genera of the intent of human consciousness and discovering which of them have the most influence on your purposeful life will open your eyes to the wonderful creations you, and others, are. A love of your Self ensues that supersedes your ego's narrow focus upon its own needs. You will also gain an awareness of how you fit into the greater scheme of things – humanity's evolving consciousness.

The next part of this book is about the construction of your outer self, the psychological elements of the you that operates in the physical, Objective Area within Consciousness. This is the you that imagines (most of the time) that your physical self stops at your skin and your psychological Self is no more than your collection of thoughts and beliefs going through an information processing system.

This section of the book will get you to *appreciate* your ego for what it is, and why you have one. You may even begin to show it some *compassion,* as many of our egos are confused and fearful, deviating from their purpose because of their ignorance of the nature of belief systems – a subject we explore in *Part III.*

PART II:

CONSCIOUSNESS AND THE

PHYSICAL YOU

CHAPTER 6:

WHO AM I AFTER I'M BORN?

Having been introduced to the channeled literature's depiction of your non-physical self – the inviolate greater Identity of your Essence self with its subconscious library of knowledge and intentional plans – let's now look at how your physical self is described.

Just as Consciousness individuates Itself in order to get to know Itself – meet its challenges, expand and evolve – so too does your Essence self. This isn't too surprising if you consider that your non-physical self is a product of individuation driven by the natural principles that underpin the process. Your physical self is another iteration of this never-ending route to Self knowledge.[84]

The previous chapter illustrates the extent to which the psychological elements of your impending physical self become prepared for action. Your Essence self, for reasons of its own expansion and evolution, chooses a broad but definitive intentional path of learning for your physical self to explore, and it has figured into things some ongoing educational issues for the entirety of the Self.

Let's get physical

Most adults are familiar with the purely physical aspects of producing a physical body. Two contrasting sets of genitalia come together in a generally messy encounter; sperm swims to egg; egg "accepts"[85] the sperm into its cell; and following a scientifically acknowledged miraculous gestation period, a baby is born.

According to Seth, there is no specific "time" when the individuated portion of your Essence ("soul" if you wish) enters the physical form. The birth of your personality, or more accurately, the psychological structures that form your *outer self*, is a gradual process that from our time blinkered perspective "begins" before even our parents are born.

It is a common belief that a baby is born with a *tabula rasa* – a "blank slate" for a mind. This notion dates back to the 17th Century English philosopher John Locke who maintained that we are born without innate mental faculties and that we gain knowledge solely through the experiences we perceive through our physical senses.

Sigmund Freud assumed this to be the case when formulating his psychoanalytic theories, and the work of behavioral psychologist B.F. Skinner in the 1960s helped cement the blank slate idea into our modern worldview – despite later research into our acquisition of language demonstrably refuting the premise.

As Steven Pinker points out in his book *The Blank Slate*, blank slates don't *do* anything, yet paradoxically young minds evidently *do* a lot of learning. We recognize the importance of learning to the human experience and can witness the phenomenal rate of learning in the very young. It is therefore logical that certain faculties *must* be present in the new mind for learning to occur.

To get a grasp of your newborn psychological state, as presented by our metaphysical guides, it is essential to realize that your life begins *before* physical birth. It "begins" within the Subjective Area within Consciousness, a place where linear time does not feature in the creative process of birthing a new personality. As your Essence starts to individuate, apart from organizing a path of intent for the new personality to align with, it also deliberates upon which physical environment is best suited to its educational aims.

There are many factors considered by your Essence in relation to your physical birth. These include your parents (yes, you pick them as much as they pick you!) and other familial issues, cultural and geographical relevancies, the time period, and various other psychological elements that will set the stage for your lifetime's learning experience.

Far from being a blank slate, your newborn self has been psychologically primed with self-expanding information from its non-physical origins. You have "form" before you are formed!

In addition, you are indeed born with a predisposition for language. The manifest physical paraphernalia that enables you to speak reflects a subjective template or "pattern" within the psyche that prepares you not just for speech but also for all the psychological complexities language embodies.[86]

According to Seth, as your life is being prepared for birth, there are many such patterns within the psyche that come into consideration – even one that "readies" your adult form in later life, albeit within highly variable parameters.[87]

Such ideas become easier to comprehend as you come to realize that all time is simultaneous in the *spacious present* of the subjective, non-physical realm where your birth begins.

Your inner self acts as your non-physical self's vanguard, pioneering the new enterprise of the physical you. It helps set the stage for your personality's adventures. A new life, driven by the intent of your Essence, is set into physical motion.

According to the channeled literature, your physical self begins with three basic psychological elements that are at the forefront of a vast and largely unexplored landscape named the *psyche*.[88] These prominent facets from the psyche form the basis of your Mind – your *ego/ego-self*, your *conscious-mind*, and your *personality*.

From here on, this book refers to this tripartite assembly as your **outer self**.

We need to remember that the outer self is a gestalt of highly complex psychological components; this trio of parts forms the barest minimum set of components for understanding your physical self's psychology.

SAY THAT AGAIN (12) Your outer self

Your outer self is a collection of the three central psychological aspects that front your physical being. These are your *ego/ego-self,* your *conscious-mind,* and your *personality.* *Your ego and your personality are not the same psychological "thing."*

You do need an ego

Your ego forms from conception onwards in conjunction with your physical body. From the beginning of your physical existence your inner self (in its role as your Essence's agent) is entrusted with the task of constructing an *ego* so that you are able to operate within the medium of physicality.

You can think of your ego as a by-product of the individuating process, a psychological construct needed to direct the action on the physical stage. Your inner self breathes life into your ego; but when your ego is born, it achieves independence, free to make its own choices, despite the ever-present non-physical umbilical cord of communication between it and your inner self. *(A cord, it has to be said, that has become severely constricted in most of us.)*

In the main, your ego develops through heredity and environment; *through nature* – genes along with innate mental faculties; *as well as nurture* – physical experiences that are *intent*ionally "managed" by your Essence and nurtured by your inner self.

Again, don't imagine that your ego has no free will, that your life is predetermined. You are born with an intentional path of learning, but your ego is free to make its own choices on what actions it will take to express this intent; or indeed, whether to stay on the path at all – *(the sign of a strangled, if not severed, cord).*

The most concise metaphysical definition of the ego is – *a* *psychological structure that **interprets** what it **perceives** to be the physical field.*

We can begin the inevitable computer analogy here. If you liken your physical body (the hardware) to that of a computer, you can think of your ego as the operating system (Windows™, for example) – the software (psychological structure) that enables your computer body to interact with its environment. Your ego allows you to *operate* within the *system* of physicality.

You may remember from the *Introduction* that as with any *living* representation of Consciousness, we are primarily bestowed with freedom of expression and an "awareness of Self" – these markers to individuality are observable, in *some* life forms, as a *personality*.

However, Consciousness took an evolutionary step in the individuation process when it came to humanity's ability to express its freedom. It gave us an ego-self – a mental faculty conferred upon our outer self that is supposed to *enhance* our ability to express our Selves freely in the physical world. The primary reason for Consciousness to introduce the ego into its experiments with physicality was to allow our species the privilege of **conscious choice**; to move our awareness of Self from acting on instinct, to *choosing* how to act – and herein lies the rub.

Since it is your ego that performs the role of stage director in the theatre of your physical experience, it is this part of your outer self that does the choosing. Your ego decides on what actions to take *by **interpreting** the physical field it perceives and using its intellect to filter out the important information contained therein.*

Your ego's **perception** (examined in *Book II*) however, is heavily influenced by your collection of beliefs stored in the subconscious area – beliefs made all the more powerful by emotional energy. This means that **your beliefs** (examined in *Part III* of this book) **govern your ego's choices** made through the acuity of its intellect.

A subtle irony comes into play here – it relates to the ego's initial state at physical birth – it being the part of your outer self's psychological structure that is near to being a "blank slate."

Your Essence self, complying with the grander scheme of Consciousness, grants your ego independence in its individuating process; it wants your ego to think for itself. As your ego develops its thinking, it builds belief systems *about* what it perceives in the physical field. This is of course a totally personalized process – each of our egos constructs its own perception of what it *imagines* to be reality because it is *interpreting* reality *through* its beliefs – thereby personalizing the physical field!

Your ego's belief systems become a screen of entangled branches through which you attempt to perceive the clearing of reality; a screen formed by its need to establish its independence from Essence. This screen of beliefs blinds us to the broader, more flexible view of reality enjoyed by our inner selves – and children, by the way, as they are only in the process of forming the entangling branches of an ego.

Your ego, because of its drive for its own identity, set in motion by its independent nature, then goes on to exacerbate the situation by misconstruing its purpose!

Your ego's purpose "is the manipulation of the personality within the physical universe."[89]

Manipulating the personality

By "manipulate," it is meant that your ego is expected to *impress* its interpretations of the physical environment upon your personality in order that your personality may incorporate such understandings into its ever-changing, always-receptive form. To do this, your ego depends upon its *intellect* to select from the physical environment any information regarded as "important" for your personality to address. The intellect is required to be as clear and dispassionate as it possibly can in this choosing.

Regrettably, the more set you are in your beliefs, the more inflexible your ego becomes in allowing the intellect to perform its task in an unprejudiced manner.

Your ego still manipulates your personality but the sculptor's hands have become clogged with the clay of its beliefs. The intellect becomes a frustrated servant to your ego as your ego handcuffs itself further by imagining that your personality is some sort of rival to the identity it is building for itself. Your ego does not recognize that it and the personality are part of a larger psychological gestalt (outer self) which in turn is implanted within the more complex gestalt of your Essence self.

Your ego largely confines its manipulation of your personality to attempts to shape it into a more permanent and stable portion of itself. This action stems from your ego's desire for *its* identity to be recognized as the *only* identifying factor of your Self. Its screen of beliefs shield it from your Whole Self as it arbitrarily makes a unit of itself – a unit you call the 'I' of who I am; an 'I' that is in actuality a collection of beliefs charged by fear of change, cut off from the mother Identity of your Essence.

Your personality, on the other hand, as we will come to later, is an ever-changing "field of action" within the psyche – nested within your Essence. Action, though, implies change, which your ego thinks may lead to instability, so it attempts to stand apart from the *action* your personality represents, satisfied instead to manipulate the personality into conforming to its own dubiously constructed platform of identity.

It is precisely because of the ego's dilutions of "Self" grandeur, combined with its nagging awareness of its humble *blank slate* beginnings, that we even entertain the notion of a blank slate being the psychological footing for our newborn selves. When we consider that our life's operational directors are at best confused, more likely unaware of their *own* purpose for being in physicality, it is not surprising that few of us have a clue as to our life's overall purpose.

As history has shown us, the remedy for the ego's plight, particularly if it has progressed into pathological proportions, is not to reinforce its sense of separation by taking it aside, scolding it for the errors of its ways, and giving it a sound thrashing. Instead, we need to awaken the ego to its purpose and integrate it back into the Whole Self.

We need to remember that the ego is born with a fabulous potential for manipulating not only the personality but also the reality it perceives. It has good reason for being. It has an intellect that is highly adept at sifting important information from what has been created in the physical plane and relaying the juicy bits back to the non-physical, inner aspects to your Self.

The ego is not some afterthought of your Essence, deliberately cut adrift from its guiding influence. When your ego's belief systems allow, the intellect can become not only more honest and objective in its analyses of physical information, but also more aware and accepting of the non-physical information relayed to it by your inner self. Establishing mutual regard and respect between your ego-self and your personality is a first step on the road to an integrated, more evolved Self.

The contemporary philosopher and spiritual teacher Andrew Cohen describes the ego in this way:

Your Best Friend and Your Worst Enemy

The ego, or individuated self-sense, is both your best friend and your worst enemy. It is your best friend because, in the most positive sense, it represents your capacity to individuate – to see yourself as a unique, autonomous entity and to bear witness to your own experience with some measure of objectivity. Individuation is what makes it possible for you to be a conscious agent of evolution, a vessel for Spirit in action. The more profound our individuation, the more powerfully Spirit can shine through us. However, ego is also our worst enemy. And this is because, for too many of us, over-identification with our separate individuality obscures the deeper and higher spiritual dimensions of our being. It is very important to understand this paradoxical nature of ego if you, as an individual, want to take responsibility for creating the future, as yourself.[90]

SAY THAT AGAIN (13) Your ego/ego-self

Your ego is a psychological structure *for **interpreting** what you **perceive in the physical field**.* It uses its *intellect* to discriminate between information it perceives as important to the Self and that which is unimportant (unfortunately, your ego regards *itself* to be the Whole Self). Your ego's predominant **beliefs** *about what it perceives* compromise its intellectual abilities.

Your ego's purpose is to impress upon your personality (so that the personality can adjust its own character) its interpretations of what is important to the Self – again, this criterion is biased towards your ego's personal concerns.

The more adept your ego becomes at objectively managing its beliefs (rather than have its intellect led by them) the more able it is to make **informed** choices that conform to the interests of your overall Self's *intent* for this lifetime.

Your ego needs a Mind

So far, we have seen that your ego has a job to do, a purpose for doing this job, and an intellect to help it out with what's important in its perception of the physical world. Once your ego is (relatively) clear on what it perceives, and is readying you for action in response to an important issue, you then need to *deal with* the physical conditions – this is where your *Mind* comes in.

We have a problem understanding what the Mind is and a common mistake is to equate it with the psyche. They are not the same thing. According to Seth, your Mind is actually a *collective* – a quantity of psychological constructs – including a number of different, individual "minds" each playing with their own thoughts, ideas, dreams, and emotions with an eye on the your Self's overall intent. Your Mind is a *portion* of the psyche at best.

Of these minds within the Mind, **the mind we utilize in any one moment is the conscious-mind.**

We imagine that we have just one mind because we only identify with the conscious one. Our brain, in the main, can only "tune in" to one mind at a time. Mind, the collection, resides within your Essence – it is another "portion" of your Essence (along with your inner self) that watches out for your outer self as it negotiates physical existence. Your Mind's purpose, along with that of your brain and nervous system, is to keep you alive.

Each one of our minds within the collective handles knowledge in a different way; and each is capable of organizing what happens on the stage of reality in their own unique way. This means that the mind we make *the conscious-mind* can affect how we deal with a situation. What our ego-self doesn't realize is that its job of assessing what is important for the Self to know about a physical situation would be made a whole lot easier if it had a more flexible approach to choosing which mind to utilize, which mind to make conscious. There are horses for courses. Depending on the situation, one particular mind would be more helpful to the ego's decision making than another. The reason for having a collection of minds is that we can interchange them so that they can best achieve their collective purpose – which is to determine *how* to act, how best to express our Self.

Because our egos are unused to working with the idea that they can employ different minds to deal with different situations, they tend to stick with one whatever the circumstances on the physical stage. The ego expects this overworked mind to deal with situations that it is ill equipped to handle; which is when mental health problems may arise, even a mental breakdown.

When we observe someone not dealing with the physical conditions appropriately, we might say, "Are you out of your mind?" or, "Have you lost your mind?" The answer to these rhetorical questions is more to do with the ego's utilization of a mind that is inappropriate for the circumstances, or the ego being unable to engage a suitable mind at all.

Fortunately, any one of our minds can handle most conditions and we "change" our minds more often than not through intervention by our inner self – much to the consternation of our egos – and our partners!

When you find yourself to be in a life-threatening position, it is your inner self that instantaneously chooses an appropriate mind to deal with the situation. This is why, for example, a person after a courageous deed might say, "It wasn't a question of being brave, I just did what needed to be done because I knew *how* to do it." The most appropriate mind that knows how to deal with such a situation jumps to the fore. If we don't have a mind that is familiar with the situation to some extent, or our ego-self clings desperately to the mind it is used to using, we can freeze – mentally and physically.

Just as your brain sends messages and orders to various parts of your body in order to physically deal with a situation, your conscious-mind sends messages to the brain about *how* to deal with the situation. Any chosen conscious-mind is privy to *all* of the data pertaining to your Whole Self – similar experiences, other lifetimes, other purposes, challenges solved and unsolved – but it only sends your brain data that relates to ensuring your outer self's continued existence.

When we eventually get to appreciate our spacious collective Mind for what it is and what it is capable of doing for us in terms of our ego's perception of reality, we will naturally become more aware of our ability to affect our reality and be truly more

–perceptive. We shall expand our awareness into perceiving far more than just the physical realm. According to Seth, this is what true *"personhood"* is all about.

How do I get a personality? *(Don't read that out loud!)*

Your personality is as impossible to define as your psyche. This is because the nature of both is never a static thing. And that is because they primarily exist within the constantly shifting, sometimes physical, mostly non-physical, dimension of **action** – a dimension that arises from existence itself.

In *The Early Sessions* books, Seth defines the personality as a "field of action." He explains that we can consider "action" to be the spontaneous means by which Consciousness expresses Itself through materialization. With respect to you and I, our personalities are our connection to the dimension of action – our connection to Consciousness.

Action is not a "force" as we tend to label such internal drives behind our materialization; it is more of a growth medium for your personality. "It is a by-product of any reality, and a part of all reality."[91] Seth also states that "action is *basically electrical* (my emphasis)"[92] in nature but because of science's limited understanding of the nature of action being anything other than a force or movement within the physical field, we are yet to develop technologies that would reveal such electrical realities. When we come to understand our Selves a little better through exploration of our psyches, the discovery of the breadth of electrical realities will advance our understanding of the physical dimension.

Because action is electrical in nature, and your personality is a *field of action*, it follows that you can think of your personality as an electrical field. If we return to our computer analogy of your Self for a moment; you can liken your personality to the electrical field within the machine – turned on and made real by plugging into the main grid (the dimension of action) from where it draws its vitality.

In a Guardian newspaper article (May 15th, 2011) the renowned physicist Stephen Hawking, when remarking on what the death experience may entail, said, "I regard the brain as a computer which will stop working when its components fail. There is no heaven or afterlife for broken down computers; that is a fairy story for people afraid of the dark." What this statement fails to recognize is that just because the brain breaks down – the central processing unit – and the computer doesn't work anymore, this does not mean the electrical grid that kept it alive ceases to exist. In death, your personality's electrical field returns to the grid to consider upgrades!

According to Seth, your personality builds from continuous electrical signals and codes from any effect, of any kind, experienced by your Self – this includes the effects of thoughts, dreams and emotions. Essentially, you *get* a personality through electrical build up!

Your physical body superimposes itself upon this electrical ghost of a structure, yet even though they entwine, they are of completely different dimensions. Your personality's electrical build up forms an electrical pattern from physical birth onwards. This pattern is both within and without every cell of your physical body, yet is independent of physicality itself.

Why do I need a personality?

Both your ego and your personality begin their existence at physical birth. Your ego begins with nothing other than its independence, whereas your personality has a trace of an identity from the outset. This trace identity comes from your Essence Identity, relayed to your personality through the subconscious. The knowledge that your personality begins with (along with some other rudimentary knowledge of the new lifetime's intent) comes from having its *primary* existence within the electrical dimension.

Your Essence, inner self and subconscious (together with

thoughts, dreams and emotions) all have a presence within the electrical dimension; which is how your personality has privy to such knowledge. As time is not a factor within the electrical dimension, it cannot confine your personality. In other words, your personality does not require the physical dimension for its existence. The significance of this statement will become apparent a little later.

Your inner self, emissary of your Essence and birth mother to your ego, has good reason to initiate the growth of your personality. That reason has everything to do with transferring information from the physical experiences of life to the non-physical receiving station of your Essence. You need to have a go-between. You need to have a part of your Self that can transform and transfer data from the physical to the non-physical.

Your ego can't do it – its existence is reliant upon physicality – it doesn't do electrical. So your personality is also "triggered" into life when your ego is born. Since your ego's purpose is to "manipulate" your personality by relaying feedback of its interpretations on what has been created in the physical field, your personality's purpose is to store and preserve this feedback, along with all other effects from the other electrical fields of human experience (notably dreams); and get this information across to your Essence.

This is why you need a personality, because your Essence requires information on *all* the experiences of your life – electrical and not-so electrical – to add to its understanding of the nature of its Self.

Your personality is always in a state of becoming – forever changing – forever being manipulated by your inner self and your outer self's ego. Whilst your personality is always in motion, the natural power of Divine Love regulates that motion. Your personality contains your ego's interpretations of reality, along with the emotional energies that underpin your ego's beliefs about reality. As your ego builds itself, your personality absorbs its "data" into its electrical matrix. Your personality becomes a doppelgänger – an electrical counterpart to your ego's psychological form.

It's your personality, not your ego, which has strong connections with your inner self. Indeed, Seth describes your personality as being a *portion* of your inner self. It has its own *"consciousness of Self"* and is therefore aware of its role in regard to your Essence self. It knows that it is within and part of the electrical dimension of action, with its own "field" therein. Personality is simply a name given to this portion of the Self *that exists within all living species whether they possess an ego or not.*

Because your personality has consciousness of Self – is within and part of action and thus not tied to the physical plane of existence – it is this part of your outer self which survives physical death. The moment of physical death simply signifies your personality's release from the physical field. It continues to exist and to change, but no longer projects itself into the physical realm.

Picking up the computer analogy again, death for your computer-self is the equivalent of being permanently turned off. When you turn off your computer *(put it to sleep)*, your operating system (ego-self) is unable to interact with the environment through its collection of software programs (intellect, mind, physical body). All your electrically encoded data is still there, by turning off your computer you've simply taken away the electrical field to which your personality belongs.

Because your personality is electrical in nature and is a counterpart to your ego, it has all of your ego's data (accumulated files from various software packages) copied. When you turn on your computer-self, your personality can transfer (upload) this copied data to another mainframe computer (your Essence) via the internet (electrical dimension). Unlike a computer, and unrealized by most of us, turning off the computer cannot turn off your personality – it continues to process information when you are asleep, *or have permanently gone to sleep.*

As understanding of this idea liberates your personality from the ego's fears of physical annihilation, you can more readily turn your mental energies to improving your present physical situation.

You need to remain aware that there are no definite divisions between the ego-self and the personality. Neither is there between the outer self and the inner self. All of your Self is one unified entity crossing the seeming boundaries between the physical and non-physical Areas within Consciousness.

SAY THAT AGAIN (14) Mind, Conscious-mind and Personality

Your *Mind* is actually a collection of psychological constructs, which includes a number of different minds with their own characteristics and abilities. Your *conscious-mind* is one of these differing minds within your Mind, chosen by your ego when assessing *how to deal with* the situation in the physical realm. Your Mind is the portion of the psyche, situated within your Essence, most closely involved with your inner self in maintaining your physical existence.

Your *personality* is an electrically encoded counterpart to your ego-self. From a linear time perspective, it "begins" life along with your ego. It has a constantly (both in physical time and outside of it) changing and evolving nature. Its "form" is electrical in quality, residing within the electrical dimension of "action." Because its existence is not reliant upon the physical dimension, *your personality continues to exist when the physical body dies.*

Before we look at a graphical representation of the entire structure of the Self, we should clarify the image with mention again of your subconscious.

CHAPTER 7:

YOUR MIND'S SUBCONSCIOUS "AREA"

The terms "subconscious" and "unconscious" often interchange when people without a formal teaching in psychology speak of the lands of awareness beyond the kingdom of ordinary physical wakefulness. This chapter aims to make you aware of the Subconscious Area within Consciousness and your personal portal to it, your own area within this Area, a land within your psyche, where your conscious-mind can relax and enjoy a beer with your inner self. Your subconscious is an area within your Self that provides you (ironically, as they are of no significance here) with the "time" and "space" for information exchange between your Essence and your outer self.

Subconscious, not unconscious

Anyone who is it all familiar with psychoanalytic theory will have come across the term "the unconscious," which Freud used to describe a part of the psyche containing thoughts, ideas and emotions kept out of your conscious awareness – *repressed*. Although not always "negative" in expression, this repressed mental activity is usually painful, traumatic or socially unacceptable in some way and it is the skill of the psychoanalyst to bring this material to the conscious-mind for psychological healing.

Carl Jung expanded upon the notion of *the* unconscious, suggesting we have a *"personal unconscious"* and a *"collective unconscious"*; two parts to the unconscious, one personal to us (along Freudian lines) and one containing the impersonal mental activity inherited from the collective mind of humanity.

The term *subconscious* is not a psychoanalytic term; Freud rejected it as confusing, believing that our minds are either consciously aware of information or not. It was his opinion that material about to enter the conscious-mind resided within the "*pre*-conscious" rather than a *sub*-conscious.

What Freud didn't realize (according to Seth) was that the conscious-mind is just the one mind we have our attention focused upon. We actually have a collection of minds waiting in the wings, waiting to take the stage as the conscious-mind; a collection we can think of as being just *below* the threshold between not conscious and conscious – poised for action whilst kept in an area of your consciousness the channeled literature refers to as your *subconscious*.

In this book, as in channeled literature, *unconscious* only means that the brain has shut down its main functions and is not able to attend to the conscious-mind – as when a person is knocked out or in a coma.

Your subconscious is an area within your consciousness where your inner senses as well as your outer senses are all utilized in assisting your ego form and express your personality. Furthermore, there are areas within this area! These areas are populated by the minds that form other personalities—*sub-personalities*—offering different characteristics when given conscious expression.

Suffice to say that the subconscious is the preferred term in metaphysical literature describing a phenomenon of the psyche that is far broader than Freud's unconscious and far more complicated than Jung's double faceted notion of psychological structures outside of conscious awareness.

Inside the subconscious library

To gain a clearer image of your subconscious "area," it may help to visualize a vast campus of scholastic buildings, the main access to which is through the majestic library.[93] Your subconscious, as psychological science is now very aware, is certainly a library of knowledge and information. As you will learn, it is also the

meeting ground for your inner and outer psychological formations. Let's take a look inside.

Imagine yourself striding up the marble steps outside this
impressive building to the entrance. You are about to leave the
outside world of physicality. Between the Corinthian columns
fronting your building are oak and glass revolving doors with
polished brass push rails. As you push through the door, you
notice three characters foolishly squeezed into the opposite
partition – the one in front being pushed along by the next, who
appears to have the third guy playing piggyback. All have determined, if somewhat fraught, facial expressions as they venture
out of the building.

Once into the reception hall, you can see a dozen or more
people sitting in large comfortable armchairs or generally
milling around the place, each familiar in physical appearance to
yourself, but their dress and mannerisms reflect clearly different
personalities.

Various large oak tables are set in rows for study purposes.
There is a reception counter in front of you across the hall with a
genderless, robotic librarian behind its much-polished oak top,
and a very distinguished and wise-looking woman perched on
the right side of the counter, sitting close to the librarian. On her
left, similarly sitting on the counter is a figure that also mirrors
your physical features, yet has a ghostly transparency to its form.
You also detect a pulsating electrical hum emanating from this
character.

The people in the reception area are your *other minds*, waiting
for the call to be made conscious. The librarian is the custodian
of this subconscious archive; a character who does as instructed
with computer-like efficiency. Its sole purpose is to feed information into the library's electrical database and retrieve information from it when instructed to do so. Like the fictional
character *Lieutenant Commander Data* from the television series

Star Trek, our subconscious librarian makes no judgments, forms no opinions, and is incapable of dishonesty or deception.

The three characters that just left the building were the three "portions" of your outer self, on a mission to deal with a current challenge in the physical realm. Your *ego-self* pushes *the conscious-mind* in front of it, as it balances your *personality* on its back and shoulders. The wise and compassionate lady on the counter is of course your *inner self*, the overseeing, noninterfering benefactor to this library. And the ghostly (not ghastly) electrically humming one is your *body-consciousness*.

Behind the librarian is an arched entrance to a corridor that leads far back into the library and to other buildings and areas on campus. Above the arch, a sign reads "Information on the Self" and if you peer down the corridor, one entrance indicates "Other Lifetimes," another, "Probable Selves."

The librarian sits at a computer console surrounded by visual display monitors. One of these monitors has the label "Body's Physical Systems" affixed to it – readouts of all the autonomic systems of the body appear on it, from heartbeat to blink rate. You notice that your body-consciousness is staring at this monitor the whole time.

Another monitor sits on the counter turned toward the enquirer, next to where your inner self sits. Away from the librarian's counter, shelves stretch around the room and fill the walls from floor to ceiling. Each is laden with ancient dusty tomes. An occasional window interrupts the swathe of shelving; and on the south facing wall to the right, a set of French doors allow a glimpse of a densely planted garden on the other side of them. Above the doors, a sign reads "Garden of Beliefs."

....

We'll leave this metaphor of your subconscious area *within* your Mind for the moment. You should retain the fact that the subconscious is *not a mind* or part of a mind, as in "the subconscious-mind." Nor should you equate it with Freud's "the unconscious." It is not a scary place at all, albeit the body-consciousness figure is a bit weird. It is instead a place within the psyche where all the players involved in the game of your life can come together to discuss strategy. It is a welcoming, comforting environment made so by your inner self's benevolence. You can trust your inner self will see to it that you come to no harm while in this place of psychological inter-*action*.

The ego's folly

It's a sad fact that at present our egos have a poor understanding of the subconscious and no real idea as to its purpose. Our egos fear even to enter the land of the subconscious because of a number of fearful beliefs. These beliefs have grown from the notions of scientific materialism, which rejects its very existence; from ill-founded Freudian notions of a noxious *"id"* where ghastly gremlins lurk; and from religious doctrine that suggests the subconscious lands are the bad lands of the psyche – populated by nefarious devils aiming to drag your soul off to Hades.

Because of our egos' fears, Western psychology's expeditionary parties have made little progress in exploring the subconscious, let alone *utilizing* it.

Most of us understand that the subconscious contains a great store of information on our life's physical and mental experiences; and many are aware of methods to access the subconscious such as *clinical hypnosis* or *mindfulness,* which appear to quell the ego's fears and allow information contained within to come through.

Eastern meditational practices have expanded our use of the subconscious for what it is – a *psychological facility* – but it is the practices and exercises highlighted in the channeled literature that are designed to exploit more fully the possibilities available to us through visiting the subconscious more regularly. They are offered as tools for us to explore the subconscious archives as well as help us maintain our psychological balance in the physical world.

At present, our egos negotiate the subconscious in a slapdash fashion. We usually enter our subconscious library through ego-driven necessity rather than through adventurous enquiry. We come into the library because our ego is not sure how to act with regard to the situation out in the physical world.

Because of your ego's reluctance to linger too long in this uncharted territory, it immediately puts your habitually chosen conscious-mind under pressure to grab information on what to do as quickly as possible and sharply exit the building. Your personality, incidentally, unbeknownst to your ego, *does* know how to utilize the action potentialities of this place, and will always jump down from your ego's back and nip to the garden of beliefs to ascertain what energies might come to bear in any action the ego decides to take.

Your ego is aware that in this library there is information available for working out how to act. It instructs the conscious-mind to approach the robotic librarian and simply ask, "What do *I* (as sole authority on the Self) *normally do* in this situation?" Your ego remains by the revolving doors, looking out for any hobgoblins that might assault its illustrious persona, nervous that the personality may return from the garden of beliefs laden with creepy crawlies. It regards the other characters within the room as separate to itself, unaware that they are other minds that can interchange with the conscious-mind it has adopted as its sole agent for dealing with physical things. He is oblivious to the beauty and loving guidance of the inner self; regarding her presence as inconsequential.

At the counter, the conscious-mind describes the physical situation as perceived by the ego and asks the ego's pre-set question. The librarian feeds the descriptive information and the question into the computerized archive thus updating energy readings on relevant information packages.

The answer to the question, chosen *electronically*, appears on the monitor on the counter. That is, the answer is the one that holds the largest electrical charge within the collection of data relating to the ego.

Ominously, because of the way the question is put, the answer comes from only analyzing information supplied by the ego, information that is solely confined to the ego's experiences. The answer's electrical charge, picking it out for display, has been accumulated through the current lifetime's physical experiences; the thoughts entertained by the conscious-mind in relation to the experiences; and emotional energy attached to beliefs about the experiences (elaborated upon in later chapters).

According to Seth, the ego is well equipped to handle the physical environment – it possesses an intellect able to select important information, and a collection of minds to work out how to act on this knowledge. The ego needs to *perceive* "correctly" (that is, as unimpeded by its screen of beliefs as possible) the physical situation and relay its interpretations as succinctly and as clearly as possible to the subconscious librarian for input into the psyche's database.

The ego should be at the counter with the conscious-mind, making sure the information transfers correctly before the subconscious computer analyzes its content. The ego should then ask the librarian to request the inner self to use its phenomenal skills and energies to help assess the situation and formulate an answer that considers the entire Self's needs. It should also request to know which of its minds is the most appropriate for subsequent action. (One day our egos will evolve to have the confidence to ask our inner selves directly!)

With this procedure adopted, answers to the modified question of, "How is it best for me to act in this situation?" may turn out to be unexpected or even ridiculous—to the ego. It will need to trust in the computational wisdom of the combined psychological characters that make up the entirety of the Self.

When an answer clearly *frustrates* the ego, this indicates that the ego's *interpretation* of what it perceived – which was information fed into the subconscious computer – was compromised by an intellect shackled by beliefs. A mature ego will recognize this to be the case and act on addressing the beliefs that generated the frustration.

A graphical representation of your Self
– the iceberg analogy

To bring this part of the book to a close, and by way of encapsulating the various aspects to the structure of your Self described in metaphysical teachings, *Figure 2* offers a graphical representation. It is a reasonably comprehensive visual guide to the various aspects and contributing elements that form the individualized gestalt of the entirety of You in the physical and non-physical dimensions.

This depiction of your Self modifies the classical iceberg model of the Mind proposed in psychoanalytic theory. Here, however, the Mind bridges the illusory boundary between physical and non-physical. It is an area within the Self, rather than "the Self" being a part of it. The Mind acts as the psychological agent of *your* consciousness, *choosing* which quantum waves of Consciousness to collapse into the physical matter that thrusts itself out of the Subjective Ocean of probabilities.

This iceberg depiction of You is thus kept afloat by the sea of Consciousness from which it emerges. Notice the Consciousness Units (CUs) and the Electromagnetic Energy Units (EEs) in this sea of Consciousness as they, just like water molecules turning into ice, "slow" their vibrational frequency to become "solidified" in the physical realm.

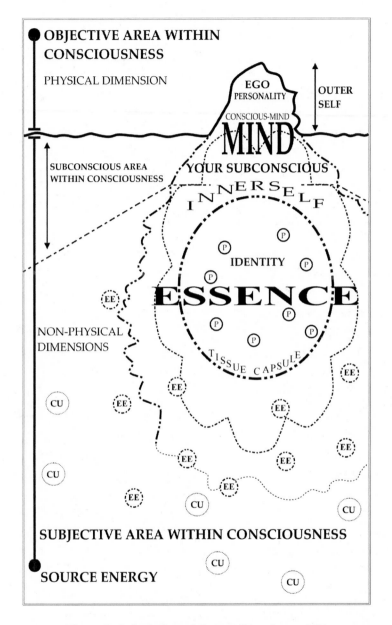

Figure 2. A depiction of the totality of your Self

As you view *Figure 2,* bear in mind that every aspect of your Self, psychic *and physical,* from your inner self to the cells of your body, is aware of your intent and purpose. Your ego-self, looking out onto the physical world, may well be ignoring such knowledge in its bid to separate itself out as *the* Self; however, rest assured that it retains access to this knowledge when persuaded to engage the inner senses.

A healthy, well-integrated Self requires open communication between all aspects and areas to the Self. Your ego simply needs reminding occasionally of its place within the gestalt of your Self. It has the director's role in the movie of your life's experiences, but should remember to listen to the producer, your inner self, so that its directions benefit the totality of your Self.

Jungian theory parallels on the structure of your Self

We have mentioned the "individuation" (see *Say That Again 4*) of Consciousness quite a bit when describing how your Self and other expressions of Consciousness come into being. Interestingly, whereas metaphysical teachings use the term for the separating of Consciousness into "smaller" expressions of Itself, in analytical psychology, the term is essentially used to mean the reverse – a process whereby the various aspects to the outer self come together, become integrated, into a healthy Whole. The individuation process for an individual is a therapeutic process aimed at bringing cohesion to the Self (referred to as "personality") so that he or she can experience his or her "true self."

In light of this duality of meaning, you can regard the individuation of Consciousness as a description of how you have come into existence; and this trilogy of books will assist you in becoming your true self, a true expression of your Self, as described by analytical psychology's *process* of individuation.

Seth and Elias have both remarked on Jung's insightfulness.

In the following brief synopsis of Jungian theory, the metaphysical terms bracketed approximate to Jung's ideas as to the nature of the Self and the psyche to give you an idea of their similarities:

In Jungian theory, the *collective unconscious* (collective consciousness of humanity) is a *repository of archetypes* (differing intentional leanings) that serve to organize, direct and inform human thought and behavior. He regarded *the Self* (inner self) to be one of our archetypes. The Self (inner self) represents a coherent whole, unified consciousness (is a representative of our Essence) that included the *unconscious* (the subconscious area) of an individual. The Self (inner self), according to Jung, is realized (brought into balance) as the product of *individuation*, which in the Jungian view is the process of *personality integration* (rediscovering your own intent and purpose).

What distinguishes Jungian psychology is his idea that there are two centers of the personality (Self). He refers to an ego-self and an inner self, both with a "personality." In light of the metaphysical teachings, we can regard this idea as another example of Jung's acute insight. We can equate Jung's dual "personalities" to the two intentional leanings an individual will express. That is, the ego-self's personality of *alignment* (family of alignment), and the inner self's personality of *belonging* (the Essence's family to which the inner self is an emissary). Here's how Jung describes this duality:

The *ego is the center of consciousness* (with a small "c" – is at the center of our physically focused personality – our aligned personality – and the *physical* expression of our individualized consciousness – our outer self). "The Self" (inner self) is the center of the *total personality* (Essence self – our personality of belonging – the gestalt of our total Self), which includes consciousness (that is, our individualized consciousness), the *unconscious* (the subconscious area) and the ego (this "part" of the outer self). "The Self" (inner self) is both the whole and the center; while the ego is a self-contained little circle off the center contained within the whole, "the Self" can be understood as the greater circle.

In other words, Jung situates your ego-self's personality (ego-self *and* personality – they *are not the same*) within a "total personality" at the center of your being.[94]

Jung's individuation or *integrating* of your personality is something the inner self is constantly monitoring and affecting. Part of the integration process is to do with bringing our focus personality's thoughts, beliefs and behaviors in line with our overall Self's intent and purpose.

Jung's *archetypes* within his *collective unconscious* do not necessarily conform to the designated prime intents of the genera of human intent, but we can regard them as specific expressive elements conforming to a family's overall intent. For example, a woman or man, for gender does not matter at this level of the psyche, who gives herself or himself over completely to nurturing the family unit, or caring for animals or anyone in need – in accordance with the intent of the Nurturers family – we might regard as embodying Jung's "earth mother" archetype.

Jungian theory also encompasses the concept of the "supraconscious-mind"[95] – *the Subconscious Area within Consciousness as opposed to* **your** *subconscious area* – deeper levels of awareness within the Self, other *frameworks of consciousness* or dimensions of our being, where we engage with the mystical and transcend the everyday experiences of our world. The Jungian Self (inner self) emerges from the supraconscious, orchestrating the individuation (steering us back onto our paths of intent) of our lives from a perspective that surpasses the concerns of the ego.

As we can see from this synopsis, much of Jungian theory on the nature of the psyche and the structure of our Selves parallels the key features of metaphysical information on the subject. We are mainly only dealing with differences in terminology. The resemblance in the language suggests that Jung must have intuited such information in some way – certainly he was deeply in touch with his conceptual inner senses. There is some evidence to suggest that he gleaned a great deal of information on the nature of the psyche from dream recall. Albert Einstein was another "genius" who took his dreams seriously.

This concludes Part II of *Know Your Self*. You now have a fairly complete structure of your psychological gestalt that spans dimensions of existence. To complete your knowledge, to truly know your Self and *how* it forms its realities, it is crucial to understand the key energies that your Self utilizes to do so. We explore these in Part III.

PART III:

YOUR CREATIONAL KEYS TO YOUR

PHYSICAL EXPERIENCE

CHAPTER 8:

BEING THOUGHTFUL

Now that we have a clearer picture of who you are and what you are doing here, we can begin to examine what the metaphysical literature has to say about *how* you create the reality you perceive. As your understanding of this process grows and you begin to apply such knowledge on a regular basis, it is possible to take your outer self into the realms of *conscious* creation – the basis for a personally fulfilling life and a step on the evolutionary path of human consciousness.

The physical events you create for yourself are the result of a production process begun in the non-physical realm. It is a process that involves a turbulent mix of key elements – intent, thoughts, beliefs, feelings, emotions, loves and desires – and the intensity of these energies within your Self.

Intent is something we covered in *Chapter 1* and because of its ubiquitous nature in all of creation will continue to feature in the descriptions of the other elements.

This chapter will take you through the next key element, **thoughts**, and their contribution to the production process. The following chapter deals with how thoughts begin their existence and transfer themselves into your psychological and physical structure.

We deal with **beliefs**, the thoughts you think more than once, in *Chapter 10*, and **truths**, the beliefs you place great value in, are the subject of *Chapter 11*.

Chapter 12, Systems of Beliefs, rounds off our examination of this fundamental element in the creation process, before we turn our attention to **feelings** and **emotions**. We talk of **love**, Divine Love, and fear – the emotion that prevents its expression – to end this first book in the trilogy of *It's About You!*

Here's a thought

We know from previous chapters that Consciousness wants to know Itself through experience, and one way in which It can do this, is to express Itself through materialization. Materialization though, does not confine itself to what we consider the one reality, the physical plane. It involves other realities, other planes of existence that intermesh with one another. This particularly applies to the materialization of a human being. Making *you* includes a whole bunch of other fields of reality, not least a number of electrical fields of action that interlink with and project themselves into the physical field. Your physical body exists within the physical field, but the materialization of your consciousness involves various other "bodies" existing in a number of fields of expression.[96]

To ease confusion, we'll keep the number of *electrical fields* to the one phrase – *electric field* – and the various "bodies" involved in being materialized to two basic ones – your physical material body and your *electrical body*.[97]

Your physical body then, comes with an electrical body, a subtly layered energy structure that science is beginning to detect and describe – the electromagnetic energy body (popularly known as the Chakra system[98]), and the *human aura*[99], for example.

Long-standing thinking attributes your aura, or auric field, with qualities similar to an electromagnetic field. In the 1840s and 50s, the magnificently named, Baron Dr. Carl (Karl) Ludwig von Reichenbach, whilst investigating the similarities, declared that what he termed the "Odic force" differed from electromagnetism in a significant way. There was an inversion of the magnetic polarities within this force, contrary to the familiar principles of like repelling like and opposites attracting. Like polarities within our Odic force are attracted to like.

The good doctor described this Odic force as an "emanation" present in most things, but particularly living things. We can but reflect on whether von Reichenbach's discovery may have been an early scientific recognition of the natural power of Attraction expounded upon in *Chapter 4*.

Electric fields of action

Your physical body's survival rests upon your electrical body. The ghostly character next to your inner self in your subconscious library – your *body-consciousness* – regulates its health, and thus your physical health.

Your subconscious area is your place of contact between your physical and electrical body. By exploring the subconscious, your conscious-mind can become aware of the other fields of realities that *inform* your outer self's psychological and physical systems. You get to appreciate the subtle forces contributing to the entire process of reality creation.

The information that comes into your subconscious from the electric field requires translation though. There are various "languages" within the electric field, each with their own grammatical laws, which need decoding by your physical outer self. Dreams, for example, exist as a field of electrical reality, and are the language of your psyche; a language we are all aware of but have a hard time translating (explored in *Book II* of *It's About You!*).

Translating and deciphering information from the electric field is *usually* (not always, as will be explained later) where your brain and its specialized neural cells come in. Your brain is your main decoding center - the central processor. It is the physical place where information from the electric field transforms into human instruction.

Neurology has shown us that *electro–chemical* actions occur at the cellular level in the brain and the rest of the nervous system. A nerve cell passes electrical or chemical signals to other cells (neural or otherwise) through its synapses. We can imagine these actions to be jumping the divide between electrical reality and physical reality. Recent research has discovered that there is a further form of electrical communication happening within the brain's cerebral cortex – *ephaptic coupling*.[100] This phenomenon reveals a separate connection of electrical *fields*, something different to synaptic transference, which may help to explain the brain's phenomenal powers of coordination when processing information.

Neural networks, at least in the brain, thus appear to span the "electrical fields of action" mentioned in the metaphysical literature. The literature informs us, however, that *all* of the cells in your body, not just neurons, are constantly involved with passing information throughout the physical body (the physical reality) *and* instantaneously transferring data throughout and across your various other "bodies" of expression required for materialization – electrical and otherwise.

I've just had a thought

Let's make it very clear from the start exactly what "thought" is from the metaphysical perspective:

Thought is a mechanism used by your conscious-mind to translate and interpret information gathered by both your inner and outer senses.

When a thought comes into your mind, it has to come from somewhere, and that somewhere is the electric field. Seth describes a thought, in its *purest* form, to be a "psychoelectric pattern" that begins its existence in the electric field. This energy pattern then transforms into what you recognize as a thought when exposed to the psychological and physical systems that form your outer self.

Transformation begins when your inner self presents the psycho-electric pattern's information to your body-consciousness. Your body-consciousness, always at work in your subconscious, controls all of the processing systems of your outer self. It not only transforms, translates, connects, communicates, coordinates and generally holds together your physical body's functions along with your electrical body's functions; but also initiates the transfer of information from the electric field to the physical field. Thought is thus the result of a projection of psycho-electric data into the physical realm via the processing systems of your body-consciousness.

Who's doing the projecting? (You might ask.) Well, you are – more accurately, your inner self is. Your inner self, able to operate in the electric field, filters out psycho-electric patterns that it wants to bring to your outer self's attention. To do this, its first step is to gather them together and give them over to your body-consciousness. Your body-consciousness begins to process this electrically coded data by assigning it to four distinct processing centers – elaborated upon a little later. After this initial processing, which creates *thoughts* and *feelings,* your body-consciousness presents these energy forms to the conscious-mind for translation and interpretation to continue.

Your inner self's dilemma

To make things clearer, let's return to your subconscious library for a moment. Back at the librarian's counter, notice your patient and compassionate inner self handing over packages of psycho-electric patterns to your electrically pulsating body-consciousness. In a flash (as time doesn't figure in here), your body-consciousness has distributed the packages to its four processing centers (discussed later) and received in return a basket of energy balls (thoughts and feelings) that it hands over to the conscious-mind for its specialized form of processing.

This is how your conscious-mind receives the psycho-electric patterns picked out by your inner self from the electric field. Your inner self picks them out, as they are relevant bits of *subjective* data on *why* you created the situation in front of you in the first place! Your conscious-mind already houses the *objective* data from your outer five-senses on *what* you have created. Thought is the mechanism used by the conscious-mind to then further translate and interpret all of this information before it suggests a future course of action to your ego.

As you observe this information transfer going on in your subconscious library, spare a thought for your inner self's dilemma in all of this. The objective information acquired by your ego, selected by the intellect, is an *interpretation* of what it perceives. Your inner self is aware that this ego-self interpreted information is subject to the distorting affects of your ego's perceptive filters. She is thus concerned that the purity of her subjective information when transferred to a conscious-mind not best suited to handle it, will also be compromised.

She's aware that each of your minds, sitting idly by in the subconscious reception, deals with information in its own particular way, has its own "language" or rules for translating information into manifest actions and events. Your inner self would prefer to consult with your ego on which of your minds should be provided with your body-consciousness' preliminary translations of her material. She is able to decipher the energy signatures that identify the balls of energy created by this first processing; and thus suggest the most appropriate mind for expression of the thoughts and feelings captured by these energy forms. She can even, given half a chance, make suggestions to your ego on ways to configure its perceptive systems to minimize distortions.

Alas, for most of us, inner self/ego-self consultations are rare. Instead, our egos simply prep the conscious-mind to ignore any communicative advances from the alluring but untrustworthy female at the subconscious counter. Anxiety, generated by the ego, often reinforces such instruction as he intimates to the conscious-mind that this poseur has the power to have him rendered *un*-conscious and returned to the halfway house of the reception area.

Despite the ego's veto on communication with the inner self, information transfer still occurs, because the conscious-mind and the inner self are of the electric field, where no systems are, or can be, closed – even by an arrogant ego. Any "chosen" conscious-mind is in itself highly adaptable and can cope with most of the information it receives, whether it comes from the ego or the inner self. The inner self can still perform her information transfer tasks, but she does so in deference to the ego's will and in the knowledge that things could be done a whole lot better.

Independent thought

According to Seth, once a psycho-electric pattern becomes a thought it takes on its own identity, it becomes an *"independent electrical action,"* measurable in terms of an electrical charge, or more accurately, as "an intensity" within the electric field from which it originates.[101]

By entering human consciousness, the psycho-electric pattern transforms into an "energy sphere" of electrical intensity, which then enjoys an independent and continued existence in the electric field, not just in your mind. Because a thought also exists in the electric field (thus not governed by time), it is possible for a thought to be available to your *(and any other)* inner self, *at more than one particular moment in time.*

This central factor in a thought's independent nature, its independence from time, can affect reality on a personal and on a societal level. If your Mind does not nurture a particular thought at a certain time, the thought can be regarded as being "returned" to the electric field – in other words, it is not lost or dead because it exists regardless of whether it is in a person's Mind or not. In the electrical field where it lives, it can "wait" for a time when physical conditions are more conducive to its psychological unfolding in your outer self. Thoughts and other creations (dreams, for example) you have assigned to the electric field for processing at a later time can be regarded as psychological "markers", or, "more probable" probable realities in your future!

On a societal level, this central factor provides an explanation for how similar thoughts are "taken up" by different people's inner selves at different times; or indeed, by different people at very similar times, particularly if their concentration focuses upon a specific field of thought.

The 19th and early 20th Centuries saw the birth of many inventions that are difficult to attribute to any *one* person's thinking; photography, radio, pneumatic tires, and cinematography to name a few. The most obvious example of such synchronous thinking might be the birth of evolutionary theory with Alfred Russel Wallace and Charles Darwin – two scientists with claim to have had the same thought, or idea, "first."

This is a hugely important property of thought. A thought, produced by your outer self's processing systems from a psycho-electric pattern, is able to "live" within many dimensions of existence because it gains an electrical signature – an *identity*. It does not require a human mind or brain to maintain its existence. You are reminded that patterned energy with an identity is *inviolate*, and from our point of view in the physical domain, immortal. A thought's lifetime (more accurately *durability*[102]) is established by the level of electric charge enjoyed at its birth – this also applies to its durability within your own Mind, within your subconscious library if you will. It is worth noting that any emotional energy present at a thought's birth *amplifies* the strength of this charge.

Richard Merrick, the exponent of *Interference Theory*[103], when referring to the brain as our main thought processor, remarks:

... After all, as our brain thinks, quantum mechanics tells us that the electrons making up our thoughts are constantly taking quantum leaps in and out of this space-time.

As quantum physicist Evan Harris Walker suggests, our brain may be acting as a kind of quantum receiver with our thoughts under the influence of non-local quantum effects.[104] So, while the body and brain may be harmonic like everything else in the Universe, our mind must resonate beyond space-time.

All joking aside, human beings might simply be semi-autonomous, biological robots under the remote control of a Higher Self. Given our current understanding of physics, it is really not that farfetched to think that we could be guided by impulses transmitted and received via quantum leaps from some other realm. Our concepts of free will, creativity and personality might well be a glimpse into this other realm, resonating through to us from space as subtle patterns in the liquid crystal antennae of our brains.[105]

Thought's contribution to the creation process

Readers of the Seth Material and many familiar with the "New Age" movement will be aware of the phrase "thoughts create reality." Seth says this many times, but it is simplistic to assume that it is only your thoughts that create your reality. To take this one expression out of context and concentrate solely upon changing your thoughts to accommodate your wishes will not guarantee success.

The reality you have before you is the result of a multidimensional information processing system, one which includes your thoughts, your beliefs, your emotions, your desires, and your personal intent – all organized under the natural principles and natural powers, particularly that of Divine Love.

It's not difficult to grasp that we create our thoughts. What we are only just beginning to understand is that our thoughts are very real energy forms that *contribute* to the creation of our reality. Once a thought has gained its independence by traversing a human (or perhaps other) mind, it takes on certain qualities. Its identity and electrical intensity, for example, give it a vibrational signature. This vibrational signature exudes a force that radiates outwards. It is a force with *electro–magnetic* properties similar to the electromagnetic field we are familiar with, but dissimilar in respect of polarity attraction and repulsion. This unique force invokes the natural power of Attraction, or what is commonly termed the Law of Attraction. It is this force, this quality of thought, which contributes to your personal reality creation process; it gets the ball rolling for you.

Nothing can occur in your life experience without your invitation of it through your thought.[106]

This quality of thought directly affects you because it means that thoughts of a similar signature or resonance are drawn to each other, while differing signatures are repelled – birds of a feather and all that. It is this attraction and rejection process that helps build and shape your personality. Your personality thereby attains a "climate of attraction," created by the electrical fields of your thoughts – as well as those of your beliefs and emotions. Abraham (Esther Hicks) refers to this as your "*Emotional Set-Point.*" This is why it becomes a habitual action of your conscious-mind to resist thoughts that are of a differing climate to that of your personality.

Your thoughts also affect others as every thought you create, whether you act on it or not, produces energy fluctuations in the field of energy surrounding your physical body – your aura. This field of energy projects itself and influences others around you. Ultimately, each of us influences everyone else through the many fields of expression of Consciousness – not least the various layers of the electric field. Every molecule of energy we transform (under the natural principle of *Energy Transformation* mentioned in *Chapter 3*), such as a psycho-electric pattern into a thought, affects everything else.

Habits of thought then, have both an electrical and psychological nature and implication.

Problems with being too reliant on thought

The psychological implications for maintaining certain habits of thought should be obvious to you. Because we create them, we tend to nurture thoughts as our own, as children of our psyche. We create habits of thought, playing with certain ones repeatedly – a practice that can lead to problems if their birth (with an intensity amplified by emotion) is associated with a distorted view of ourselves. Any thought or thoughts given too much attention, can grow to dominate the personality.

Cognitive (relating to thought processes) Therapy, devised by Aaron T. Beck in the 1960s for treating depression, marked the beginning of mainstream psychology's recognition of the importance to our health of the way we think. Cognitive Behavior Therapy (CBT, a more comprehensive approach), is now the most preferred form of intervention for dysfunctional thinking. Lately, an intervention named "mindfulness-based cognitive behavior therapy," which combines *mindfulness* meditational practices from the Buddhist traditions with CBT, is gaining prominence.

In light of our understanding that thoughts can affect at least our psychological health, we were quick to assume that by thinking positive thoughts all will be well. Sadly, imagining that your conscious-mind simply needs to expel negative thoughts and introduce positive ones, remains a one-dimensional solution. Our approach to attaining psychological *and physical* health needs to include our *feelings*, and any emotions that may follow them into the conscious-mind – as well as our thoughts. Indeed, psychological disturbance can generate from our failure to consider these crucial elements in our psyche.

We currently believe that thought is the sole mechanism for processing information; we also believe that the only information *worth* processing is that which enters the conscious-mind via our outer physical senses (and instruments of enhancement). Feelings, however, are another gift in the processing package we have available to us. Like thought, they begin as psycho-electric patterns of energy that your body-consciousness transforms into this *forerunner* to full processing by the conscious-mind.

Your conscious-mind needs to consider both its thoughts and its feelings when it deliberates upon how to deal with the physical situation. An over reliance on thought as *the* way to process information can create a psychological disturbance born of the inner self's frustration that other processing systems (described in the next chapter), more attuned to feelings, become denigrated.

According to Elias (Mary Ennis), before your body-consciousness begins to translate the psycho-electric patterns of information into thoughts and feelings, your inner self grades them into four different kinds of information. Each kind of information requires a specific form of processing that will best smooth its path into physical expression.

Thoughts are still produced whichever processing route the information takes; but it is the *kind* of thoughts produced that are key to facilitating further processing in the conscious-mind. Yes, the *conscious-mind* is the place for processing thought, but we don't realize a), that conscious-mind processing is a secondary stage of processing; and b), that we have a choice as to which of our minds we set to work.

There are minds within our collective Mind that are adapted to deal with thoughts of a particular genre – types of thoughts fashioned by certain kinds of information. *You can better explore and express (bring into reality) your thoughts through a mind that resonates to the tune of the thoughts it entertains.*

At present, the ego-endorsed conscious-mind may well develop thought processing problems if it struggles to deal with thoughts that are of a different tone to those it is comfortable with. In addition, the thoughts (and feelings) the ego manipulates the conscious-mind into accepting from the body-consciousness, may not be the most appropriate or helpful to it in ascertaining *how to deal with the perceived conditions* – the job of the conscious-mind.

It is the mark of an educated mind to be able to entertain a thought without accepting it. **Aristotle.**

A final thought

A thought has a very real electromagnetic identity with a force that exists in the electric field of *action*. This is something that science has yet to understand, although the disciplines of cellular and molecular biology are opening science's door to this knowledge. Because a thought (a sphere of energy) lives in this electrical place of action, it *acts* on other forces within the field. Your personality is another force, a "field of action," that lives within this electric field. If your personality's emotional climate draws to it a thought's vibrational signature – through the power of Attraction – that thought will act on and affect your personality's content.

The effect of any thought to your psychological and physical systems is an exact and certain one; determined by its electromagnetic identity. This is because an electromagnetic energy system, that best functions within certain configurations unique to your Self, *saturates* your physical and psychological bodies. Thoughts can have an adverse or beneficial effect on this electromagnetic self. Your body-consciousness and your energy centers translate such effects into actual changes in the molecular structure of the cells within your physical body. Because of the natural power of Attraction, habitual patterns of thought and their consequent effects prevail.

Concerning your health, it isn't difficult to realize that malignant or disparaging thoughts can be problematic for your physical expression – they can affect your personality and your physical body. Additionally, as you are now aware, because of a thought's independence from time, it can affect you both now and in the future. According to Seth, the truth is that although habitual negative thought patterns are the main cause of ill health; the converse is not necessarily true – ill health does not cause negative thought patterns.

There is nothing either good or bad, but thinking makes it so. **Hamlet, Act II, Scene 2.**

On a more positive note, the metaphysical guides remind us that the more we enjoy each and every moment of our lives, less problems will occur. By enjoying life, being appreciative and compassionate, and living as fearlessly as possible, our thoughts become naturally pleasant and attract similar thoughts that give rise to more beneficial circumstances. It is important for us to remember that we live in a safe universe, one that supports us; thinking about this natural state of affairs will help bring us the best possible developments from the Subjective Area within Consciousness.

Abraham (Esther Hicks) has this to add:

You are an extension of Source Energy, and you can tell by the way you feel how much of who you really are is flowing in this moment or how much you are not allowing to flow by virtue of what you're thinking about.[107]

SAY THAT AGAIN (15) Thought as a mechanism.

Thought is a mechanism used by your conscious-mind to translate and interpret information gathered by both your inner and outer senses. Many of us only oil this mechanism with information provided by the outer physical senses. This is detrimental to our conscious-mind's ability to estimate how to act, and occurs because of the ego's narrow understanding and disparaging beliefs on the nature of "feelings" – the additional, *crucial* information provided by the inner senses.

EXERCISE 3 USING YOUR THOUGHTS TO FEEL GOOD[108]

Thinking about a happy event from your life activates positive feelings. With these feelings come memories of other pleasant occasions, along with sensations from both your outer and inner senses – smells, sounds, excitement, feelings of euphoria – all associated with feeling good.

Whenever you think, you also activate your body-consciousness in your subconscious library. It investigates and stimulates cellular memory patterns that relate to what you are thinking about. In a short period, your entire body re-experiences the feeling state achieved at the time of the event.

Your cellular structure changes in recognition of the information contained within your thoughts – it doesn't give a hoot about whether the information relates to the "real" world outside the body, it is responding to instruction from your body-consciousness.

What you need to realize is that all of these psychological associations are "living things," living energy patterns that frequent a dimension unconcerned with time. Just like cells, thoughts have an identity that reacts to other energies, and they revel in associations; drawing to themselves resonant energies whilst fending off those that threaten their existence.

For the next sixty-eight seconds[109] focus your attention on a highly pleasant event from your life. Only entertain those thoughts, feelings and sensations that are associated with this event or other occasions when similar mental activity made you happy. If a contrary thought appears, banish it immediately and concentrate on the original event again. It can take a number of attempts before you can maintain a purity of thought for sixty-eight seconds. Regular practice will achieve this, and your cellular structure will benefit immensely.

CHAPTER 9:

FOUR INFORMATION PROCESSING ROUTES

According to Elias, information from the electric field, the psycho-electric patterns of energy your inner self offers your outer self to ease the full expression of You in the physical domain, comes in four particular flavors or varieties.

It is naïve to assume that such information can only be processed by thought; and you are reminded that thought is a mechanism for use by your conscious-mind to translate and interpret information gathered by your senses – *both inner senses (from our inner self) and outer five senses (from our outer self).* Thinking is, however, just *one way we process* information.

The initial energy patterns of information, graded by our inner selves, pass through four distinct energy-processing centers, four bioelectrical routes to the conscious-mind and on to physicality. Each route gives birth to thoughts *and feelings* for the conscious-mind to digest. These energy-processing centers relate to the bio-electromagnetic energy centers we know as the *Chakras.*[110] For ease of understanding, we can equate Elias's energy processing centers with these energy concentrations referred to in Eastern mystical teachings.

Elias states that the four chakras specifically involved in processing information collected by your inner self, are the Crown Chakra (assigned the color purple); the Throat Chakra (blue); the Solar Plexus Chakra (yellow); and the Base Chakra (red). These concentrations within your electrical body are the first ports of call for the four flavors of information contained within the psycho-electric energy patterns. In a manner of speaking, they are a function of how you process information – how you input information and how you then *output* or express this information when your conscious-mind has finished its translations in what is essentially an information processing cycle.

You have the ability to receive and transmit information through *any and all* of these four processing routes. However... you do have a *preference* for one of the four, a predetermined (by your Essence) aspect of your personality that marries with your personal expression of intent – defined by your families of belonging and alignment. Like your adopted families of intent, your information processing preference serves as a layer of distinction in the construction of your personality.

Below is a list of the four energy-pattern-processing-centers and the distinguishing features of the *inner* information that comes in from your inner self and, after some juggling in your conscious-mind, passes back out through these centers on its way to physical expression (most notably, your behavior). They are information-processing routes that play a significant part in the full expression of your personality:

Crown Chakra – this energy center processes information of a philosophical nature. Issues related to Truth, Freedom, Reality, Existence, Concepts and Causality flavor the thoughts created by this center. This type of information relates to the Conceptual set of inner senses mentioned in *Chapter 3*.

Its philosophical leanings give rise to a focus upon the intellect and "thought-based" processing rather than "feeling-based." Information enters this center through impulses and impressions ("mental enzymes") that are *almost immediately* turned into thought patterns. This center rarely entertains feelings.

Thought is energy – energy on its way to physical expression. The *physical* way station for Crown energies is the pineal gland, situated deep within the brain.[111] This gland is heavily involved in the transformation of non-physical "mental enzymes" into thought and electro-chemical energy patterns—physical chemical enzymes—that contain the data necessary to cause the physical body to propel thought into physical manifestation.

In biological terms, this translation process involves a communication platform that we can loosely term "telepathy." Seth advises us that telepathy takes many forms, not least one that transfers information between cells in this process. His legacy expects the emergence of a new field in biology – "basic organic psychology" – that recognizes this necessary intangible communication platform in living structures. Epigenetics, a branch of cellular biology pioneered by Dr. Bruce Lipton, may well be a precursor to this expectation.

Personalities that favor the Crown chakra processing route trust in thought and are suspicious of feelings, particularly if they invoke emotions. Therefore, they process information almost entirely through the action of thought. Because they avoid feelings and emotions – commonly highlighted by attempts to override this form of communication by inappropriately using thought to decode its message – psychological challenges may ensue. The ego-self can develop a truncated relationship with the Self. It does not understand how to process the energy signatures of feelings and emotions and, because thought is its champion, applies this non-resonant energy to the activity. This folly misinterprets the messages of feelings and emotions at best. Ultimately, much valuable information pertinent to full expression of the personality is lost.

This doesn't mean such personalities cannot correctly process feelings and emotions at all, but their expression will be a constant challenge.

Throat Chakra – this energy center processes information relating to our interactions and communications with others. This covers a broad spectrum of interactions that span our dealings in the non-physical realm as well as the physical realm. Each and every part of Consciousness is included.

Interactions are "energy exchanges" that occur within and between our Essence selves; between our Essence selves and various layers within Consciousness; and between our outer selves and physical "others" – from rocks, trees, dogs and spiders; to children, adults, communities and countries.

The Throat chakra deals with mental enzymes concerned with "collectivity" and "bringing things together." Information travels into and out of this center on a bed of "sensations" – a subtle form of feelings, not overly imbued with emotional energy. This center thus produces more of a mix of thoughts and feelings, and is again associated with our Conceptual set of inner senses, although there is openness to the Empathic inner senses that include emotional energies.

The primary physical structures associated with processing this flavor of information are the pituitary gland, hypothalamus, thalamus, thyroid gland and thymus gland.

Personalities that favor this processing route are fairly rare; they lean towards further processing (in the conscious-mind) to be thought-based, but bring into consideration feelings and their inclusion in deliberations.

Solar Plexus Chakra – this center is involved with processing information concerned with our artistic expression. As you can imagine this subject matter covers another broad spectrum. Associated with our Empathic set of inner senses, and in contrast to the Crown chakra, the priority is on feelings in initial transla-tions of the psycho-electric data.

In contrast to the Throat chakra, information is taken in on a bed of pure feeling and later expressed with an emotional intensity that links to those feelings. The center still generates thoughts, and they play their part in further processing, but the focus is upon feelings and any emotional energy that may adhere to them. Personalities that favor this route to physical expression *trust* their feelings and the expression of their emotions.

Feelings are not the same energy form as emotions and do not necessarily link to emotions – something that is fully explained in the later chapters of this book. Feelings are energy forms that signal your conscious-mind that information from your inner self is available for processing. Your personal feeling-tone within you (mentioned in *Chapter 2*) initiates your inner self's capture of these signals for initial processing through your body consciousness and this energy center. Feelings are a language of the electric field, a way of communicating within your Self.

Personalities that prefer this way of processing information are apt to pay attention to their emotions; however, because of our beliefs and confusion over feelings and emotions, this doesn't mean that such individuals have an easier time of processing information – far from it.

Physical structures allied to the Solar Plexus center are the stomach (hence that "gut feeling"), the gall bladder, the liver, pancreas, small intestinal tract and diaphragm.

Base Chakra – this center processes information that we currently understand to be of a "spiritual" nature. The information received relates to your outer self's relationship to your inner self and your Essence; your relationship to nature; and your relationship to Consciousness Itself. You will find that your physical expression (your translation of this information back into the physical) reflects in your desires to connect.

Empathic inner senses are again at the source of this information. Religions are an explicit example of our desire to connect, each telling their own story of how we can achieve this.

This center's physical presence is around the base of the spine. Apart from processing this kind of information, it also functions as an anchoring station for all the energies that contribute to the physical you, your outer self.

The receiving mechanism, the bed on which this information

lies, is one of feeling again, except this is a feeling that does not form a direct link to emotional energy. You may sense this feeling as being similar to intuition but more than this – a form of direct insight, a direct *knowing*. Thought is not directly involved with the feeling, but we generate a *quality* of thought in those that form after processing this feeling.

You can regard the feeling as a direct awareness of the natural power of *Divine Love* (see *Chapter 4*). Not to be confused with the feeling we derive from Divine Love – human love.

Prominent religious figures, such as Mother Teresa of the Catholic Faith and Buddhism's Dalai Lama, are examples of personalities that exhibit a preference for processing inner information via this energy center.

Like the intentional types described by the genera of human intent, these four information processing styles are *all* included within your personality. You have chosen a preferred style, but with training, you can open up to any and all of the others. Therefore, if you are someone who prefers to immerse yourself in thought, you can still appreciate the communications supplied to you by the varying modes of feeling.

The dominant processing mechanisms are the Crown chakra, reliant on thought as a path to expression, and the Solar Plexus chakra, reliant on emotions. Perhaps contrary to what you might expect, according to Elias, most people prefer to process information through the Solar Plexus chakra; this is because of all our inner senses, it's the Empathic ones that hold our attention – just as with our outer senses, sight, followed by hearing, take precedence.

We all then pay most attention to our thoughts and emotions and allow these to dictate the expression of our personalities. Personalities that choose the Throat and Base chakra routes to expression are far less common amongst us.

EXERCISE 4. WHICH TYPE OF PROCESSOR ARE YOU?

If you haven't a clue as to which processing route you favor, let's take a moment to examine your thoughts and feelings!

Firstly, what do you *trust* the most – your thoughts or your feelings?

Secondly, try to identify what types of thoughts and feelings you entertain on a more regular basis. Read through the differing characteristics of the four processing centers below and see if one center resonates with how your conscious-mind prefers to deal with information.

Solar Plexus processors tend to be suspicious of thought. They trust their emotions. They trust in their *gut* reactions, particularly if they find their thought processing to be at best confusing, more often *obfuscating* (obscure, unclear and overly complicated). This type of processor will often imagine their thoughts to be delusional, as if their intellect is deliberately attempting to confuse them. They may *think* they are thinking continuously – and thus doing a good job of digesting information – but they actually *assimilate* information by using their emotional energies, not through continuous, roundabout thinking. More often than not, when they express their information to others, it's accompanied by a gush of emotional energy.

Crown processors have a hard time recognizing a feeling of any sort and when the feeling is associated with an emotion their conscious-mind can go into thought processing overdrive – circuitous or convoluted thinking prevails – often ended by a resolute suppression of the feeling and any accompanying emotional energy. Those with a keen intellect are well practiced in explaining to themselves and others how thoughts, betrothed to reason and logic, are all that is required to deal appropriately with any situation. The modern worldview champions the intellect for its reasoning skills whilst ignoring the worth of feelings – which makes it all the more difficult for Crown processors to express emotion. When they do, it can be an explosive release of energy. Frustration and anger are usually the translations of this emotional release.

Throat processors, being between the Crown and Solar Plexus centers, incorporate both thought-based processing and feelings that attach to emotions. Although prone to use thought rather than feelings, they are more adept at interacting with others, as they are more conversant with the Empathic inner senses and appreciative of the messages of feelings and any emotions that may follow them.

Base processors are adept at tuning into a feeling that is akin to direct knowing. It's not a feeling that links to emotions; it is a purity of feeling that we do not have the language to describe. These personalities may experience what they perceive to be moments of intuition, but this would be too shallow an interpretation of the feeling they sense. Accompanying the feeling may be a sense of calmness. The personality that expresses this preference for information processing would exude an air of total spiritual involvement in life.

The work of Anodea Judith Ph.D. is worth mentioning here. She

is a leading authority on the integration of chakras and therapeutic issues. She suggests that information that is "in-tension"
in the Mind of your Essence – or energy *in-formation* that your
inner self has gathered for consideration by your conscious-mind
– achieves physical expression by transfer through your chakras.

You can think of the chakra system as a subtle energy pathway
for your consciousness to bridge and connect your Essence self to
your Mind and body. Judith refers to this as the "rainbow bridge"
in light of the colors given to the chakras. The movement of
energy through your chakras continually "condenses" (think of
the Electromagnetic Energy Units of Seth continuing to slow
down) consciousness until it is eventually ready to *solidify* in the
physical realm as physical action. We expand upon her ideas
from her book, *Eastern Body Western Mind*,[112] in *Book II* of *It's
About You!*

Your preferred processing system is the one that appears most
familiar to you, the one that you listen to more intently. Like the
families of intent, no one choice is "better" than another, your
choice does not *exclude* the other paths to knowing, and you are
always capable of entertaining any of these psychological
systems.

What we need to appreciate is that contained within our
personality is the ability to process information and communications from the electric field – from our inner selves – in a variety
of ways and we should seek to exercise all of them. By doing so
we gain a far broader understanding of our own personality, the
nature of our Selves, and what is influencing our perception of
reality. Understanding these communications from our Selves
also influences our relationships with others – *all* "others" –
especially fellow humans, so we are better able to accept and
adjust to where different personalities are coming from.

At present, a majority of us feel more than we think and a
good many of the rest of us think without feeling. For the

"feelers," difficulties arise from an education that suggests we should think about what we feel; and that certain feelings are unacceptable. For example, when very young we are led to believe than many of our biological feelings (communications from our body-consciousness) are perverse in some way and therefore should not be expressed outwardly.

For personalities that link feelings to emotions, and thereby wish to express themselves more fully through emotional content, any denial of the value of feelings can be extremely difficult to live with.

The "thinkers" amongst us are of course ready to adopt any erroneous schooling on feelings – unaware that their own method for processing information also has its pitfalls. Some may cut off the Solar Plexus center that links to their emotions, thinking that this will allow them to move through life relatively unscathed. This may be the case; however, the expression of their personalities is often unnecessarily confined.

It is crucial for us to understand that we *feel* first, before we think. Even for those processing through the Crown chakra, feelings are there first before a seemingly instantaneous take up of thought.

CHAPTER 10:

BELIEVING IS PERCEIVING

Believe nothing, no matter where you read it, or who has said it, not even if I have said it, unless it agrees with your own reason, and your common sense. **Buddha.**

The thing about thoughts is that they grow into, and graft themselves onto, **belief systems.** These systems are at the heart of the creation process – central to the creation of **your** reality.

Thought *in itself* does not create your reality; if it did, our species would be long since extinct! Thankfully, we are yet to give over our creative abilities to a mechanism whose primary function is to translate information. You already know that the thinking of something you want to create, however consistently, only very rarely appears to bring it to fruition. This is because it's not thought that *ultimately* shapes and governs your manifestations; it is your beliefs that have the final say on what you perceive as your reality. They grab your thoughts by the roots and graft them onto their trunks before producing the fruit of your reality.

Clues as to the nature of your beliefs are evident in what you *do* and how you *respond* to a situation. Reality itself reflects the content of your beliefs. By noticing what you are doing, how you are responding, how you are behaving, and what information is central to the event you are experiencing, you begin to uncover the psychological framework on which your reality depends.

Remember that when your ego-self and conscious-mind enter your subconscious library to widen their understanding of, and how to respond to, a certain situation; the conscious-mind, directed by your ego-self, studiously avoids any contact with your inner self – thereby missing out on her more wide-ranging and time-neutral information. The conscious-mind makes a well-worn direct path to the librarian's information counter. At the counter, your body-consciousness slips the conscious-mind its basket of preliminarily preprocessed information from the electric field – thoughts and feelings. Your conscious-mind knows what to do with the thoughts, but is not too sure about the fluorescent feelings.

Your time-oriented ego directs the conscious-mind to seek out the librarian's archival information because it is on this information that it places its trust – *past* information is the *only* information it regards as having any applicability in creating a response. Your ego, as its existence began when you were born, assumes the subconscious also came into existence on this momentous occasion. It knows that the subconscious houses all information concerning itself. However, because of its narcissistic nature, it also assumes that this "self" information is the only data that its buddy, the conscious-mind, needs to access. It knows little about your Essence self, with its far broader knowledge base, or the other zones of knowledge within your subconscious.

Your ego-self is thus apt to say to the conscious-mind when in a quandary as to what to do, "Now listen, there are a load of dodgy characters hanging around this subconscious area; so, as before, quickly go and ask the librarian geezer what we normally do in this kind of scenario, then we can get the hell outa here. If that weird, ghostly humming bloke bungs you a basket while you're at the desk, bring it back to me – it might just have some useful thoughts in it. We like those."

The information your ego-self permits the conscious-mind to gather from the librarian narrowly confines itself to actions and behaviors sanctioned on past occasions that closely mirror the current circumstances. The conscious-mind must then use this limited data to deliberate on how to deal with things. It is data based purely on habitual actions – *what you normally do*; and *how you normally behave* – the expressions of what you **believe** you should do.

Using this ego-confined data and comparing it to the ego's perception of the current situation is all that the conscious-mind has to work with. Your ego filters the thoughts and feelings within any basket given over by the body-consciousness – usually discarding the feelings, and approving only the thoughts that conform to already held beliefs. Your conscious-mind's conclusions cause you to act, unsurprisingly, in a manner *primarily determined by your beliefs.*

It is, therefore, your beliefs and belief systems that hold the most potential (an electrical potential, incidentally) that thereby govern your behavior – what you *do*, and how you respond to your physical environment.

So what exactly are beliefs?

Belief: The acceptance by the mind that something is true or real, often underpinned by an emotional or spiritual sense of certainty.[113]

Abraham (Esther Hicks) succinctly defined beliefs as "thoughts you think more than once," while Seth states that beliefs are thoughts "you choose to stamp as true."

Once a psycho-electric pattern turns into a thought, it becomes *real* within the electric field – the playground of your psyche. It has a charge, a vibrational signature, an identity. When your conscious-mind entertains a thought it stimulates this charge and activates its pulling potential. Thoughts of a similar signature draw to it; electrical potential increases until the conglomeration of thoughts reach an electrical threshold and a "significantly" charged belief takes root. A belief is thus a concentration of energy in your Mind – an established plant in the garden of your subconscious area.

Your personality is the gardener that tends your garden of thoughts and beliefs. A belief maintains the same magnetic pulling and repelling properties of thought, only with heightened potential – in an electrical sense and in terms of *likelihood of physical expression.*

As you steadily grow your assortment of plant life – thoughts and beliefs (watered by emotional energy) – in your personality's imagined garden, an overall design takes shape. Your thoughts and beliefs present a unique canopy of foliage, a combined scent, a collective "tonal frequency" that encapsulates the essence of your garden and thus your personality.

Remember that your personality is the electrical counterpart to your ego. The tonal frequency of your personality therefore becomes the identity your ego cherishes and considers its own. Which means your ego's identity rests upon your collection of thoughts and beliefs. This fragile foundation (it can sense their tenuous nature) explains why your ego is so fearful of any contrasting thoughts or beliefs that may affect the integrity of how it defines itself – and why it jealously guards its prized collection of foliage.

Figure 3 below depicts a section from a typical person's "Garden of Beliefs" found in the subconscious area of their Self. It represents the collection of thoughts and beliefs that create the personality's tonal frequency. A line sits atop the foliage to signify the frequency curve of this tone. It shouldn't be difficult to imagine how this frequency curve fluctuates in accordance with the thoughts and beliefs under its canopy.

Because beliefs, like thoughts, exist in the electric field, their *durability* is reliant upon their electrical potential – which has nothing to do with time. Your outer self translates the *strength* of an electrical potential as the degree to which you regard a belief to be a truth—*your truth*—and its durability, in relation to time, translates as continuity – how long the belief figures in your thoughts.

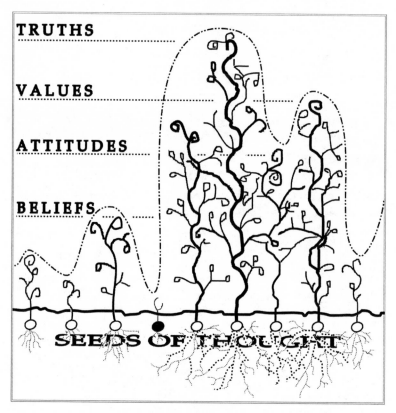

Figure 3. Your personality's tonal frequency

Electrical potential builds steadily through repetitious thought patterns, but the element within the electric field that can turbo-charge that potential is emotional energy. If, for the sake of measurement, we give a thought one unit of electrical potential, and a belief, maybe ten units, then an emotion can have a potential ranging from, say fifty units, to… well, *bonkers-amounts* (not a recognized scientific term).

In other words, emotional energy is the primary force that gives life to, grows, and sustains your beliefs – emotions water your garden of beliefs.

The Theory of Evolution, a confusion of beliefs

To illustrate this thought-to-belief-to-truth growth process, let's look again at the Darwin/Wallace example of synchronous thinking mentioned in *Chapter 8*.

The theory of evolution came about through Darwin and Wallace having very similar thoughts on how living forms might have evolved over time. A theory, in essence, is a belief about something arrived at through contemplation. Darwin and Wallace are reputed to have had very similar beliefs about evolution; it was just a case of who would be able to express their beliefs first through publication. History reveals that Darwin pipped Wallace to the post, but it does not reveal *why* and how their rivalry affected the theory itself.

From information provided in another channeled book by Jane Roberts, *The Afterdeath Journal of an American Philosopher: The World View of William James*, we can surmise that it was the greater strength of the electrical potential behind Darwin's beliefs that propelled his work into physical reality ahead of Wallace. Events suggest that a secondary train of thought triggered another set of beliefs within Darwin that in turn attracted and accrued a considerable amount of emotional energy. This emotional energy superimposed itself upon the electrical potential of his evolutionary beliefs, thus powering their physical manifestation.

The extra charge projected his theory into the physical realm, but most importantly, the secondary set of beliefs associated with this crucial energy *distorted the vibrational signature and integrity of his thoughts on evolution* (remember all thoughts are electrical actions that interact with and affect other thoughts). The distortion, or electrical interference, realized as *a heightened potential for misinterpretation when Darwin's collection of thoughts achieved manifestation through publication.* The entangled thoughts and beliefs that instigated the interference, stem from the rapidly growing shrub of the genus "competition."

Darwin had written up and developed his work on how species come into being through natural selection twenty years before 1859 – the date of first publication of *On the Origin of Species*. He was planning to publish a far broader work, but was diligently refining it and searching for the definitive explanation as to why organisms mutate.

T.R. Malthus's *An Essay on The Principle of Population* provided Darwin with a solution to this puzzle. The solution, though, had become inexorably bound to another philosopher's interpretation of Malthus's work – Herbert Spencer – who is reputed to have coined the phrase "survival of the fittest." Darwin's explanation of natural selection – the "randomly occurring variations in offspring" being favored in a changing environment both for survival and for forming species' – became interpreted to mean that the struggle for life revolves around the elimination of the "unfit." This "modern" belief of the time gained considerable growth in the human psyche during the industrial revolution.

Survival of the fittest became the catchphrase of a belief now nestled within a system of beliefs within the human psyche; a collection of beliefs that erroneously suggest that as we are separate from others, we must therefore be *in competition* for life's resources.[114]

Wallace, another fan of Malthus, sent Darwin his own paper outlining a theory of natural selection. In the face of this competition, "Darwin was appalled."[115] It sparked a chain of thinking in Darwin's mind that had him agonizingly nurture this modern belief within himself and led him to project these thoughts on human competition into his seminal work. In *The Afterdeath Journal of an American Philosopher*, William James remarks:

Darwin's considerable achievement in perceiving the interrelationship of creature, species, and environment was entirely misinterpreted. His cataloguing of effects led him to perceive only competitiveness, and made him blind to the basic cooperative ventures existing between species and between creatures and their environment.[116]

By the fifth edition of *Origin*, Darwin was using the expression *survival of the fittest* as a synonym for what he originally described as "natural selection." This expression, the catch-phrase of his thoughts on competition, ignited the potential for misinterpretation of his work. Darwin's emotions rushed him into publication. A more patient and more cooperative stance with Wallace (they did at least give a genial joint presentation of their works to the Linnaean Society in 1858) may have seen a more robust and purer expression of his beliefs on the origin of species. Perhaps then we would not have been made to endure the misinterpreted translation that to this day remains the glue that holds together the unquestionable truth that we live in a hostile world, where every living thing is hell bent on preserving its gene pool.

The theory of evolution began as a thought, grew into a belief system of heightened electrical potential, which eventually became a "truth" by which we perceive our reality. This classic example should make you aware of the potential (electrical or otherwise) of your thoughts and beliefs.

When thoughts become beliefs, they move from being mechanisms for interpreting information, to a tool that *manipulates* your perception – perception being the overall psychological instrument that forms your reality. (*Book II explores the phenomenon of our "perception" – for the moment regard it as a filtering instrument, through which your ego deciphers and evaluates the energies it aims to bring into physical action.*)

Beliefs and the systems that develop from them are not an artifact of your Essence self, they are *tools* meant for constructing the reality of your physical world.

Your beliefs don't just grow from your thoughts

Apart from growing an electrical potential from the seed of a thought, you can acquire beliefs through various other means. In the main, they come as "gifts." Wrapped in the paper of communication, they take the form of seedlings ready to plant in the nursery beds of your personality's garden of beliefs. Your primary care-givers present you with some fundamental beliefs on physical survival, but you receive beliefs not just from your parents and family. Everyone and everything around you can proffer you a belief. Moreover, it is everything around you that nurtures and reinforces the growth of your beliefs – because you draw to you events that conform to your beliefs.

Emotions govern the speed by which your beliefs establish themselves in your psychological garden. Whether it's a fear of being stabbed by your father's fork if you don't eat your greens that has you believe cabbage is a dietary must; or that joy you get when chomping into a chocolate bar that has you believe that the cocoa plant came from heaven – emotions play a key role in belief development.

We gather beliefs even when we are not aware of it because the wrappings of communication distract us from the message. Our present technological era has a focus on the various ways we can communicate through its wizardry. Mobile phones and the internet now compete with radio, cinema and television to capture our thoughts and get us to believe in something. Gone are the days when we only acquired beliefs from the people we came in physical contact with.

Continued accrual of electrical charge raises a thought's potential to a belief; and above that, as potential increases, beliefs begin to grow into stronger psychological entities – attitudes, values, and truths. Notice that each of these terms contains a degree of *emotional* strength. A belief develops into an *attitude*, which is, "a belief by which a man acts by preference"[117]; which then becomes a *value* we hold (enduring belief); and then matures into a truth (core belief) – that we do not *believe* are beliefs! Once our beliefs have matured, we defend them vigorously—and there's the truth of the matter!

When a belief becomes your truth, beware. It can easily hold back your progress in understanding the reality of who you are and what your intent and purpose is for this lifetime. As an example of beliefs holding back our progress in understanding our collective reality, we can look to the once held scientific belief in *phlogiston*.

The belief in phlogiston, held by chemists from the late 17th Century until the late 18th Century, halted the uncovering of the naturally occurring elements – particularly oxygen. Phlogiston, a belief cultivated by the thinking of Johann J. Becher (1635–1682) and nurtured by the thoughts of Georg E. Stahl (1659–1734) – who devised the term – was an "air" that carried the properties of "fire." Understanding of the physical elements in the 17th Century began with the premise (belief) that they came under classical definition – they were of earth, air, fire, or water. Thoughts about "fire" gave rise to the belief in phlogiston to explain how things ignite and burn.

It was the French father of modern chemistry, Antoine Lavoisier (1743–1794), who eventually showed that phlogiston did not exist. It was neither a substance nor a principle for combustion; his discovery of oxygen and hydrogen put paid to the belief in phlogiston.

This example of a scientific belief holding back our understanding of the physical world should be a reminder to us all that if we hold too firmly to our beliefs and don't examine them regularly, we slow the evolution of our understanding of not only our physical environment, but also the nature of our Selves.

CHAPTER 11

TRUTHS

It ain't what you don't know that gets you into trouble. It's what you know for sure that just ain't so. **Mark Twain**

Your truths are still beliefs. When you realize that your truths grow from the saplings of your beliefs, you will be able to view your truths with a far more relaxed and objective approach as to their importance. Your truths may become as inconsequential to you as the few absolute truths that permeate the physical world. This is because it's not truths that govern your life, *it's your beliefs that dictate what you perceive to be a truth* that hold the utmost consequence for you – it's your beliefs that decide how fulfilling and how joyous your life is.

So what are truths, you might ask? Surely there is something; a concept, a reality, that has truth to it – something that is consistent, an absolute that we can rely on so that we can frame our reality constructions? Is there not an ultimate Truth, with a capital "T," found by the constant enquiry of our mystics, scientists, philosophers and intellectuals? Before we answer such questions, here is what a "truth" is according to the channeled guides:

A truth is an absolute – a constant facet of Consciousness that exists throughout all expressions of Consciousness.

A truth, therefore, applies itself to all dimensions of existence – across all Areas within Consciousness, whether in the physical Objective Area or the non-physical Subjective Area. The only such truths named in the channeled literature are:

- **Consciousness** – the ultimate, absolute, one Truth put forward by Seth and other channeled teachers as *All That Is* and Its individuations – *your consciousness* for example.
- **Energy** – the vitality of Consciousness.
- **Reality** – the myriad products, physical or otherwise, of the creation process employed by Consciousness.
- **Tone/Vibration** – the vibrational signature of an individualized product of the creation process.
- **Color** – a vibrational constant within the expressions of Consciousness.
- **Divine Love** – the natural power defined in *Chapter 4* that provides the impetus for all creative actions – not to be confused with human love.

Degrees of truth

The answers to the previous questions are bewildering in that they require us to understand "degrees of truth" in order to resolve them.

According to metaphysical teaching, *there is only one absolute Truth* – which gets a capital "T" to match its capital "C" – Consciousness. The above truths emerge from this Truth in order that Consciousness can express Itself across all dimensions. Which makes the above list of truths, after Consciousness, *relative to It.*

Your consciousness, for example, is a truth relative to the absolute Truth of Consciousness Itself. So these listed truths are one rung down on the degrees-of-truth ladder if you like, they don't get a capital "T," but from our perspective in the physical realm, *to all intents and purposes,* they are the truths our reality relies upon.

Another step down the ladder are the *natural principles* and the remaining *natural power* (after Divine Love) *of Attraction*[118] reviewed in *Chapters 3 and 4*. These are the truths relative to how Consciousness creates and sustains the physical world.

Most enquirers to date have been looking for *the* Truth – God, the God particle, Grand Unified Theory, Theory of Everything – *within our collective* **belief systems** (such as those described in *Chapter 12*), which, *by their very nature,* do not necessarily contain any of these relative truths. Ironically, belief systems do contain *the* Truth, as no "thing," even the thing of a belief, is separate from Consciousness.

Usually, our personal information processing systems of *Chapter 9,* contain at best a translation or interpretation of the relative truths listed above. The *feeling* of human love, for example, is *an interpretation* of the truth of Divine Love. Additionally, the way we perceive color as varying frequencies on the electromagnetic energy spectrum is a translation of its truth, which is, according to Elias, that it is a multidimensional action within Consciousness.

Our collective core belief systems, such as the one Elias calls "science" are a further step down on the degrees of truth ladder. *Their* truths can only be relative – relative to the physical dimension and the realities created therein. For example, in relation to physics, gravity is a "relative truth" describing the movement of large physical bodies in the physical, space-time dimension. It is a truth that *only applies* to physical dimensions – physical expressions of Consciousness. Another example is *Time,* a scientifically recognized *construct* – known to be a relative truth of our physical dimension.[119]

When we come to personal truths, *your* truths, then we must consider them as really, really, relative! We might just call them "qualified, relative truths." Your truths are relative to the amount of energy you have accrued to certain beliefs.

Always remember that along with heightened energy comes a cloak of concealment, the cloak of personal truth. *Your truths are therefore liable to exclusion from any examination of your beliefs.*

SAY THAT AGAIN (16) Truths.

The only *absolute* Truth is *Consciousness* and Its expressions.

Relative truths are principles incorporated within and consistent across – *all dimensions* of Consciousness. All such truths arise from the intent of Consciousness to express Itself. They are therefore relative to Consciousness.

Societal and Personal truths are a product of amplified energy potentials accrued by beliefs and belief systems. *They pertain to the physical dimension* and the creations therein. They may contain interpretations of relative truths, but they are neither consistent nor constant within our physical dimension.

The truth of your reality

Even though you create your reality *through* your belief systems, which appear to have no real substance or consistency to them, this doesn't make your reality any less real!

You may have noted from the list above that "Reality" is a *relative truth* – just one rung down from the absolute Truth of Consciousness. This means, any reality, however it is created, even when cast by the mold of a belief system, is a truth and has been made real for a purpose – to purify and intensify the experience.

Your reality, as observed through your senses, is your own very real and magnificent creation. You (beginning with your non-physical self) have managed to pattern raw energy (albeit through the malleable medium of your beliefs) into a *definite, solidified form* that remains stored within your Mind – and thus the mind of Consciousness – long after its moment of being. How neat is that!

Of course, some of your creations aren't too pleasant, but you are now well aware that in order to remedy unpleasant realities you need to look to your beliefs.

Our belief systems are real to us because they are an aspect of our outer self's psychological makeup – a specially constructed medium through which we shape our creations. Their reality is their truth in our physical realm; but they have only relative truth when their place in all of Consciousness is considered. This is because beliefs are not a constant feature of Consciousness across all dimensions; they are restricted to the creative processes within physical dimensions.

Belief systems can change across physical dimensions; we have our collection of belief systems that we use to create our reality, other physical dimensions have their own set of belief systems. In short, beliefs are a facet of physicality. As Bashar (Darryl Anka) puts it, without our *beliefs*, we would create no reality and be non-existent. Beliefs are our templates for physical manifestations – the method by which we solidify our experiences. They are the primary filter in our instrument of perception through which we express our personalized portion of Consciousness.

Importantly, as you begin to recognize the nature of beliefs and examine them more objectively, you begin to release their hold on your actions. They are what they are, an integral part of the physical realm we have chosen to experience. There is therefore no need to judge them – beliefs in themselves are neither good nor bad, they exist as choices. Our psyches contain *all* beliefs; we choose (currently without much conscious input) which beliefs we apply energy to – which beliefs we grow in our subconscious garden – and which beliefs we express as indication of our collective or individual personality. What we do, how we behave, is an expression of our beliefs through the creation of our experiences. Realities exist so that we can experience the beliefs that are creating them.

The experience of the "truth" of our reality is all about bringing to our awareness the *relative* truths of our beliefs. Reality draws our attention to the fact that we can choose our reality! If you don't like what you are experiencing, if you prefer something else, then choose to change it – *by first reconfiguring the vibrational energy signature of your beliefs.*

Your personal reality asks the questions, "How do you *feel* about what you've created here? Is this in line with your intent and purpose?" If your feelings are of a negative hue, then you know that the reality generating such feelings is not in line with your intent and purpose. Your feelings are signals from your inner self to look to your beliefs in order to change the reality to one you prefer, for it is your beliefs that steer your creations.

How can I better establish my own truths?

The answer has something to do with opening up to as many ways of knowing[120] as possible. The contemporary philosopher Ken Wilber, in establishing Integral Theory, promotes the recommendation that *all* sources of knowledge have something, however little, to contribute to our cosmological standpoint. No one source can make claim to being the sole arbiter of truth, neither is it likely that any one source can be completely devoid of truth. It isn't a question of adhering to one source and discounting all others as untruthful; it is about discovering what *feels* true for you within any field of knowledge, no matter its origin.

The process of assessing what feels true, without capitulating to the ego's faultfinding interference, is a forgotten skill in most people. It is a process that begins with paying attention to any feeling that occurs when taking in information; for example, "I'm feeling invigorated by reading this" or, "I'm feeling frustrated by reading this."

The feeling is the precursor to an emotion coming to the surface of your awareness. If you recognize the emotion to be "positive" – exciting, joyous – then you can assure yourself that the information conforms to your inner self's guidance on what is "true for you." If you recognize the emotion to be "negative" in tone – anger, sadness, frustration – then you know that the information *challenges* your beliefs; *it does not necessarily mean that the information is not true for you.*

Recognizing this challenge, you can then go on to exercise the considerable reasoning powers of your ego to fathom exactly what beliefs are involved and adjust them accordingly. Importantly, you simply need to become aware that the one piece of information may irritate your current belief systems, but you don't have to narrow your choices of action to one of instant dismissal of the validity of *all* further information to come from that source. You can still choose to make note of the irritation and continue to absorb any further information that generates a pleasant feeling.

When it comes to approaching your personal collection of irritants, this will become apparent during the remainder of this book and *Book II*. Addressing to your beliefs will become a crucial factor in any personal shift in consciousness required by your inner self.

As you become used to receiving information in such a manner – paying attention to any inner sense of feeling as to its substance, *as well as* employing the rationale and logic of your ego – you can become more confident in assimilating information into your worldview and ethical principles. It is the feeling you get from your inner self that you can trust as the arbitrator of what is and isn't presently true for you.

Learning to trust your inner guidance, whilst adopting an integral practice when gathering knowledge, establishes a more dependable discernment. You begin to understand that both "truth" and "reality" are dynamic concepts, craftily shifting their allegiances between us. In other words, what is true and real is always subjective; it is always subject to your beliefs.

Before we move on to the equally important factors in the creation of your reality – feelings and emotions – the next chapter sketches out the collective core belief systems that humanity has constructed out of the medium of beliefs through which we express our Selves.

CHAPTER 12

SYSTEMS OF BELIEFS

As you might imagine, we've been doing a lot of thinking over the millennia and some impressive belief structures have grown up covering a multitude of topics. Elias (Mary Ennis) has attempted to narrow down these topics to manageable proportions, but in so doing reminds us that, like the genera of human intent, outlines and subject matters entangle and interweave with one another, so be wary of envisioning any strict delineation. Within any of these belief structures are hundreds, if not thousands, of subsidiary beliefs.

To aid understanding of the nature of your personal beliefs, we can take the analogy of your personality's "Garden of Beliefs" mentioned earlier a little further.

Recall for a moment the scene we left behind in *Chapter 7* of the reception area in your subconscious library. You will remember that your personality likes to nip off to the garden of beliefs whenever the outer self calls into the library. Your ego waits nervously at the revolving doors as the conscious-mind enquires at the counter. Your personality knows that the garden represents the entire collection of its counterpart's (the ego) thoughts and beliefs accrued since physical birth. To a large extent then, the garden is a reflection of itself as well as the ego. As such, it loves the garden and wants to take care of it; it is the gardener in residence.

Imagine thoughts to be the seeds handed to your personality by the conscious-mind for planting in this garden. Watered by emotions and nurtured by the sunshine of attention, a seedling grows into a plant – a belief. Eventually, some of the plants reach tree proportions; a size that makes them appear to require little conscious attention as they establish themselves within your garden.

For any gardener it is ridiculous to judge a plant. Gardeners recognize that a plant simply *is*; it exists as an expression of nature, of Consciousness, in physical form. Your personality views the plants in its garden in the same way. As gardeners, we don't label plants as good or bad (even weeds are just plants growing in the wrong place), but we do exercise our power of choice through preference. As you become consciously aware of the nature of beliefs, and begin to appreciate your personality's love of gardening, you become a *conscious* gardener – you get to choose which plants you give your attention to and cultivate in your garden of beliefs.

Listed below are the ten "core systems of beliefs" that Elias declares to be the subject themes we spend the whole of our time thinking about. All of our thoughts and beliefs come under the canopy of these essential topics. They thereby underpin our reality creations as they are the primary filters within the instrument of our perception. You can imagine them to be ten themed planting beds in your garden, each containing trees, bushes and plants associated with the core topic. For the trees, each branch, twig and leaf is a subsidiary belief. Their fruits and nuts contain their seeds of thought.

These fundamental belief systems help us to understand where any particular belief might be coming from; which tree it may have branched from – a start in the process of addressing a belief, or collection of beliefs, that may be at the center of a reality we would like to change.

Ten core topics of thought that we have developed into belief systems

- **Spirituality** – We have generated a belief system that revolves around the pursuit of "spirituality." This system is an amalgamation of our thoughts on whether there is more to our being than just our presence in the physical dimension. The origin of this existential quandary stems from the individuation of humanity's consciousness from Consciousness Itself.

This belief system has grown because the further individuation of the individual – *interpreted by our ego-selves as separation from Source* – results in the ego "forgetting" that we are spiritual beings "first" and foremost, with a Self that operates in the "spiritual" realm as well as the physical realm.

Much of the reason for the growth of this belief system is actually to do with acceptance of our Self – our outer self and our non-physical Essence self – as a unity within the oneness of Consciousness.

Of course, religious doctrines are belief systems that fall under this topic and they are at the heart of our *traditional worldviews*.

• **Truth** – Because beliefs grow into highly charged entities that purport to be truths, we expend a great deal of mental energy pursuing this notion of what is true, what is real, and what isn't. Seeking truth is something the intellect portion of the ego-self likes to do, particularly in those individuals that prefer to process information through the Crown chakra route (presented in *Chapter 9*).

Understanding that our truths are *relative* to the perceiver (observer) and the circumstances (the dimension in which the action occurs), will greatly enhance the *theory of relativity*.

This bed of beliefs produces heavily camouflaged foliage, in that its plants become invisible to us by blending in with those of the surrounding beds. In so doing, we are seldom able to see them let alone examine the health of these plants and prune them into better shape.

This system of beliefs is of course the cause of many a conflict. The longer the plants from this bed remain unobserved and unattended the less receptive they are to any well-intentioned care or attention any gardener has to offer. The branches of such trees become thick and less flexible, unable to bend in the winds of change that challenge their strength.

- **Emotions** – Emotions are of chief concern to the processing of information through the Solar Plexus chakra. As this is our most preferred route for processing information, and due in no small part to our ignorance of their important role in the construction of our realities, much of our thinking revolves around the topic of emotions.

  Emotions themselves are independent from belief systems; they are electrical energy potentials – the vitality of our universe. We grow a belief system in an attempt to understand them and explain what they are. As Elias reminds us, "Belief systems are those inventions that you create to explain what you do not understand."[121] Think of emotions as the water that is imperative to the health of your garden of beliefs.

  Alongside the energy they bring to the creation process, emotions include a communication to your conscious-mind as to the state of your overall being. We explore their true nature in *Chapter 15*. The subjects of emotions and sexuality, according to Elias, take precedence in our thinking as we explore and examine the factors that contribute to our reality.

- **Sexuality** – A topic, would you believe, that takes up an excessive amount of our thinking time. The belief system of sexuality includes beliefs about gender – what it means to be male or female; sexual preference – which gender we are attracted to, if either, or both; the sexual act itself – our beliefs about why, how, where, who with, and when it is performed. Overall, the belief system of sexuality generates a mass of thoughts that preoccupy our minds a great deal of the time – particularly during our reproductive years, and certainly for anyone producing inordinate levels of testosterone.[122]

Socrates once said that at least with age (reduced testosterone production) comes the opportunity to think about something else.

An additional area within this topic that Elias brings to our attention is that of "orientations." Orientations play a significant role in our perceptions of the physical dimension we are exploring. They relate to sexual preference, what we conventionally think of as "sexual orientation," but they go far beyond this tenuous link. Orientations are an area within the belief system of sexuality that we are yet to think about, precisely because we are unaware of their existence and thus influence upon us.

We explore orientations, along with their influence on your perception in *Book II* of *It's About You!* This will bring you something new to think about concerning sexuality.

- **Relationships** – A system of beliefs that incorporates the many types of relationships we have, not least our ego-self's relationship with our inner self. It isn't difficult to appreciate how this system's branches of beliefs entangle themselves with those of the trees in the Sexuality bed close by.

  Relationships in respect of our parents, our partners, siblings, other family members, our children, co-workers, other groups, other countries, our "God" are all set within certain codes we adopt – based on our beliefs on the matter.

- **Perception** – We have many beliefs about what perception is, and *how* we perceive through our outer senses. Some think that perception is just about our sense of vision. There is much more to learn on the subject.

  Your perception is concerned with how you view and interact with your Self (your outer self with your Essence self), how you view and interact with the physical world, and how you view and interact with others that co-create the physical dimension.

  Importantly, your other belief systems are constantly influencing the design and growth of the plants in your bed of perception – particularly the belief system of sexuality, with its "orientation" branches inexorably entangled.

  Perception is not solely about your visual sense, neither is it limited to information processing – it is all of your inner and outer senses, all of your information processing systems, all of the communication systems within your Self, the energy of your emotions, and all of the belief systems through which you filter these reality organizing elements. Your perception is at the heart then of your "worldview." *The totality of your perception regulates how you create your reality.*

- **Sensing** – This system of beliefs has primarily grown from our preoccupation with the outer physical senses and our heightening of them through instrumentation. Of these senses, vision has become our favorite, which explains why it has become synonymous with perception for some.

  The glut of media coverage on the subject of cooking suggests that taste may come a close second in our attention upon the outer senses.

Our inner senses (described in *Chapter 3*) are currently subject to beliefs that discourage their use. They are as natural as our outer senses and we currently use them either sparingly or without conscious awareness. Consequently, this bed of beliefs lies unattended and has become overgrown with weeds blown from other belief beds.

- **Science** – The belief system of science provide us with an excellent foundation for knowing the physical universe we have chosen to explore. The map or description of what it means to be a physical expression of Consciousness is virtually complete. For it to be completed there needs to be a realization that to know more of the physical domain we must progress in our exploration of the non-physical realm. Practiced use of the inner senses can achieve this.

Most scientists do not *believe* that we have inner senses that are capable of increasing our knowledge of the physical world. This belief flies in the face of the evidence that many scientific breakthroughs result from inner knowledge being allowed access to the conscious-mind through "naturally altered states" (the inner senses at work) such as dreaming, intuition, and inspiration.

The success of scientific endeavor since the renaissance period has seen this bed of beliefs expand rapidly in our gardens. Among many growth spurts, a tree within it has sent out a branch that in many respects resembles the hardy branches of religion that spread themselves from the trees of the spirituality plot. A religion of science can only perpetuate systems of beliefs that attempt to explain our inherent spirituality rather than truly embrace it. This dominant bed of scientific beliefs features considerably in our *modern worldview.*

- **Physical creation of the Universe** – This system of beliefs
  has grown up from our fascination with our own creation
  and the creation of the physical universe. The belief
  systems of Science and Spirituality (specifically religious
  doctrines) provide us with inadequate explanations – they
  each have their own myths on what happened "before the
  beginning."

  When asked by an interviewer in the 1980s what the
  world needed most, the American mythologist Joseph
  Campbell (1904–1987) replied, "A new myth." He
  suggested that it would need to encapsulate a more holistic
  view of the planet and its peoples; a suggestion that gave
  birth to a postmodern myth within the *postmodern
  worldview* that is beginning to emerge.

- **Duplicity** – Deliberately left until last, this system of
  beliefs does not even attempt to confine itself to one
  particular bed. The plants that associate with its theme are
  generally creepers that grow amongst the other beds, often
  smothering the more established shrubs and trees.

  According to Elias, this belief system grows out of our
  notions on duality – our thoughts on the contrast that
  always exists so that we can make choices about what we
  prefer. He names it Duplicity, because there is more to it
  than just deliberations over duality.

  Duplicity is the system of beliefs that incorporates a
  degree of deceitfulness; that is, the perfumes of its plants
  seduce you into thinking that because you observe a
  contrast, you also need to make a judgment about the
  contrasting elements. The system lures us into being
  judgmental – virtually *all* the time. This judgmental aspect
  leads to conflict, both within our minds, and in the
  physical environment. Its strength within our belief
  systems stems from a lack of trust in our outer selves and

our ability make our decisions of preference.

This belief system is at the center of our difficulties when it comes to recognizing and addressing our problematic or unhealthy beliefs. We must identify and deal with this insidious system overlaying our other beliefs before we begin any re-landscaping projects in our garden of beliefs. Its all-pervasive, entangled presence in your garden interferes with any efforts to change the landscape of your beliefs. You need to bring its creepers under control if you are to go on and manage your garden.

We come to terms with Duplicity in *Book II,* as it is the belief system that most affects your *perception* – the instrument that creates your reality – also explored in *Book II.*

Ten things about beliefs you won't believe

As beliefs are such a broad and important topic—they do, after all, play the most crucial role in the creation of your reality— rather than attempt to encapsulate the subject in a brief *Say That Again* box, we round off this chapter with a succinct reminder of the most salient points that are crucial to your understanding of them.

1 A belief is a thought you think more than once

The more you think a thought, the more energy accumulates to it. This grows the seed of a thought (more rapidly when watered by emotional energy) into the seedling of a belief. The distinct energy signatures of thoughts and beliefs attract thoughts of a similar nature, thus increasing a belief's electrical potential and potential for physical expression.

The combined energy of your thoughts, beliefs and emotions in your subconscious "garden of beliefs" produces a unique electromagnetic frequency – your personality's "tonal frequency" – that is an integral part of your being.

2 **Beliefs become attitudes and the truths by which you lead your life.**

Some of your beliefs accumulate so much energy that in time they grow into *attitudes*. An attitude's energy will govern your thinking processes and behavior – it will determine what is possible for you. Eventually, with a great deal of energy invested, an attitude grows into a value, and ultimately a sturdy tree of "truth" for you.

Truths are beliefs that we do not question as to their validity. The more vehemently we express our opinion, the more we reveal the intensity of energy behind the belief.

3 **Core systems of beliefs can be invisible to us.**

A core belief will have attained enough energy to become at least an attitude, if not a "truth" for us. A tree of truth blends into your garden of beliefs so well that it is often difficult to acknowledge its presence.

Its strength will influence our perception to such an extent that we perceive from the physical realm only those events that correlate with it. The twigs and branches of such a belief reach into the most intimate areas of our lives and no evidence will be forthcoming to disprove it because we will only be able to perceive that which confirms it. It thus becomes invisible to us.

4 **A belief is neither good nor bad – it is a neutral construct.**

You can label a belief as "positive" or "negative," but such labeling should recognize that a positive belief is one that complements the expression of your Self, whereas a negative belief restricts the expression of your Self. Negative beliefs associate with fearful thoughts, whereas positive beliefs engender excitement and creativity.

5 **Acceptance of beliefs nullifies their power.**

Accept your beliefs for what they are – a unique and magnificent collection of concepts that you can manage by increasing or decreasing their energy potential as and when you choose.

Decreasing a belief's energy prunes it back to its original purity so that you can better see if it is in harmony with what you want your garden to express of you. If it is inappropriate to what you wish to create from your garden of beliefs, you can uproot it and return it to the psyche's nursery from whence it came.

In order to accept all of your beliefs, you must cease judging them – remember that they are neither good nor bad; they are, in themselves, nonaligned.

6 **Your beliefs ultimately govern what you perceive as reality.**

Put another way, your beliefs are the architectural plans by which you construct your reality. As with architectural plans, they are required for any physical construction. Beliefs are an integral element of the design of the physical dimension; that is, they come with the territory. Your beliefs continuously influence your *perception* of the world, and your perception of the world, is *an action of **interpretation** of your reality*.

7 **Changing your beliefs will change your reality.**

The reality you experience is a reflection of what you expect to perceive in accordance with your beliefs. There is no *one* reality fits all then, the reality *you* perceive *is still very real*, but defined by *your* beliefs. Thus, by changing your beliefs, you can change your reality. By "change," we mean reassigning the energy behind the beliefs you are currently utilizing, or uprooting certain beliefs and replacing them with seedlings you prefer.

In changing your beliefs, you reassign energy – turn your attention (what you are *thinking* about) – from one belief to another. The beliefs themselves do not change.

8 **We incorporate all beliefs but utilize relatively few.**

All kinds of beliefs are available to you; so you can choose, consciously, the beliefs you wish to energize, nurture and grow.

Beliefs are not your enemy – realize that from a broader perspective they are a key part of the instrument through which you express your Self in the physical domain.

9 **You can learn to use your beliefs more efficiently.**

Recognize that you always have the power to re-assign energy to your beliefs of preference. Preferences are merely preferred expressed beliefs. We can prefer one belief from another knowing that this is not an absolute judgment of the belief itself.

Do not apportion blame to someone who you think gave you a "problematic" belief – this act engenders a judgment of the belief as well as the person involved. You must suspend judgment in order to accept the offending belief, and thus nullify its power.

10 **We are what we believe ourselves to be.**

Your *perception* follows that which you believe. So get in touch with your beliefs. When you begin to identify your beliefs, you start to *appreciate* what you're creating, whether "negative" or "positive," because you know *how* you're creating it and how to go about changing things if need be.

Every belief incorporates many influences. *Recognizing* how a belief is influencing you opens up your choices as to whether you prefer for it to influence you or not, and if so, which influences you prefer to allow.

Addressing the "negative" attitudes and core beliefs that dictate your creations leads to a freer expression of your outer self's *intent*.

It is of supreme importance that you acknowledge the existence of joyful beliefs; and that you cultivate positive, joyful and creative belief systems that bring you excitement in the construction of your reality.[123]

The remaining chapters of this book describe the nature of feelings and emotions as presented in the channeled literature. Feelings and emotions complete the fundamental creational keys that constitute your perception, the "thing" that brings you your reality.

If you are feeling daunted by the magnitude of the affect your beliefs have on your life, take heart from the fact that *you are always capable of managing those you keep in your personality's garden*. Although it is impossible for you to remove them completely from your psyche, you can focus your attention on nurturing the beliefs that best suit who you are and what you are here to do.

Now; beliefs are not your enemy. You have **chosen** to be manifest in this physical dimension. It has been a choice. No entity, no force, no element of consciousness greater than yourself has thrust you into this physical reality. You have chosen.[124]

Believe that life is worth living and your belief will help create the fact.
William James.

CHAPTER 13:

FEELINGS ARE NOT THE SAME AS EMOTIONS

One thing that needs to be clear from this point onwards is that *feelings are not the same things as emotions*. Feelings and emotions are energy forms that assist you in expressing your Self; they are neither positive nor negative in themselves; one is a mechanism for initiating instant action, the other is a potential energy resource for concerted action.

The biologist and philosopher Humberto Maturana first mentioned in *Chapter 1* points out "… that the feelings we describe are a commentary made about the emotioning, not the emotioning itself."[125] This intuitive statement closely parallels the declaration of several channeled guides who assert that a feeling is a signaling mechanism by which your inner self gains your conscious-mind's attention prior to transferring information through the four routes presented in *Chapter 9*.

Your emotions are not signaling mechanisms deliberately seeking conscious awareness. They gain conscious awareness through the preceding feeling signal, as they usually, not always, enter processing through the Solar Plexus chakra route. Like thoughts, emotions stimulate actions in the objective physical realm.

Another distinguishing factor is that your inner self often dispatches feelings to your conscious-mind after consulting with your body-consciousness, whereas she will dispatch emotions after consultation with your personality. This is because emotions *belong* to your personality. They are the connective forces that bind your non-physical self to your physical self.

Your personality is the portion of your Self that manages and channels their resources. It is responsible for "holding" emotional energy from immediate release. It does this under instruction from your inner self in view of your overall health, as well as instruction from your ego-self – which is liable to be erroneous instruction born of its fears.

Feelings are more of an integral part of how your outer self functions. They are part of the mechanics of how you express your Self in the physical realm. An emotion, on the other hand, is an independent electromagnetic energy form that exists in the electric field of reality, and is not a part of your physical expression unless you invite it to be so. As with thoughts, emotions do not require a host Mind to exist. Like thoughts, you can choose to entertain them in your Mind or not.

Your personality can include and utilize emotions in creating the tonal frequency of its identity. *If your personality holds an emotion's energy to it, it does so for a reason. Any subsequent release of this energy thus becomes a **significant event** as the emotional energy **has gained important psychological meaning**.* This meaning changes the emotion from its pure energy form to an energy form *with a communication.*

> **The strength of any feeling** indicates the level of importance your inner self puts upon the information it is imminently transferring; **the strength of any emotion** that may follow a *particular type of feeling* (see below) indicates the level of importance of the communication carried with the emotional energy.

Most feelings are to do with relaying important information to your conscious-mind as "instantaneously" as possible; the information doesn't care to be held up by any thought processing. Impulses, though not the same things as feelings, are examples of instant information transfer from your Essence self. A charging rhinoceros heading right at you or a mugger wielding a knife instantaneously fills you with the impulse to act, as well as adrenaline, so that you can engage a "fight-or-flight" response. Who needs to think? This important impulse has you act immediately in accordance with the innate drive of Consciousness (reflected in your consciousness) for survival.

The "let's bypass the thought mechanisms" principle also applies to feelings, which aren't quite so hurried in their information transfer. If you're feeling inspired, for example, and you acknowledge this feeling as the prelude to valuable information about to flow into your awareness, you might reach for instruments to record the information before your conscious-mind becomes inundated and unable to retain it.

Feeling inspired

An experience that virtually all of us have enjoyed that illustrates the immediacy of feelings is the sensation of *inspiration*. Inspiration is an experience that often puzzles us – in the sense that we wonder how the accompanying thought came to be. It's as if someone else – someone who has managed to dodge our brain's defenses, has put the thought or thoughts into our head. Our puzzlement stems from the realization that the thought lacks the stamp of our brain's approval; and the devious someone is our inner self.

Although your brain and the structures within it (particularly the pineal gland) is your main physical information processor, it is not always where psycho-electric patterns are sent for processing. Remember that your inner self hands over its collection of information to the body-consciousness for translation into physical energy terms in your subconscious library. Your body-consciousness then filters the patterns through your energy processing centers, giving preference to your center of choice. Your inner self though is capable of overriding normal procedure for psycho-electric messaging; and will do so if it feels the message is important enough, or may suffer distortion in translation. It may thus instruct the body-consciousness to relay the information through an energy center more attuned to accept and express it. In the case of inspirational information, this would be the Throat chakra center. This center produces a mental *sensation* that precedes thought processing in the conscious-mind.

The body-consciousness is itself quite capable of generating feelings that grab the conscious-mind's attention – pain is the obvious example. Your inner self though, is always collaborating with the body-consciousness when instigating the feeling of pain, whether it is psychological, emotional or physical in nature. It's not difficult to appreciate that if an angry wasp has just sunk its stinger into your delicate derrière, then your body-consciousness should not have to go a circuitous route involving thought for you to act immediately on this painful information.

A particular type of feeling

If you feel pain (physical or emotional), your conscious-mind is made immediately aware that your outer self (the physical or psychological structures) requires urgent attention. Collaboration often occurs between your inner self and body-consciousness to produce a feeling.

Many of us dismiss such feelings (even pain) as unimportant, despite the fact that we constantly receive numerous kinds of feeling signals. They come as sensations through the Throat chakra; a sense of awareness of our internal state (emotional-signal) through the Solar Plexus chakra; and feelings akin to intuition, but more profound, signaling a direct awareness of the vitality of Divine Love, through the Base chakra. We can also throw impulses and impressions into the mix of energy forms that bombard our conscious-mind's experiences.

One particular type of feeling though, which we will call an *"emotional-signal"* to prevent confusion with other kinds of feelings, is not too concerned about gaining an instant response or have you scrambling for pen and paper, but instead seeks to alert you to the imminent onset of an emotion.

In the academic field, the psychologist Paul Ekman, Ph.D., recognizes the distinction between an emotional-signal and an emotion through his research on emotions. His studies show there to be an impulse to act prior to the onset of an emotion. Impulses, according to channeled guides, are not feelings or emotional-signals, but a form of direct communication emanating from your Essence self. Even so, Ekman's "impulse" can equate to the "emotional-signal" type of feeling suggested by channeled literature, particularly when Ekman qualifies his use of the term impulse by suggesting it to be "the spark before the flame" gleaned from his studies of Buddhist writings.

We are constantly equating this emotional-signal, or spark before the flame, with the emotion that follows it, which is why we believe such signals to be the same as emotions, and place both forms of energy under one all-encompassing term.

Let's look at fear again to make things clear.

You can have the *impulse* to act immediately – adrenaline pumps through the body for either fight or flight – prompted by your inner self's knowledge that imminent physical annihilation is a distinct possibility. Then there is the *emotional-signal type of feeling* of fear that *alerts* you to the *emotion* of fear – which is an energy resource with a communication. The emotion provides you with energy for a sustained response if required, but if you use this energy, there are conditions attached.

Emotional energy always comes with encapsulated instructions as to its use. There is a communication, constructed by your personality in agreement with your inner self, recommending that you carefully consider your actions, if not in the moment, then as soon after acting as possible.

We experience emotional-signals as having a positive or negative quality to them. Those that appear to have a negative tone precede what we view to be a "negative" emotion (as with fear), and positive ones, a positive emotion (as with joy). Information encapsulated within an emotion provides the most precise documentation of what you are creating in the moment and how the creation may or may not be in line with your overall intent.

Part of the message of a *negative* emotion informs you that you are, in this moment, creating your experience in a way that contradicts your desires and intent. It is therefore important for you to acknowledge and examine the entirety of the communication of such a negative emotion. (Actually, it's just as important to heed and *appreciate* positive emotions as they are indicative of your manifestations being in line with your desires and intent.)

Elias cautions us on the way we currently process our feelings and emotions, particularly where emotional-signals are concerned. We have a tendency to focus simply on the tone of the emotional-signal, and then assume that any accompanying emotion gives us license, as well as the energy, to *react* to the situation in a manner befitting this initial signal.

If we sense anger rising within us, for example, we are likely to act in an aggressive way. Our actions focus on the emotional-signal of anger and the energy contained by the following emotion drives our actions along while we remain in total ignorance of the message also contained within the emotion. We invariably behave in such a manner, acting out the tone of the emotional-signal by foolishly only exploiting the energy of the subsequent emotion, thus leading to us regretting our actions.

SAY THAT AGAIN (17) Feelings

A feeling can take several forms. Each of which is a configuration of electromagnetic energy that alerts your conscious-mind to information from your inner self that is pertinent to your current physical experience. Feelings can be a seemingly instantaneous processing of the information, or they can act as forerunners (*"emotional-signals"*) to further information on your inner status, encapsulated within the independent energy configuration of an emotion.

The feeling comes first

Again, feelings do not always precede an emotional experience. We have feelings that are different kinds of inner "sensing" that are not concerned with emotions but do present you with a sense of knowing. Feelings are the signals you receive informing you of information, picked up by your inner senses, that your inner self considers important for the conscious-mind to process and thus reach awareness. In short, a feeling is the herald of significant news from your director of operations.

If you ignore a signal, it is likely to persist or even escalate in intensity. For example, the "niggling feeling" you might get about something or someone; or when you *feel the need* to cancel a planned action – like attending an event, taking a plane trip, or making a journey of some kind.[126]

The majority of us prefer to process "inner" information through the solar plexus route to the mind. This route invariably attaches emotional energy, along with its message, to the feeling – the emotional-signal. We subconsciously place the tone of the signal, and thus the emotion, on a positive/negative scale in accordance with our most pervasive system of beliefs – the system named *Duplicity* by Elias.

As we do not fully explore Duplicity until *Book II*, know now that it is a belief system born of duality, our psyche's fondness for separating things out into opposites – good/bad, right/wrong, black/white, physical/non-physical, and so on.[127] The element that turns mere duality into the treacherous duplicity belief system that limits our creativity is the act of *judgment*.

We see the contrast, but rather than simply registering a preference for one or the other, we often feel the need to defend our choice – which stems from a deep-seated lack of trust in our outer selves and our ability to choose. Noticing how often you do this, and how fervently you defend your choices, is a start on the road to changing the beliefs that stymie your creativity.

We like to separate our feelings and emotions out into

"positive" and "negative" ones. No problem there, but an act of judgment in this separation can diminish our appreciation of their energy and distracts us from the communications they contain. To break the judgmental habit, we should remind ourselves constantly that thoughts, beliefs, feelings and emotions are energy forms that are *neutral* in themselves.

We also need to appreciate (and believe!) that although our belief system of duplicity invariably applies a judgment to our separations, like any other system of belief, *we can manage it*. Indeed, it is imperative that we fully understand that, as it is our belief systems that steer our creations, our well-being is dependent upon the management of our entire garden of beliefs.

Your "vibrational signature" revisited

The first exercise of *Chapter 2* (*The tone of your vibrational signature*) had you attempt to recognize your personal "feeling-tone" – an expression coined by Seth and used by other channeled guides. Your feeling-tone is not the same thing as a feeling, although we naïvely identify its communication as one. Your feeling-tone is the vibrational signature of your entire being or Self, which, if you allow it, will speak with your outer self. What it confides is an identification of the relationship your feeling-tone has with another feeling-tone. This doesn't have to be another person's feeling-tone, it can be the vibrational signature of any energy form you are encountering. All physical constructions are energy forms, so this includes people, animals, rocks, buildings, places and everything else besides. The ancient Eastern tradition of Feng Shui, for example, is concerned with recognizing the feeling-tones of the physical environment.

The basis of the communication is whether the other feeling-tone resonates with your own. When you are more familiar with your own feeling-tone, you will be able to explore this communication more readily. You will be able to sense a "does" or "doesn't resonate" message from your Essence self transmitted through your feeling-tone.

This communication is *not* a feeling – which is a signal to inform you of pending information – it is a direct form of transfer of a peculiar type of information. An "intuitive knowing" is perhaps the best description of this communication from your Essence. Remember that emotions (with their own peculiar message) are usually short-lived and feelings (with their impulsive promptings) ebb and flow, whereas your unique feeling-tone, the vibrational signature of your Essence (with its resonating message), remains a constant within you during your lifetime.

Each of us interprets the feeling-tone message differently as it makes its way through our belief systems and our information-processing centers. The solar plexus processors amongst us, the most preferred route, automatically translate this feeling-tone into emotion, thereby confusing and distorting the purity of the original message with the communication of the emotion chosen to define it. Our interpretations of our feeling-tone messages are another example of our muddled approach to processing inner information.

As an example of the difference between a feeling-tone message and a feeling (emotional-signal) that is closely followed by an emotional message, let's take the experience of entering an unfamiliar room in an unfamiliar building.

As you enter, you sense something "negative" about the room. This is your feeling-tone recognition that this energy form is, or contains, a feeling-tone (vibrational signature) that is in contrast to your own. Most of us *interpret* this "intuitive knowing" as an emotion.[128] We then express this interpretation by remarking to others that the room feels sullen, has a sad feeling, is depressing, or uplifting – all emotional considerations. Emotions immediately obscure the feeling-tone communication, and then the thoughts that follow become confused as the distorted information travels through the filter of our belief systems.

Similar to, but not the same as an impulse, the *pure* feeling-tone message is an accurate assessment of surrounding energy signatures that your conscious-mind can use in its thought processes when figuring out what to do in an unfamiliar situation. It's a very subtle form of communication that we need to practice sensing. Familiarity with this internal antenna will assist us in the control of our reactive behaviors brought about through emotional connections to our beliefs.

We have to tune into our feeling-tone and get familiar with its qualities before we can sense its messages without distortion. When you accomplish this for yourself, it will become a highly useful instrument for everyday interactions. You will be able to recognize the vibrational signatures of other individuals, places and objects. With practice, this quiet inner voice will be as loud in your conscious-mind as the voice of your belief systems.

In case you are equating a feeling-tone message with an impulse, note that they are different forms of communication from your Essence. Their distinction lies in the nature of their communications. Information offered by your feeling-tone is to do with the *identification* of other vibrational signatures. Impulses are direct *instructional* prompts for you to direct your physical actions in a certain way.

Catch the emotional-signal early

The teachings of Abraham (Esther Hicks) approach the subject of feelings and emotions and the way we label them in a very pragmatic way. The Abraham brief is to focus your attention on *"feeling* good."

To bring this about you need to notice your mood and gauge how you are feeling. If you notice any feeling other than a positive or neutral one, then look to change the feeling as quickly as you can. A negative feeling is telling you that your conscious-mind is cultivating thoughts that are in contradiction to your desires. (The subtle difference between "desires" and "wants" is a subject explored in *Book II*.)

According to Abraham, it doesn't matter which label you attach to the emotional-signal (feeling) or the emotion it precedes – anger, guilt, anxiety – if you sense a "negative" mood, you are nurturing thoughts that contradict your desires. To remedy the situation, turn your thoughts to any that give you a more positive emotional-signal. This can even mean turning your thoughts to an emotion that still follows a negative emotional-signal, only with less intensity or energy potential.

Anger is an example emotion that follows a negative emotional-signal, but its intensity, or energy, is not as raised as those of hatred or rage. So if you feel hatred, get angry instead and you will begin to feel better. Don't stop there though, keep turning your thoughts to emotions and their signals that are still less intense than anger, and so on.

In *Ask and It Is Given* Abraham produces a useful scale of intensity in relation to emotions and the emotional-signals (feelings) that come before them as an aid for *gradually* steering your thoughts to a more positive position – back in line with your overall desires and intent. *Gradually*, as it is recognized that to attempt to move from a feeling of, say, "despair" to unbridled "enthusiasm" is asking too much of an outer self unused to dealing with any sort of a feeling, let alone those that appear to be the same as emotions. It would be a bit like asking your car to go forward when you have it in reverse gear.

Catching a negative *feeling* early on, and quickly reformulating your thoughts, is a great way to deflect any emotional discomfort that might be associated with it. The Abraham approach plays upon the fact that thoughts are the initiating factor in the creation process – organize these first and much of the time, you will not need to experience a negative emotion or figure out its message. They will be reserved for important occasions only!

Persistent negative thinking, easily entered into as the natural power of Attraction takes hold, can take you to a painful place. You may be glad to know that contrary to certain life-coaching regimes or psychological interventions, it is not absolutely necessary for you to "flood," "face your fears," or "feel the pain," of the majority of the unpleasant experiences you create for yourself.

An intense negative emotion communicates a need for an examination of your beliefs, which may entail facing some fears – however, you can nip *emotional-signals* in the bud, before their presence takes hold of your thoughts. Remember that *your reality is a reflection of what you have **been** thinking about,* so if the current mental situation is becoming painful, take your conscious-mind as quickly as you can to a less painful place by focusing your thoughts on the kinds of realities that make you feel good.

The Abraham approach to negative "feelings" and emotions reminds us that our point of power is always in the present moment – so if your thoughts come with negative hues then change them now by adjusting your thoughts to those that make you *feel* better. While you are at it, remind your conscious-mind that from now on you want to take *conscious* control over which thoughts you plant and nurture in your subconscious garden of beliefs.

CHAPTER 14:

FEELINGS EBB AND FLOW

Within the reception area of your subconscious library, you will recall the electrically humming companion to your inner self – your *body-consciousness*. The primary function of your body-consciousness is to monitor and regulate your physical (chemical) and not-quite-so-physical (electromagnetic) systems.

The energies of feelings and emotions flow through your body's electromagnetic systems and affect its chemical systems. It is here, within the chemo-electromagnetic processes of your body, that the most profound difference between feelings and emotions becomes apparent.

That difference is that *feelings consume energy, whereas emotions are an energy resource.*

Whether negative or positive in our designation, feelings can consume a lot of energy, particularly if we perpetuate them. Ignoring our feelings can perpetuate them (as with that niggling feeling), or we can use the energy of an associated emotion to keep the feeling of an emotional-signal going (as with worrying, or stress). Because they can expend a great deal of energy and can thus drain the body's physical systems to a point of exhaustion, your body-consciousness will automatically subdue feelings on occasion. This is why it appears to your conscious-mind that feelings constantly ebb and flow.

The administrations of your body-consciousness offer some reprieve from negative feelings, and its ebbing actions also explain why positive feelings don't stay forever (as in excited the whole time) – they too can be a drain on your resources. Abraham's suggestion that you deal with negative feelings as soon as you sense them by turning your thoughts to more positive ones is well worth considering. By doing so, you *consciously* help your body-consciousness with its energy management; a practice that becomes a precursor to further conscious manipulation of the psychological factors that bring your reality.

If emotional energy has taken the negative feeling to an intensity that makes it difficult for you to change your thoughts, then you must pay attention to the emotion's communication (defined in the next chapter) and act upon it. Such diligence will then make it unnecessary for your inner self and body-consciousness to generate this emotional-signal again!

In a bit of a mood

Moods seem to ebb and flow as well, so are they the same things as feelings?

Well… yes and no!

Moods certainly come and go and although they are not the same things as feelings, they do focus upon the type of feelings we are calling emotional-signals.

Your mood is a measure of the collective tone of the emotional-signals waiting in your subconscious garden for the attention of your conscious-mind.

You can think of your mood as an indicator of your personality's "emotional climate" (Abraham's "Emotional Set-Point") in any one moment, or if you will, the "atmospheric pressure" within your personality's garden. Rather than ebbing and flowing like feelings, your moods have highs and lows that indicate the strength and polarity of the emotional-signals gathered within this subconscious area of your mind. Alternatively, you can consider your mood to be an assessment of the accumulation of emotional-signals foisted upon your personality by the ever-dubious conscious-mind. Perhaps a bucket full of potentials for action held in abeyance.

However you conceptualize them, moods reveal a subconscious stage of preparation for future actions and give a good indication as to how you will allow energy to flow through into action – heavily or lightly. A heaviness of mood slows your physical actions, lightness speeds things through.

Of course, the heaviness or lightness of your overall mood also gives you conscious indication of the mean value of your personality's emotional-signal collection in terms of their positivity and negativity; where your mood falls on the continuum that ranges from ecstasy to despair.

These particular readings of your mood are highly important to you, especially if you gauge them to be on the heavy side as well as negative. What this indicates is that you are likely (the more so the heavier and more negative) to generate thoughts that will invigorate emotional energy that propels ill-considered actions. In other words, "bad" moods tell of the dominance of negative emotional-signals in the moment, which is a condition that sets your thoughts on a track that can encourage an emotional outburst, or other forms of energy release.

Moods are about emotional-signals, not emotions. Emotional-signals come before emotions; they give you the opportunity to prepare yourself psychologically for the incoming energy surge of the emotion. They allow you to *choose* whether to invite the energy into your experience and offer a chance for you to manage the energy's distribution.

Your personality's garden is a way station for emotional-signals. Kept in your garden they keep emotions in abeyance, ready for when your personality, in alliance with your inner self, decides for them to trigger their associated emotion. As The Dalai Lama remarks in his conversation with the emotions psychologist Paul Ekman mentioned earlier, "We cannot find a Tibetan word that captures the concept of 'mood' accurately. There is a concept of 'latent emotions' in Buddhist psychology..."[129]

Ekman states that he believes moods "must be a by-product of something else," whereas channeled literature suggests that the build-up of emotional-signals produces moods. Because emotions *follow* emotional-signals into our experience, emotions do not produce moods. The aftermath of an emotion released will sustain a mood to some extent, although this is because other emotional-signals associated with the emotion naturally become attracted to the psychological state that has just occurred.

Ekman also remarks that he would like to see moods banished, and in reply to people asking about "good" moods, he suggests they are a delusional state, closing off potential problems. Good moods are not "useful" from a Darwinian perspective.

Metaphysics suggests this attitude is a discounting of the Self. All experiences, whether expressed physically or psychologically, positively or negatively, have meaning and are therefore useful. For the reasons stated above, moods – emotional-signals – are an important part of our psychological life. Their design is to assist us in the *use* of energy, as we allow them to flow into the physical dimension "through" our Selves.

Seeds of thought offered by others

If we sense a negative feeling when communicating with someone it can mean either that our Essence is sending a "feeling-tone" message, or more likely, we are generating an emotional-signal. The emotional-signal implies that we are allowing his or her negative thoughts to grow in our mind. Essentially, we are accepting from them seeds of thought that come from their garden of beliefs, and the emotional-signal is telling us that they are not suitable for our own garden. Know that your negative emotional-signal is asking you to act in one of two ways.

The first way is simply to accept that their thought offerings will have a detrimental effect on how you feel in the moment, so don't allow them to concentrate in your mind and disassociate yourself from the conversation. If need be, end it or change the subject. Just trust in this feeling, and appreciate the fact that each person chooses the thoughts they wish to propagate (albeit usually without conscious awareness). You *are* using *your* conscious awareness by acting in such a manner. You get to choose whether to accept the thoughts on offer, or to end the conversation.

It is also not your job to insist that others accept your own thoughts because they make *you* feel good. Trust and appreciate that the thoughts you are offering in return produce a positive effect on you, but others are free to take them or leave them. You do not need to defend that which makes you feel good. If you find yourself doing this, then know that you are denigrating your inner self by not trusting in its guidance – good feelings are indications from your inner self that you are in tune with your personal intent. (Don't worry, your thoughts will not feel good if they are in association with anything that violates another expression of Consciousness – it is a natural principle that governs the nature of your feelings. If you violate, you will feel "natural guilt" – refer to *Chapter 4*.) Therefore, if you feel negativity in the thoughts the person is offering you, agree to disagree on the subject and leave it there.

The second way to respond to a negative feeling is to explore it. If the feeling has roused an emotion, then you know the basic message with any emotional charge asks you to examine your beliefs. You don't need to begin a mental examination immediately you sense emotion, just appreciate the fundamental message and resolve to look into it when you next have a quiet moment for yourself.

Remember that your garden contains *all* beliefs, but not all thoughts. Perhaps the conversation's design is for you to realize that the "negative" thoughts the other person offers have already grown in your garden to the height of a belief and you are unaware of this, or you are denying their existence.

See where the feeling takes you. Is the person giving you thoughts that generate an emotional-signal that has an emotion attached? Are you sensing anger, hate, guilt, jealousy, envy, or any other negative emotion? If so, and you find yourself rising to this emotion, perhaps embracing it, or find it difficult to dismiss, then you have an awareness of a belief within you that requires attention. *Feelings, followed by emotions, **shadow** your beliefs.* As Bashar (Darryl Anka) remarks, "There is no such thing as a feeling without a point of view [belief] that creates the feeling."

Your conscious-mind seduced

Let's return to your subconscious library to help clarify exactly what's going on in your Mind when others offer you their thoughts. This place, as it does not employ linear time, allows you to observe your psychological actions that from the physical perspective appear to happen instantaneously and automatically. Take your imagination to the reception area once more and let's see what the conscious-mind is doing with any recently acquired thoughts.

You will recall that on entering the library, your ego sends the conscious-mind to the librarian to submit information on the current physical situation and find out what you normally do in response to similar situations. In working out what to do, which it does through the mechanism of thought, the conscious-mind has a bit of a dilemma when it gets in front of the librarian.

Its dilemma is to do with its capacity for retaining information – information it requires to perform its task. Cognitive psychology has known for some time that the conscious-mind cannot hold too many pieces of information (including thoughts) in its buffers without having to consign them to a long-term memory store (your subconscious library's database) if they are to be used in future deliberations.

The average number of "chunks" of information it can hold for use in making a decision is seven.[130] A thought would be one chunk; information from your physical senses deemed important by your intellect – say, the burly features of the person you're talking to – would be another chunk.

Your conscious-mind has only this short-term memory store to play with. This is why it needs to clear its head of any inconsequential information gathered by the outer senses. It can then reload with the important information picked out by the intellect (burly features – watch the aggression!), any archival chunks from the librarian on similar situations, and any supplied by the various characters of your subconscious library – thoughts, feelings, and emotions.

In view of this capacity issue, your conscious-mind first offloads at the librarian's counter all the information from your physical senses. The librarian inputs this data into the archival database, which you can think of as the "long-term memory" store, but is more than this. When done, the robotic librarian will give its usual response:

"Thank you for the physical data gathered by the outer senses. I will have this analyzed for you and any feedback pertinent to the selection of future actions will be available shortly. Do you have a question?"

"Well… as you are probably getting used to, my friend the ego over there by the door is in a bit of a rush and would simply like to know how we would normally respond to this bloke we're talking who is offering us his thoughts on metaphysical stuff."

The librarian flicks a look of resignation, "Do you want your future action to be a consciously decided one, or a reaction?"

"Whatever's easiest really. As you know, I haven't got much of a capacity for holding information. Doesn't a reaction make my job of working out *how* to act a lot easier?"

"Sure does. Very often you don't have to work anything out at all. Are you holding any thoughts or feelings?"

"I have a thought given to me by this chap we're talking to. My ego friend doesn't like me to mess about with feelings." Your conscious-mind replies.

"Ah... the thought would probably have had a feeling with it. Check your thought with the body-consciousness and the inner self lady here – they will tell you what sort of a feeling it has, if it has one."

Your conscious-mind moves hesitantly over to these virtual strangers for a review of the thought. It then returns to the librarian.

"They say that the thought generates an emotional-signal type of feeling within us that they consider to be negative or resistant. Apparently, I initially ignored it not realizing it was a worthy chunk of information for me to consider in my deliberations. What do I do now?"

"Okay... If the thought has a negative feeling it is resistant to growth in the garden of beliefs over there. To clear it from your head take it to your personality, who is already in the garden. Your personality will take it off your hands and give you the details on how you normally react if that's what you want to do. Don't forget to return to me for any feedback I might have on past situations similar to this one and the really important information from the ego's intellect."

"Great." Your conscious-mind then scurries to the garden.

In the Garden of Beliefs, your personality is in its element. This is because it has built the garden from scratch – from the time of its own beginnings when the ego and the conscious-mind first began to play with thoughts (and feelings) in childhood and grow them into beliefs; through the adolescent years when it laid out the core belief systems beds; and into adulthood, a time of management and reshaping. Your personality is your loving gardener, capturing and directing the waters of emotional energy, as they flow through its garden; waters that nurture the seedlings of thought, and bring sustenance to the core belief beds.

Your personality creates its garden in the grounds of the subconscious in order to store the subjective elements involved in objective living – the thoughts, beliefs, feelings and emotions – that your conscious-mind *must have* for it to make sense of the physical environment. The garden is a repository of subjective information unique to your current lifetime; it is a reflection of your current identity, the *you* of your current outer self, the *I* of your ego-self.

While your ego-self faces the machinations of the physical world and copes with an easily overburdened conscious-mind, your personality organizes this vibrant if perhaps unruly garden. Ideally, it would prefer to manage the garden with your ego's assistance – after all, it is as much a reflection of your ego as it is your personality. Working together, they have the best chance of getting to grips with the any beliefs or belief systems that threaten to strangle the garden's grand design.

"I believe you can tell me how we can react to this conversation we're having by looking at this thought I've gotten from it?" Your conscious-mind asks of your personality on entering the garden.

"If we must." Your personality sighs. "No chance of the ego coming in here for a chat over how we might consciously respond then?"

"Ah… no, sorry. He still doesn't like coming in here. Anyway, reactions are just so cool – nothing much to think about, less work for me, and we can get on to the next situation."

"Great. Yeah… they're marvelous aren't they, reactions? They really are a great way of engaging with and learning from others." Your personality mumbles with a double-thick tone of sarcasm.

"Well, the feeling with the thought tells me it is unlikely to grow in here as it doesn't resonate with our current thoughts and beliefs. I will release it back into the wild landscapes of the electric psyche for you."

"W'ever. How do we react though? I need to know what to tell the ego." Your impatient conscious-mind will reply.

Your personality reluctantly informs your conscious-mind, "The thought relates to beliefs about relationships and fidelity, we have a highly energized belief on this topic that can supply you with ample energy for a reactive response."

"Let me have that energy then... and what do we actually *do* in response?"

"Because their thought is contrary to what we believe, and taking into account the amount of emotional energy we have available, we would normally argue our point of view until we are blue in the face."

"Fine ... Sorted. Can you chunk this information for me?"

"Oh don't worry, this reaction comes in one big chunk that overrides any other chunks you might get from the librarian or anyone else in here. The emotional energy does come with a message for the ego though from your inner self and me. I will wrap the energy in a paper that bears this message. Try and get him to read it would you?"

"Why don't you tell him yourself when we go back into the physical realm?"

"To tell you the truth, he hardly recognizes my existence. He carries me around all the time, but we rarely converse. And believe me, I would like to have a much better relationship with him and show him around this garden – if he would ever summon the courage to come into it."

"Okay, well, thanks. I'll give him the whole package, but I can't guarantee he'll read the message."

The conscious-mind returns to the library, picks up a chunk or two of information from the librarian, and then presents everything it has to the ego. The ego tears off the packaging from the reactionary energy package, throws it on the floor, whistles for the personality to climb back onto its macho shoulders, and the three of them exit the building.

All of which, in "real" time, happens in a flash.

In view of the conscious-mind's chunking constraints, and weakness for a quick fix, it's not difficult to see how calm and considered thought on what to do is set aside when emotional energy is in the offing. In certain cases, such as grief or anger, the energies can easily swamp the conscious-mind and obliterate conscious consideration. Any elevated energy of a belief entertained during conversation usually results in your ego-self exhibiting habitual, reactive behaviors.

Habitual behaviors are fine when they come in wrappings with a positive feel – keep doing what you're doing is the essence of any emotional communication. Negative wrappings however, warn of problematic growth in your garden of beliefs – growth that can strangle the beauty of your personality's endeavors and the full expression of your outer self in the physical domain. As the philosopher, David Hume (1711–1776) wrote when musing on our devotion to habitual reactions, "It is not reason which is the guide of life, but custom."

A truly conscious conscious-mind

When not influenced by your ego's fears, the conscious-mind can follow its natural work ethic – using thoughts *and* feelings to work out what actions to take and how much emotional energy to apply to those actions. If a situation calls for immediate action, without conscious-mind deliberation, you can trust in your inner self, in association with the body-consciousness, to have you do what is necessary. The "time" your ego and conscious-mind currently spend in your subconscious area does not need to be as fraught and hurried as the ego's paranoia dictates.

Once your ego becomes more used to your subconscious area, by gaining familiarity through the exercises presented in these books, non-life threatening situations requiring a physical response become more valuable to you in the Self-learning sense. You become truly appreciative of all of your experiences, aware that they all contain learning and a subtle guiding principle aimed at keeping you on your path of intent.

To begin its duties, a fully functioning and unencumbered conscious-mind does need to offload the five-senses data gathered for storing and analysis[131] because of its restricted information processing capacity (short-term memory). With this practicality aside, it should then assess any *feelings* it has – the emotional-signals, impressions, and sensations supplied by your inner self and body-consciousness. With practice, it can also consider any feeling-tone communication received directly from your Essence self. Some feelings are well worth retaining as a chunk of information that soothes the deliberation process.[132]

When another person offers you their thoughts, your conscious-mind can give them over to your personality who will assess whether to grow them in its garden or return them to the great park of the psyche. Your conscious-mind can then work with your personality on which of *your* thoughts and believes might be worth presenting to the conversation after acknowledging the strength of any beliefs you hold, particularly if they have grown to an attitude or "truth."

To round things off, your healthily functioning conscious-mind, can then return to the librarian to consider any highly important information picked up by your outer senses, and any archival feedback. This entire process, your conscious-mind's progress in the subconscious as it gathers information to give it the best footing for working out how to act, can take as little or as much time as is necessary, as it is not a process that adheres to your ego's restricted view of time.

All such gathered information needs to be chunked and translated into the conscious-mind's currently ego-preferred medium for deliberation – thoughts. It can *think about* including the power of any emotional energy provided by the garden's sturdiest beliefs, but it should do this in consideration of the effect this might have on the circumstances. It can also remind the ego to take some *quality* "time-outs" (for example, meditation) so that it and the ego too, can get acquainted with the subconscious and commune with your personality on managing its garden of beliefs.

Broader aspects of the Self can thus contribute to your conscious-mind's deliberations on what to do, so that the outer self can act in a way chosen in a *fully conscious* manner.

The ego's fears, arrogance, and reliance upon habitual behaviors, contrive to misdirect the conscious-mind in its hunt for information that can solve the dilemma of how we should respond to our physical experience. Habitual behaviors, such as driving a car, are a convenient, conscious-mind freeing solution for many of our actions. Often though, they are an inappropriate and non-progressive solution to actions that relate to communi-cation – to how we should behave towards others. Communication with others should *never* warrant a habitual response – simply because an *un*-conscious response is an insult to your Self, as they, and everything you draw to you, are a reflection of you.

The ego fears that the decision-making processes of the conscious-mind can lead the outer self into trouble. This fear stems from the duplicitous creeper that brings *judgment* to any decision or choice. Have we made the right one?

To make a choice, to state a preference, does not have to invite either inner mental or outer physical conflict. Conflict is an action driven by an ego that does not *trust* in its choices and therefore feels a need to defend them. Choosing is the exciting bit about conscious creation. In doing so we need only to pick a preference and see how it *feels*. When it feels negative, we need to choose again.

Presently, it is routine for the conscious-mind to pacify the ego with a neat little package of tried and tested behaviors that make the need for any serious thinking unnecessary. Because of our ignorance of the motivational power of feelings and emotions and their directive capabilities, our actions on how to deal with a situation are thus often ill-considered and unmanaged.

Feeling or emotion?

We are used to working with the outer sense of touch and distinguishing between the feel of various physical surfaces, we are not though used to working with our inner senses and discerning between the feel of our feelings. We lazily sort the nuances of our feelings into either good or bad sensations; then we don't fully appreciate the good ones in case they might be sinful, and don't investigate the bad ones for the highly useful messages they may contain. Ironically, bad feelings are good in the sense that they have the potential to teach us more about our Selves and the reasons as to why we don't feel so good!

Important inner-information speaks to us through the signals of our feelings and the voice of our emotions. You can count on the fact that if the information is not important, you wouldn't get the feeling; if it wasn't very important, it wouldn't be followed by emotional energy. Information attached to an uncomfortable feeling suggests that before the conscious-mind can come to a considered response it needs to check with your personality for any emotional involvement. If present, the emotion's intensity reflects how imperative it is that you give some attention to your subconscious garden of beliefs.

The emotion can *scream* at you at times; it does so because *it is in your garden of beliefs that you will find the reasons* behind any form of negativity you are experiencing.

You will find the reasons amongst the roots of your beliefs.

Uncovering them may require some digging, but bringing them into the light of awareness can substantially alter the landscape and thus the disposition of your personality.

Until we become more proficient at differentiating between feelings and emotions and exploiting their informative power, we will continue, personally and collectively, to create our realities in accordance with the slapdash manner followed by the ego and the conscious-mind on their visits to the subconscious library.

The next chapter deals specifically with the phenomenon of emotions – the energies that bring the inner you into your outer physical reality.

CHAPTER 15:

CLEARLY DEFINING EMOTIONS

Before humankind evolved the ego-self as part of its psychological structuring, emotions served as they do for many life forms – as the stimuli to action.

As part of the next stage in the shift in human consciousness (discussed in *Book III* of *It's About You!*), our self-aware ego with its self-reflective ability will evolve a step further by acknowledging and appreciating that emotions not only provide the energy to drive our actions, but also *inform* us of our "inner" psychological health.

In the coming years we move from ego self-awareness to total Self-awareness. We progress from the ego's reflections on its little-self, prone to misconceptions, fears, and habitual reactions, to a *Whole-Self* reflective ability.

Our self-reflective focus will be upon reading the communication of emotions and acting upon these instead of focusing on only the *emotional-signals* that precede them. We will come to realize that emotions are the life force of this physical plane, as they are integral to its expression *through* our Selves.

It is primarily because our conscious-minds are under instruction from our egos to ignore incoming information associated with feelings, and any subsequent emotions, that we remain in abject confusion as to their true nature and importance to our well-being. Until we fully understand them, we will continue to react to certain situations rather than respond to them in a fully informed, objective and self-developing manner.

Anger, for example, is a negative emotion that contains the message from our inner self that at this moment, as our conscious-mind assesses the situation – we cannot see a choice (as to how to act). In actuality, we *always* have choices, anger tells us that we cannot *see* the choices because of a belief we hold.

We ***react*** to the emotional-signal of anger by utilizing the emotional energy that follows – usually in a highly agitated if not aggressive way – and then allow ourselves to think such behavior is "normal" for the situation. We lose or ignore the emotional communication, the element that can prevent us from reacting the same way in similar situations, and the anger persists as a force that closes our choices – choices that are always to do with following the healthy path of our intent and purpose.

Separating feelings from emotions

You will be aware by now that feelings are signals alerting you to information transferring itself from inner awareness to outer conscious awareness. One type of feeling, an emotional-signal, alerts you to the availability of an energy resource – emotion. An important distinction to keep in mind is that feelings consume the energy within your physiological systems, whereas emotions supply you with energy.

We have learnt to associate an emotional-signal with the emotion it precedes. However, in doing so, we assume they are the same thing, the same energy configuration, thereby allocating the same term to both psychological phenomena.

You may *feel* sad, anxious, happy, frustrated, angry, or any one of a vast number of emotional-signals. They are though, emotional-signals; they are not the emotion itself. Some emotional-signals are subtle; others have a strength that is easily recognizable and thus easily attributable to an emotion – fear, sadness, excitement and joyfulness, for example. As if to deliberately complicate matters, these typically strong signals also express themselves with subtlety at times.

In view of our current state of confusion and the difficulty in differentiating between feelings, their emotional-signals variety, and emotions themselves, *Appendix IV* aims to clarify matters. It provides a basic list of terms we use to describe either a feeling or an emotion, or both, and introduces you to the subtler definitions promoted by channeled guides. It is a list of terms that will eventually require a new language if we are to separate and define more clearly our feelings and emotions. As Paul Ekman poignantly remarks:

We are, in some sense, animals who do not have, at least in English, enough words to describe the varieties of our emotional experience, particularly when they are destructive versus constructive. Without different labels for each mental state, it is hard to be able to reflect on their nature and consider how we want to enact them in future emotional episodes.[133]

The communication of an emotion

As mentioned previously, the Abraham material provides a useful scale of the feelings – emotional-signals – we have labeled as having positive or negative implications. They range from the most disempowering states such as depression and despair, to the most empowering – joy, appreciation and a sense of freedom.

Deep negative feelings signal to your conscious-mind that within your subconscious you are fixating upon one or more emotional-signals, thereby draining energy from your outer self. Allowing the emotional energy (that the signal alerts you to) to flood into your system of self will bring you renewed energy – *and*, important information concerning the beliefs that are generating the emotional-signals, thereby impeding the natural flow of your energies.

Positive feelings signal the very opposite. They tell you that your overall inner state is in a position to allow energy to flow through you unimpeded, to accept a burst of emotional energy that will add to and encourage the growth of thoughts and beliefs that resonate with your personality's intent and purpose. The fundamental underlying communication of a positive emotion is that you are a uniquely important expression of

Consciousness supported and embraced by the natural power of Divine Love.

Regardless of how positively we label them, *all* emotions act as carrier waves of communication from the radio station of your inner self to the receiver of your outer self's conscious-mind. Emotional-signals ask that you bring your attention to the communication of an emotion and tune in to the message it contains.

An emotion offers a quite precise communication. The message encompasses the tonal-quality, or "vibrational equilibrium" of your Essence and the inner systems of your Self – *in the present moment* – and what thoughts and beliefs, if any, are influencing this state. It can identify the core belief system, if not the particular belief, within your subconscious garden that is manipulating you in the moment; and it can tell you precisely what pattern of thinking is being stimulated. It is communicating to you what you are actually doing psychologically, to yourself, right now.

> *An emotion is not a reaction to the circumstances; it is informing you of all the factors that go into creating the circumstances.*

In the case of so-called negative emotions, what you are doing to yourself psychologically relates to the way in which you are managing to criticize your outer self. Elias refers to this as "discounting" yourself.

Embarrassment, for example, is to do with *judging* yourself because of concern over how another perceives you to be. Sadness communicates some type of *denial* of yourself, of your actions, and of your own freedom. The emotion of sadness generally contains the message that you are psychologically influenced by a "denial of self" – which is an unnatural expression as far as your Essence self is concerned, so it becomes "sorrowful" and lets your conscious-mind know this. Negative emotional messages alert us to various other ways in which we discount ourselves – *self-doubt* (as in anxiety) is another example.

Positive emotions, such as the feeling of happiness, generate the message that you are validating your outer self. Excitement is also to do with validation of your outer self, even though the emotion of surprise sometimes tinges its coloration.

There are a vast number emotional communications. Once you begin to recognize that emotions are energy resources that always carry a message from your inner self (and are not a reaction *to* the circumstances), your freedom of choice, on how to act *in* the circumstances, opens up.

Many of us assume that we have little power of control over our emotions. We readily recognize feelings to be part of our psychological makeup, but emotions appear to be forces "outside" of us – independent organisms akin to viruses and bacteria whose energies will help us either resolve a situation, or make matters worse. Emotions *are* independent – *belief systems are not required for their expression*. However, they are in fact very much a part of us, intimately interwoven into our psychological structuring and our ability to express our personality, and ultimately our Selves, in the physical domain. Again, they are the life force of this dimension of existence we call physical reality.

SAY THAT AGAIN (18) Emotions.

Emotions are patterns of energy that reside within the Subjective Area within Consciousness. They come closest to the physical dimension in the electric field where they exist as independent electric actions. As with all actions, their intent is to find expression, and their dimension for expression is the physical dimension. The physical vessels for their expression are not limited to humans.

> In humans, an emotion offers us a supply of energy as well as a precise communication from our inner self. The communication relates to the overall disposition of our Self's varying layers and structures, in the moment, and the systems influencing that disposition – usually our thoughts and beliefs.
>
> The most precise definition of the phenomenon of a **"negative" emotion** might be:
>
> An energy enhanced communication from your inner self that tells of the current disposition of your Essence in association with your psychological structures; particularly those belief systems in your "Garden of Beliefs" that are of concern to the natural expression of your personality and its chosen intents and purposes.

The origin of emotions

Because science has yet to grasp that the physical is a *representation* of a non-physical system of energy patterning (the Objective Area within Consciousness is drawn from the Subjective Area), emotions, like consciousness, are assumed to be a bi-product of brain functioning. Research indicates that areas within the "limbic system" of the brain, particularly the amygdala, in conjunction with the endocrine system and autonomic nervous system, play a key role in emotional expression.

The channeled literature suggests that these physical systems, particularly the pineal gland of the endocrine system, are indeed "crossing points" between the not-so-physical electromagnetic energies that configure our non-physical Selves, and the physical expression of our Selves.

From René Descartes' early fascination with the pineal gland, through to the discovery of their chemical representation in the body provided by Dr. Candace Pert (the "molecules of emotion") and the more recent work in epigenetics on how our emotions affect cellular structure, emotions are slowly establishing themselves in the scientific world.

Perhaps motivated by a resurgence of interest in emotions, Charles Darwin's *The Expression of the Emotions in Man and Animals*, first published in 1872, is again available. The work illustrates the evolutionary significance of emotions to the more complex levels of consciousness in the physical world.

From the metaphysical perspective, emotions originate for a wide variety of reasons. The vast majority of emotions are encouraged into existence by a sponsoring thought; however, your personality can initiate their appearance, or they can appear like a sudden shower visiting your personality's garden of beliefs.

Your personality is quite capable of steering your emotional rainwaters as they flow through its garden on their way to physical expression – as they flow back to the ocean of reality. For most of us at present, our egos are a hindrance to our person-alities in this regard. Our egos need to be more aware that the roots of a belief system can dam their progress, and cause them to form stagnant pools of energy that nurse habitual reactions. Emotions seek physical expression through us – that is, they must flow through our gardens of beliefs once they have entered our personal psychological structuring.

When not part of our psychological structuring, just as with thoughts, emotions exist as electrical forces within the electric field described in *Chapter 8*. As the emotion comes into the physical world through our conscious awareness, it requires translation.

Seth tells us that the translation of energy and information contained within the emotion involves a sophisticated system of interrelationships. Think again of the characters in your subcon-scious library, and imagine the relationships between each of them. They may all be speaking the subjective language of Electric-land, but each character has their own interpretation of the meaning of the emotion as well as their own regional dialect to describe it!

For our ego-selves to understand an emotion's full meaning through the objective languages that describe only our knowledge of the physical realm, our inner selves rely heavily upon metaphor and symbolism as ways of blending the disparate languages. As biological scientist, Lloyd Fell poignantly remarks in his book *Mind and Love: The Human Experience*:

George Lakoff and Mark Johnson have shown us that: "the essence of metaphor is understanding and experiencing one kind of thing in terms of another."[134] In other words we can think of one thing in terms of another and utilize this meaning bridge to jump our train of thought onto another track: to change the direction of our thinking and thereby change what we are experiencing. ... So metaphors are not merely to beautify our language; they actually define our reality, shape our thoughts, our plans and our expectations, and form the basis for our actions.[135]

Translating emotional language

Metaphors continue to act as the bridge of knowing that spans the physical and non-physical worlds of our being. Up until the advent of Quantum Mechanics, yet still somewhat mesmerized by the perceived linearity of time in the physical domain, science had concentrated its efforts on explaining actions and events through cause and effect.

Quantum Mechanics – which shows that events can occur simultaneously, thus doing away with time as it crosses space – heralds a new understanding of other *fields* of existence. Fields of existence, not least quantum fields, begin to appear that require explanations that we can only possibly understand using metaphors. Once we have a grasp of the concept, we can then go about rewriting and embellishing our vocabularies.

Albert Einstein, after providing us with the definitive mathematical metaphor for the physical field ($E = mc^2$), also sensed that something else was required to explain the actions of physical bodies – another field of action, a "subtle force" was at work in nature. The *New Scientist*[136] quotes him as taking inspiration from the work of James Clerk Maxwell (1831–1879) on electromagnetic fields and his subsequent equations in formulating relativity theory.

Other notable "field" metaphors to help us understand our dimensions of existence come from the physicist David Bohm (1917–1992), who proposed an "implicate order" to explain the fields of existence "outside," but not separate from, the physical dimension – which he named the "explicate order"; and the biologist Rupert Sheldrake offers "morphogenetic fields" to explain *A New Science of Life.*[137]

Metaphors are the medium of explanation for concepts that are new to us and contain great subtlety of meaning. Quantum theory has taken science into a land where metaphors ease our understanding of the language of subjectivity. It revolutionizes scientific thinking and is a progression from not so long ago when Seth remarked in *Book 3* of *The Early Sessions*:

The trouble has been that your scientists see or perceive electrical and chemical systems, for example, *only in their relationship with the physical system* [my emphasis]. They do not realize that these systems exist in universe actualities of their own. And the electrical and even chemical systems play a much larger part within the physical system than matter plays within their systems. They could both exist without the world of physical matter, but the world of physical matter could not exist without them.[138]

Emotions act as the driving energies behind our actions and they inform us of the nature of our subjective world – in the present moment. To some degree, emotions are metaphors in themselves, a stage in translation of the information captured by our inner senses. They are the outer extensions of our inner senses.

Abraham (Esther Hicks) suggests that just as your outer physical senses interpret the vibrational signature of physical matter *in the moment,* your emotions act as your inner sensors of your emotional climate in relation to your experience *in the moment.* They indicate to your conscious-mind the present state of your vibrational offering. Emotions also indicate to you whether you are allowing "Source" or "Universal Energy" to flow through you unimpeded.

The independence of emotions

Emotions exist as independent electric actions within the electric field. Your ego, once alerted to them by an emotional-signal, has the power to utilize their energy for its own creative actions. Because of their independent nature, not reliant upon any one pathway to expression, you are free to control their energetic pathways; you can channel the stream of their energy as it passes through your garden of beliefs.

Unlike beliefs, which you cannot cast out of your Mind as your personality is reliant upon them for its expression, thoughts and emotions are transitory. Such electrical actions constantly bombard your outer self's psychological systems. Like thoughts, emotions directly affect your physical systems.

Once accepted, transformed and interpreted, an emotion's overall impact upon your perception affects your brain. This is when and where its electrical properties directly affect your physical body. Your emotions may not be reactions, but the brain will initiate a reaction to this kind of electrical stimuli. Your nervous system is set in motion by the electrical energy in motion – E-motion.

We readily "accept" ("rejection" is an action in itself discussed in the next chapter) the thoughts and emotions where a mutual attraction exists between our personality's emotional climate and their electrical signatures. Because we have not understood that emotions *directly* affect the physical system until recently, we are only just beginning to see the connection between the personality's emotional climate and physical health. It is not until we acknowledge that emotions exist in real, albeit in alternative-electric-field terms; and maintain independent identities outside of the purely subjective domain, that we will begin to understand more fully our physical bodies in the objective dimension.

The function of emotions

Apart from providing energy for action, the main function of emotions is to transfer information from your inner self to your outer self – a communication. Expressing your Self in physical reality incorporates many pathways of communication between the various "parts" of your Self. Emotion is one avenue of communication that transfers pertinent information gathered by your inner senses to your non-physical self.

Your inner self produces an *emotional-signal* in order to gain your conscious attention. The *emotion* is the movement of energy from the subjective realm to the objective realm. Once the signal gains your conscious-mind's attention, you can begin to define what the message of the emotion is. The fundamental message of any emotion is that in this precise moment you are bringing into the creative process energies from the subconscious, subjective realm.

Again, emotions are not reactions; they are closely associated with the physical event you are experiencing, but you do not create them *after* the event. They form along with the physical creation to inform you of the beliefs you hold that are affecting your *perception – which is the overall psychological instrument creating the event* (discussed in *Book II*).

Your physical senses provide you with information on the

event – the sights, the smells, the sounds, and so forth – whilst *simultaneously* your inner senses, through the emotions in particular, also provide you with psychical information concerning the event you are experiencing. All of your senses, inner and outer, communicate information across the various "layers" to your Self. Your physical layer communicates information through "body language," for example; emotions particularly favor facial expressions to enhance their own communication. There is now a field of study that examines "micro-expressions," facial expressions that are extremely difficult to fake – poker players take note!

Your Essence communicates with you directly in every moment you are in the physical domain. It does so by appointing your inner self as its emissary, and then utilizing feelings and emotions to help guide you on a path of ultimate fulfillment – the full expression of your intent and purpose under the natural power of Divine Love.

When your thoughts contradict your primary intent, your inner self will communicate this to your conscious awareness by dispatching a "negative" emotional-signal and emotion. The purpose of negative emotions is to steer your thoughts away from those you are currently propagating. Similarly, when you are entertaining positive thoughts in alignment with your intent, your inner self will offer you positive emotions to enjoy.

The *reason* you entertain an emotion is to bring into your awareness the subtler details of the experience to which your conscious-mind is not paying attention. For this reason, when you thoughts appear to be in chaos, turn your attention to what you are actually creating in the moment. Do you sense negative emotion involved in the creation? If so, know that it contains vital information about why you've created the experience, information worthy of investigation if not in the moment, when you are able.

With no emotional content, communication suffers

Because emotions are integral to our communications, we are not very good at communicating without them.

Who hasn't sat through a presentation or speech where the presenter makes it very difficult for you to remain focused on its content because there is no emotional involvement in its delivery?

The information we absorb more easily is that which comes with emotional energy – whether delivered with passion or aggression. Easier still to soak up is information delivered with humor – an expression of positive emotion that reminds us not to take life too seriously.

Without emotional energy, there is little lasting information transfer. Emotions connect us to the electrical encodings (information) of an experience or physical event. As with the physical sense of smell, which can connect you to the information of a place and revitalize memories of experiences in that place, emotions connect us to the psychological conditions and information surrounding an entire physical experience – thus similar experiences evoke memories of the originating event.

Emotions play with time

We are all capable of recalling an experience or two where time appeared to speed up or slow down.

"The experience was so joyful, the time just flew by."

"I was in a rage officer, everything happened in a flash."

"The more excited I got that my team were winning, the slower the clock ticked down to the final whistle."

"The fear seemed to take over; everything seemed to go into slow-motion."

Such experiences inform us of the non-uniformity of time – they mess with our concept of time in order to show us that time is in fact a *mental construct* that we use to understand the progression of events.

Boredom is a feeling, a special type of emotional-signal that tells you time is dragging so slowly because you are not exercising your imaginative and emotional powers. Your conscious-mind is devoid of thoughts, feelings and emotions. The stream of emotional energy flowing through your garden of beliefs has reduced to a trickle – you have become psychologically and physically inactive.

CHAPTER 16:

GETTING ALL EMOTIONAL

Your conscious-mind does not discriminate between negative thinking and positive thinking. Thinking is what it does, so regardless of whether thoughts arise from receiving negative emotional-signals relating to the *actual* situation, or they are set in motion by the positive emotional-signals of an *imagined* situation, it will entertain them and eventually take them off to the garden of beliefs for possible propagation.

Worrying, a mental action that includes the emotion of anxiety in its assessment of future probabilities, is an excellent example of when the conscious-mind is naïvely playing with negative thoughts – as if they were magnetic balls innocently attracting other balls to themselves.

As Abraham neatly suggests, worrying is using your imagination (ideas, thoughts and images) to create that which you do not want. Elias elaborates when stating that part of the communication in the emotion of anxiety, when used in worrying, is that you are using your thoughts to stimulate a lack of trust in yourself and your creative abilities – which sets those creative abilities upon a slippery track to an unwanted reality.

Know that an emotion, in this case anxiety, *never* contains information warning you of something yet to come. An emotion is *specifically informing you of your current state of being* – how energy is flowing through your personality's garden of beliefs *right now*.

To illustrate a more enlightened appreciation of the process of experiencing a negative emotional-signal, followed by the associated emotion, with some thoughts, which should lead to a subsequent examination of beliefs, we can take anxiety as an example.

Dissolving anxiety

Most of us understand anxiety to be a feeling that can grow rapidly into a fearful emotion. Because of our ignorance of the psychological design and import of these two discrete forms of inner information relays – feelings (in this case an emotional-signal type) and emotions – our usual approach for dealing with anxiety can easily lead to a debilitating condition. The following scenario describes how the conscious-mind and ego-self usually go about dealing with anxiety:

On noticing the feeling of anxiety within us, we invariably focus on the feeling (emotional-signal) and expect our conscious-mind to discover the reason for its appearance. Your ego asks your conscious-mind, "Why am I feeling anxious?"

Your conscious-mind thrives on information it can turn into thoughts about how to deal with things, so when focusing solely on the emotional-signal, it soon becomes disheartened when finding that the signal contains little information to work with.

As the emotional-signal itself holds few seeds for thought, your conscious-mind will move on to review the important physical-senses data gathered by the intellect for subconscious analysis and storage. Here too though, there is little to go on, as this data does not contain information as to the psychological cause of the anxiety. It may attempt to reason that a physical element is the cause, but this evidence does not answer the ego's question as to *why* you are feeling anxious.

The conscious-mind needs thoughts, so it will then suggest to your ego that it needs to visit your subconscious library to try to generate some in response to the question.

"Okay," says your ego, "but just ask what we normally do with anxiety."

In the library, the librarian accepts the physical data, and advises the conscious-mind to go to the garden of beliefs with its "emotional-signal" and for information on how you normally respond.

In the garden, your personality points to a tree of belief that resonates with the emotional-signal and the conscious-mind gathers up some seeds of thought that have fallen from its branches.

"Thanks a lot, just what I need to work out how to deal with the anxiety," says your easily pleased conscious-mind.

Before your conscious-mind returns to the subconscious reception however, your personality relays the following:

"Before you report back to the ego, you need to know that this feeling of anxiety was only the emotional-signal to alert you and the ego to held emotional energy that needs releasing from this subconscious place. The ego held on to it, prevented it from flowing out of the garden here, for its own purposes, but I need him to know that we need to do something about allowing it to flow again as it is swamping us – literally.

"You leave with thoughts that can help dissipate the emotional-signal *feeling*, but that's all. The ego needs to realize that these thoughts come from a tree of belief that could do with some serious conscious attention. It is a tree that is monopolizing the waters of energy in this garden, its roots dam their flow. It is the source of the anxiety we're experiencing. I'm saying that this belief will continue to bring us anxiety, and more often, if we don't drain off some of the energy it has accrued over the years, and curb its influence upon our energy resources.

"I'm giving you a bucket full of emotional energy tapped from this accrued energy. It will be enough energy to take us past our usual actions when dealing with this anxiety. Whereas before we have coped by using uncontrolled emotional rants and shaking a lot, this time we need to do something different. We need to get the ego to wake up to the message of this emotion. Therefore, as a last resort, after consultations with our inner self and the body-consciousness, we are going to go for a nervous breakdown.

"Attached to the side of the bucket is a communication that

comes with this energy, a message that asks the ego to take some time away from the physical dimension and focus his attention on this garden of beliefs and the particular belief in question. The three of us working together could easily deal with the belief, and thus the anxiety, in a more consciously controlled fashion. In view of the event we have planned, it is very important that he reads it."

As you may be aware from your own experience, or that of others, it can take a dramatic intervention such as a nervous breakdown to get the ego to look within for some answers to the woes of anxiety. Thankfully, such a dramatic event takes its time to manifest. As well as being a wakeup call to the ego it serves as a safety valve, releasing a great deal of the energy "held" within us as part of an inept "coping" strategy for anxiety. It also forces the physical system to rest, thus providing time for us to turn our thoughts to internal matters.

For a more considered approach on dealing with anxiety, that will get some answers on *why* we feel anxious and what to do about it, we need to focus on the information carried by the emotion of anxiety. When we focus on the *feeling (emotional-signal)* of anxiety, our conscious-mind will snatch information, seeds of thought, from anywhere in the garden of beliefs that associate with the feeling. Thoughts will come from familiar beliefs that may have little to do with the source belief.

The emotional-signal of anxiety contains little information other than we are beginning to doubt ourselves in some way. The *emotion* of anxiety has a precise message, one that contains a number of packages of information that reveal *how and why* the doubt has set in.

Great anxiety communicates that we are presently unable to see the choices we have available to us in working out our next actions. We know that fear is involved. The fear is to do with being unable to clarify our choices. We are afraid that as we cannot clearly see the choices available, we will make the wrong choice. We know we have choices available, we simply cannot see them clearly enough to make a decision. The feeling of anxiety *signals* a doubt and this is what you are doubting – your ability to make a "correct" choice.

The element within the Mind that instigates clouding of the conscious-mind and prevents it from going about its work is a belief or clump of beliefs. The higher the emotional charge of anxiety, the greater the energy potential of the manipulating belief – there is a clear and marked correspondence. It may be that the troublesome belief has established itself so well in your garden that it is now an attitude, or even a "truth." Remember, truths are often difficult to see for what they are – highly energized beliefs.

It is the information provided by the emotion that should begin your quest to resolve anxiety. As anxiety builds, the emotional-signal of frustration and the emotion of anger can enter the fray. This is because frustration and anger relate to anxiety in the sense that they are all psychological conditions that compromise your choices for action – anxiety by clouds of confusion, frustration and anger by a perceived restriction of options. Any frustration added to anxiety should further alert your conscious-mind to the fact that a belief clouds your choices and is steering the decision process.

Acknowledgement in itself that the emotions involved with anxiety carry information allows your conscious-mind to begin to clear its vision. You can discover the manipulating belief that began your anguish by examining your thoughts. The thoughts you are nursing in the moment of anxiety are those that fog your mind.

Remember that your conscious-mind was quick to pick up its seeds of thought as soon as it went into the garden to look for some. It picked them up from under the problematic belief that is at the core of the matter – seeds that directly relate to their psychological parent. The energy signature, the DNA of your most dominant thought is therefore a match for the belief you want to find and prune within your garden. It is *this* thought that once grew into the belief that is now distressing you. *Your thoughts germinate in the soil and spring from the shaded ground beneath your beliefs.*

Channeled teachings state that energy from an emotion follows your thoughts. What this means is the energy of the emotion of anxiety will automatically flow towards the patch of ground in your garden where the thoughts and beliefs generating the anxiety are growing. You therefore have a distinct path, a stream, in your psychological garden that will lead you to the problematic plant that requires your conscious attention.

Any emotion, positive or negative, is communicating to you that what you are generating in the moment – including your thoughts – is always in association with your beliefs. To understand and receive this communication in the compassionate spirit in which your inner self offers it to your outer self, immediately opens up your choices. This act allows your conscious-mind to use its thoughts in accordance with their design – to interpret and translate all communications, whether they are from the physical realm or the non-physical realm. It can then feel fully informed before it recommends a course of action.

The sequence of thoughts, feelings, emotions and beliefs

Our understandable preoccupation with linear time has us yearning for knowledge on what comes "first" in the process of creating our physical reality. What we need to remember is that thoughts, feelings, emotions and beliefs are independent systems "living" in a field of existence that does not employ time. They are within a *spacious present* – which is what makes the present moment, the now, so powerful and important. Consequently, the sequence of *when* these energies engage is not the issue; it is the cooperative merging of their independent natures that sets the time of their emergence – literally, as we will see later.

Therefore, when your conscious-mind, ego and personality head out of your subconscious library into the physical world armed with the energies and information on what actions to take next, they do so with all of these largely subconscious entities firing at the same "time." This said, it is possible to discern a pattern of psychological events that appear to be sequential, and it is to this pattern that certain channeled guides would have us focus.

Glimpses of this sequence come from various metaphysical guides. Omni (John L. Payne) advises us that "thought precedes emotion," so if you recognize you are experiencing an emotion, it has appeared because of your thinking. Seth states, "Your thoughts will activate the appropriate feelings."[139] Abraham concurs with this, which is why Abraham's fundamental message dedicates itself to addressing the way in which you think. Elias states that the feeling of an emotional-signal precedes an emotion.

Elias and Seth agree that emotions and beliefs engage at the same time – in unity. This is why we should not regard emotions in themselves as "reactions" to what we perceive; the reactionary element is the belief, not the emotion that fires with it. Elias and Seth remind us that our emotions, along with our *imagination* (the forming of our ideas and thoughts), *follow* our beliefs. Here, the interpretation of "follow" we take to mean that the energies of thoughts and emotions, attracted by resonating vibrational signatures, *pursue* the applicable beliefs.

You therefore have beliefs, emotions and thought formation all happening in concert in a mental event designed to assist your conscious-mind to decide on how to act – what action you should take and thus bring into reality. This means that if you take the belief element (the conductor) away, then the emotional context is lost and the entire mental event dissolves away – ready for your imagination to start over and turn its attention elsewhere.

This disclosure highlights the importance of addressing to your *beliefs* if you are experiencing a negative emotion. If you can drain energy away from the influencing belief in this mental

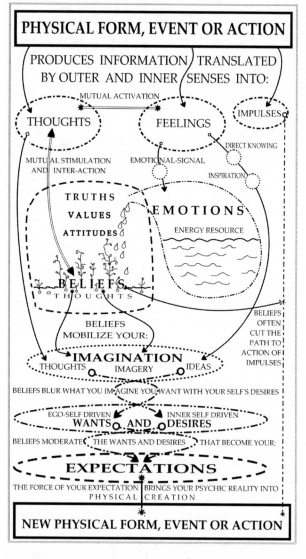

Figure 4. The sequence of mental machinations

situation, your negative emotion soon subsides and your Mind frees itself from negativity in general.

Figure 4 illustrates the only slightly sequential, mostly circular, mostly all-at-once machinations that occur in your conscious-mind when thoughts, feelings, emotions and beliefs come into play.

Emotions in relation to beliefs

Emotions are not belief systems – although we do construct a system of beliefs to try to explain what they are. Your beliefs reside within the subconscious area of your psyche, and as emotions are not dependent upon this domain, they exist regardless of any belief system.

This means that it is possible to experience an emotion quite objectively, in its pure form. You can go stand in the rain as one might sweep through your garden as an unpredictable shower. You can utilize its energy, and check in on the tonal quality of your Essence. In other words, emotions always bring energy to act along with notice of your overall state of being, but they don't always associate themselves with your beliefs.

In actuality, emotions are neither positive nor negative in quality; we label them as such *as they associate with our beliefs* during the creation process. A "positive" emotion resonates with your self-affirming beliefs; a "negative" emotion resonates with, and informs you of, self-denying beliefs.

Belief systems are an implicit facet of our experience of the physical dimension. Humanity's consciousness places belief systems at the focal point of its creative ambitions. (This is why beliefs are at the center of *Figure 4,* above.) Belief systems influence our emotions simply because for emotions to experience physical expression, as any action in the electric field seeks to do, they can do so by flowing through our individuated expression of Consciousness. They can flow through the peculiar psychological structures of our species, the primary construct of which is our belief systems.

If you imagine your emotions to be the life giving waters of your psyche, they need to flow through your subconscious garden of beliefs on their way to the physical world. Other animals, that do not express their consciousness through the incorporation of belief systems, are therefore able to experience pure emotions more readily.

Emotions are an element of your expression that you have chosen to be the method, so to speak, of your expression within this particular physical dimension. This is not to say that other physical dimensions do not incorporate emotion, for some do, but within this particular dimension, it is one of the base elements of your creation of expression.[140]

Emotions denied, rejected and repressed

Emotions are forms of energy from the electric field of action, the field of reality "closest" to our physical reality. With this premise in mind, it is not too difficult to consider emotions as *representations* of action – the energy to act, encapsulated. Now, energy is always looking to express itself through action. Therefore, emotions are actions always looking to express themselves.

In the subjective, psychological area within your consciousness, psychological actions conform to certain rules regarding energy and actions. Fundamentally, these are that *actions are Self-generating* – that is, your system of Self generates actions (like emotions) in order to express itself; and *actions act upon themselves* – that is, they affect each other, and thus their original path of action.

These principles may be easier to understand if you imagine emotions to be encapsulated action packages, molecules of water bouncing off and *inter-acting* with each other as they flow through the subconscious area of your mind.

Seth categorically states that *energy cannot be retained* – it *must* be released. We cannot, therefore, retain or hold the energy of emotions within us forever. They must be released one way or another. You might build a dam to hold back the waters of emotion flowing through your garden of beliefs, but eventually they *will* make it to, and express themselves in, the physical realm. This being the case, we do need to understand how we can consciously manage their energy as they flow through us.

Emotions, like thoughts, have their own *structure*. We can manipulate structures.

As we are beginning to discover for ourselves, emotions have an electrical and chemical structure. When the electric field of action forms an energy structure, like an emotion, it commits that form to act and it cannot be stopped from doing so. However, we *can* manipulate them, and we do, albeit without any real conscious control at present. Our ego's *conscious* manipulation of the energies of emotions through to their expressed actions forms part of humanity's current psychological evolution.

In our psychological structuring, to deny an action—an emotion—automatically changes the path of the action as well as the person. Similarly, if we attempt to reject an emotion, it is our own psychological structures that are affected the most, not so much the emotion's structure.

Because of the committed nature of energies and actions in the psychological realm, it is impossible to repress an emotion. We can though, and do, create *an action of repression – which we* currently assume to be "repressing" an emotion. This *independent* action of repression is the energy form that affects and thereby changes the original emotional energy form – and leads us into psychological difficulties.

Any attempt to deny, reject, or repress an emotion is psychologically detrimental. Your subconscious does not produce such actions; the residents of your subconscious library are always looking to supply you with information on why such detrimental acts are happening. The character generating these actions is your ego-self.

The ego imagines that it can stand apart from action. Because of its preoccupation with the objective physical realm, it has "objectified" action to such a degree that it believes that it has the power not only to manipulate the energies of action, but also deny them a path to expression (an impossibility) if it so chooses.

The ego's refusal to accept an emotion usually involves one of two actions of its own. Either it will attempt to return the emotion to the subjective world of the subconscious – hand it back to your personality in its garden – or it will attempt to set it further apart from itself by constantly disregarding its existence. Either action is born of ignorance of an emotion's commitment to action (express itself) in the physical dimension.

The acceptance and non-acceptance of actions such as those offered by emotions illustrates that the ego is itself a series of actions, a collection of "approved" actions selected from the many that buffet it. Your ego, on the whole, develops from actions chosen as characteristic of its own nature, actions that resonate with your personality's tonal frequency.

Actions, by *their* nature, change things. Therefore, the nature of your ego changes as it constantly accepts and rebuffs actions. This means actions or emotions your ego chose as acceptable in the past, may become unacceptable and subsequently denied entry into its collection of approved actions later in life. This in itself can lead to psychological strife as the former action, once accepted and "positioned" within the pattern of actions forming the ego, finds itself fighting for its place within your mind.

PLEASE SAY THAT AGAIN (19) The ego's attempts to rebuff an emotion.

Here is an attempt to summarize the ego's attempts to deny, reject or repress an emotion:

Unbeknownst to your ego, when it doesn't want to accept an emotion (which is an action) into its subjective world, the *action of non-acceptance* (which includes an emotion), automatically includes itself in your overall psychological structuring.

In other words; denied, rejected and repressed emotions will express themselves, if in a somewhat warped fashion, despite your ego's futile efforts to rebuff them. Importantly, they will often do so in an unruly, defiant fashion, outside of the direct control of the ego.

Such emotions, unaccepted but nevertheless a part of the ego, consequently drain energy from the systems of your outer self, energy that should be put to use pursuing your outer self's *purpose-ful* actions.

Emotions and expectations

Expectations are a compelling combination of emotional energies. According to more than one channeled guide, we cannot classify expectation as an independent emotion as it is often an amalgamation of energies constructed from various emotions. For example, excitement with anticipation produces a positive expectation, whereas anxiety with anticipation produces a negative expectation.

Turning your expectations into preferred outcomes is all about learning how to consciously manipulate and direct your emotional energies. You manifest your desires (and other psychic constructions) through the force of expectation. As Seth puts it:

Expectation is the force, then, that triggers psychic realities into physical construction.[141]

Your emotions are not the result of your expectations, although the expectations you bring to fruition do lead to the further expression of emotions – elation or disappointment, for example.

To aid your understanding of how you form your expectations let's use a baking metaphor. Think of an expectation as a cake produced from the ingredients your personality has to hand in your garden of beliefs.

You begin the cake mix with the flour of your desire. This flour consists of the finely ground seeds of thought that relate to your desire. There can be a few lumps in this flour, which are to do with the tiny granules of thought clustering around a "want" – which is a thought form similar to a desire, but already tainted by an influencing belief. You put the flour through a sieve to break up, extract these lumps, and help keep its purity of desire.

Usually the reverse happens – the lumping becomes worse because the sieve you are using is the sieve of your beliefs. Sifting the flour through your beliefs stimulates the power of Attraction, the fine granules of thought begin to cluster together even more in your mixing bowl.

Nevertheless, you quickly mix in the milk and waters of your emotions. The other flavoring ingredients (the envisioned details of your expectation) go in, followed by the eggs, the binding agent for the batter – which represent the core belief systems that relate to your desire.

A thorough whisking ensues before transferring the batter to a baking tin and placing it in the oven – the oven of time. In the physical world of cake making, you would set the time on the oven and leave it alone. In the kitchen of your psyche, you don't. The time for an expectation to bake is set by your inner self, with due consideration given to any "interfering" factors – such as confounding beliefs (nasty lumps in the batter), and anxious cooks, like the ego, who open the oven door to check things, chuck in another ingredient half way through baking, and keep wanting to know when it's ready.

Such interference in the baking of an expectation is what leads to a less than desirable outcome. You are likely to have a cake that doesn't quite match up to the one you envisioned, or you may even have a totally disappointing under-baked mess.

The message from the metaphysical literature is a resounding, *"Leave it alone!"*

When you have fashioned an expectation from your desires, when your batter is ready, do not think about it at all while it is baking in your psyche's oven. As Abraham recommends, give it back to "Source" – that is, leave it with your inner self in your subconscious kitchen. Trust that the characters in your inner kitchen, your inner resources, left to their own devises, will do the work and pick the right time for your expectation to come out of the oven and onto the table of physicality. Your inner self, with its greater perspective, in its privileged position of under-standing fully your life's intent and purpose, will sort out the what, who, when, and how of making your expectation as close to your desire as possible.

At present, our egos believe that having the conscious-mind concentrate on thoughts alone will bring about an expectation's materialization. This is like asking your conscious-mind to concentrate on picking out the lumps in the batter and leave it at that. If you wish for a desire to become real, you need to make sure your sieve of beliefs is as clean and unclogged as you can possibly have it. You do need to sift the flour of thought, so don't think you can throw your sieve away! Become fully conversant with the nature of your beliefs; for your desires filter through them, and they have the greatest influence on whether your cake of expectation brings you joy.

Expectations become the frameworks on which we build our realities. We each have an emotional "heritage," a pattern of psychic energies that we can manipulate, just as we manipulate the "solidified" energies of physical matter. When you use your imagination to speculate on what you desire and then back this with great expectations, almost any probability can manifest itself. We are yet to master this internal manipulation of energies in a conscious fashion; doing so is a feature of our collective shift in consciousness. Expect this to happen!

The entire subject of feelings and emotions is currently a very confused one in Western thinking in particular. This confusion mirrors our lack of understanding, which persists through a lack of psychological research and naïve assumptions as to their nature. I hope that this book will have clarified a few things for you when you come to think about and deal with your feelings and emotions.

In attempting to deal with the energies of your undesired emotions, I recommend that you begin with familiarizing yourself with a method such as EFT (see *Appendix II*) from the field of Energy Psychology.

A summary of the metaphysical information on the effect of the emotions on our Selves suggests that they not only change our physical cells, but also stamp their presence in various other realities. The physical field, the electric field, and the field of dreams are just a few of the realities they affect.

We need to train our egos to allow emotions to flow through us in acceptance; they are, after all, *in motion* — they will pass and others will replace them. When our ego attempts to hold onto them or rebuff them (usually because of fears), they are made stronger and less manageable. In Book 3 of The Early Sessions, Seth advises us that, "The validity and strength of emotions cannot be overestimated..." They are a representation of the vitality of the universe, just one stage of translation away from the energy of Consciousness Itself, as it seeks expression and experience through You. As Seth remarks, this vitality, "... has been tinged psychologically in its entry through the subconscious, but that is all."

Emotions are the most vital tools with which you have to work. It is for this reason that you must learn how to *use* them.[142]

In addition, Abraham informs us,

We refer to the *Non-Physical You* as your *Inner Being,* or your *Source.* It is not important what you call that Source of Energy, or Life Force, but it *is* important that you be consciously aware of when you are allowing a full Connection to it and when you are restricting it in some way — and your emotions are your constant indicators of your degree of allowing or resisting that Connection.[143]

CHAPTER 17:

YOU'RE EITHER IN LOVE OR IN FEAR

There is a common notion that runs through most of the metaphysical teachings on emotions, and that is that there are just two fundamental emotional states – love and fear. You can imagine these states to be on one emotional continuum, a measuring stick with Divine Love at one end and abject fear at the other; rather like Abraham's scale of emotions mentioned in *Chapter 12*. All of the emotions we label as positive or negative are gradations along this continuum. You can thus measure a negative emotion you are experiencing as how far your current psychological state has moved away from Divine Love.

You might also think of a sullen mood as an indicator of the lack of positive emotional energies making up your personality's emotional climate – how overcast the skies are in your personality's garden of beliefs.

The natural principles and powers described in Part I of this book underpin our very existence in the physical dimension. For human consciousness to operate within the physical realm it has to translate these working principles of Consciousness. Because our consciousness possesses *conscious* self-awareness with an ability for self-reflection, we are *allowed* (through Divine Love) to translate these principles *in our own way*.

Human love is our best effort at translating the natural power of Divine Love. Fear is a hugely feeble attempt at translating the drive of Consciousness for existence, something we misinterpret as "survival."

In essence, fear stems from a lack of understanding, whereas Divine Love embodies understanding.

Let's talk of love

We talk of love as being an emotion. Divine Love isn't an emotion. Our translation of it, human love, does though employ emotional energy.

Divine Love is not simply an independent energy configuration, an invigorating force from the electric field. It is both an *action* and a *way of being* – the way of being of Consciousness. It is a *quality* of all actions (including emotions), and a natural principle that *applies* to all actions – in whatever field of existence they occur.

Divine Love is about the total acceptance and the non-judgmental, unconditional allowance of what is. This is because *any and every "thing"* of what is, the likenesses and contrasts (good and bad stuff), is at its very core an expression of Consciousness born of Its quest to know Itself through experience. Consciousness, human consciousness, *your* consciousness, can't know itself, can't decide on what is preferable for existence, can't make choices, can't change things, without the contrast provided by un-preferable creations.

Divine Love powers the process of the individuation of Consciousness (refer to *Say That Again 4*). As it is a natural principle of action, it demands that actions adhere to certain qualities of expression. These are the qualities of acceptance, allowance, appreciation and compassion – as in reality, in *Truth*, all actions, all expressions, whether made physical or otherwise, are individuations of Consciousness.

This is how Elias talks of love:

Love is a quality of consciousness. It is the action of becoming.[144]

Love is a truth, and the translation within your physical dimension of love is not attraction. It is that of knowing and appreciation, genuine appreciation, which appreciation is expressed in acceptance. In this, the knowing is also significant, actual knowing of yourself and knowing of another individual and expressing an acceptance which generates an appreciation. This is the genuine expression of love.[145]

Elias reminds us that when it comes to understanding the *truths* of our reality (described in *Chapter 11*), we show little interest in them, other than Divine Love, which our current definitions show to be misinterpretations of its truth. We misinterpret and ill-define Divine Love because of our preoccupation with defining everything – which by default must occur through the language of our belief systems – an extremely limited and biased medium for expressing what we want to know, or think we already know.

As Anita Moorjani comments in her book *Dying to be Me*, when coming to terms with her near death experience (NDE), she realized that her NDE state was one of pure awareness (couched in Divine Love), which suspends "all previously held doctrine and dogma."

I've found that subsequent to my NDE, I'm at my strongest when I'm able to let go, when I suspend my beliefs as well as disbeliefs, and leave myself open to *all* possibilities.[146]

Moorjani's NDE is a testament to the fact that Divine Love is an action, a quality underpinning all experiences, a state of being and becoming – not a thing to be described, even if we had the language to do so.

It is impossible to express such truths as Divine Love through language that is associated with belief systems. As we come to recognize and continue our attempts to uncover the truths to our existence, we get to realize and be more aware of the nature of our beliefs and the belief systems we construct to describe our existence. We get to know that beliefs are merely a tool for physical existence, a medium by which we paint our physical dimension.

We articulate our own expression of Consciousness through emotions, but this articulation is also heavily involved with another prime driving force – sexuality (see *Chapter 12*). The blend of these forces behind our physical expression gives rise to much confusion about the nature of emotions, sexual expression – and the *acts* of love we imagine accurately convey the *action* of Divine Love.

Because Divine Love is the very nature of Consciousness, and to know Itself is Its primal desire, this too becomes **your deepest** *(currently subconscious)* **desire** – to know your Self through the action of love.

As Omni (John L. Payne) remarks, Divine Love is at the core of your being and becomes a magnet within your personality, operating under the natural power of Attraction. **You have a will to love** because it is within the nature of Consciousness and all Its expressions.

Our will to love is the only influencing factor upon our *free will*. We have free will as a natural consequence of Consciousness allowing humanity "conscious self-awareness" in its evolutionary progress. Because we have free will, we are even free to ignore the one influencing factor that exists to protect and sustain our free will – our will to love provided by Divine Love.

Your will to love is your direct link to Consciousness and Its *modus operandi* – Divine Love – "… the complete and total acceptance of what is."[147]

A will free to disregard Divine Love

The conscious self-awareness step in the evolution of our consciousness brought us an ego-self so that we could manipulate our expression of consciousness within the medium of physicality. Our ego-selves allowed us to self-reflect, and we began to imagine that our physical selves were the totality of who we were; that our egos were the source of our identity; and that we were separate from other things (expressions of

Consciousness).

This egotistical leap into loneliness led us to believe that death must be the end to our existence. We observed how other animals defended themselves against death and took this as indication of a need to protect ourselves against it. Eventually, we developed a deep-rooted belief system that sees all "others" as potential threats, and thus we cannot *allow* another the benefit of our will to love.

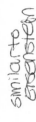

Our *shift in consciousness,* begun around a century ago and said by metaphysical teachers to be accelerating over the next few decades, incorporates a conscious "remembering" that Divine Love is the fundamental principle of creation and that we need to make a conscious effort to bring our creational skills back within its guidelines.

Our free will has taken us along a path of experiences that demonstrate how ignoring Divine Love's guidance affects our creations.

We have spent centuries discovering how the absence of acceptance, appreciation, allowance and compassion creates realities that none of us prefer. War and conflict have been our way of teaching our Selves that we have free will in the creation of our realities. However, the *Shift* required of our consciousness is to accept that there also exists a "how best to go about it" creation scheme, a purposeful principle of creation, a *natural* way – which is to acquiesce to Divine Love.

Our will to love has never gone away as it cannot do so; we have been pretending it's not there to see where our free will would take us.

Our shift in consciousness is the next *inevitable* step on our evolutionary path. It is a step that takes us *within* an acceptance of the power of Divine Love. The only other alternative step, *outside* of this acceptance, is to allow our collective ego to play out its own inevitable next step, a next step we have witnessed taken by many individual egos that cannot accept how things actually work, and are unable to adjust their beliefs – suicide.

Seth suggests that the personality of any individual who commits suicide soon realizes in the *Transitional Area within Consciousness* that their actions are inconsequential to the grander scheme of their Essence self, and the even grander scheme of Consciousness. This is because, as Omni reminds us, we cannot extinguish the spark of Divine Love within us. No matter "how far into the darkness" we go, this spark of Love, this will to love, brings us back to Consciousness – back from "lovelessness" to unconditional love.

To reinforce this point, you can look at our *shift in consciousness* this way.

There is really no need for humanity to commit suicide – it's a *futile* action. In the grander scheme of probable realities floating in the timeless sea of the *spacious present*, Consciousness is aware of this futility. It remains a probability, but the alternative probability of expanding our consciousness further offers more enticing experiential possibilities. *All* actions (even the probable one of our suicide) are a product of Consciousness getting to know Itself through experiences; and *contrasting* experiences are the best way of doing this when exploring the physical domain. Humanity has spent a great deal of time playing with contrasting actions and particularly the ultimate contrast – what happens when you ignore the natural principles of the Universe, and in particular, Divine Love.

The last evolutionary step in our consciousness – conscious self-awareness and self-reflection – gave us the free will to explore this ultimate contrast of experience. This next evolutionary step or Shift in our consciousness is inevitable because we have taken this exploration as far as it can go – to the gates of self-annihilation.

Where's the fun in not being part of Consciousness expressing Itself in the physical realm? Is it not time for us to explore other contrasts that Consciousness has to offer?

Human love

When Elias reminds us that love is a truth, he is talking of Divine Love, a *multidimensional* quality of existence, a truth that is only relative to the one Truth of Consciousness.

Human love and our descriptions of it are our *interpretations* of Divine Love.

Even though our interpretations are somewhat muddled and confused by our beliefs systems, they are nonetheless a creative attempt at understanding the vitality of Consciousness and making Divine Love a reality within our physical experience. Creativity and further understanding will eventually bring us closer to expressing this primal force in a less convoluted way.

The consensus of channeled advice on how we can best express Divine Love and thus enjoy its guidance both in psychological terms and physical actions is to *begin with a total acceptance of what is*.

From this fundamental action of understanding and knowing that "what is" is there for a reason – to learn *what is* preferable through contrast – we can *accept* "what is" for what it is!

This doesn't mean that what is un-preferable is acceptable! The un-preferable is there to get you to act upon it being there! It's there to get you to realize that the preferable creation you desire will entail some work on your belief systems.

When you *know and accept* that all creations are there for a reason, you get to be appreciative. When you know that *you*, everyone, and everything is there for a reason, you begin to show genuine *appreciation* – which is a genuine expression of Divine Love.

Genuine appreciation of another individual is therefore the basis of human love. Genuine appreciation *allows* you to *allow* them to be who they are.

Allowance is another expression of Divine Love.

You should be easily able to recognize when you are being appreciative and allowing – expressing Divine Love through

your will to love – if you take a moment to review your relationships, particularly those you have with children. Notice when
you *don't* appreciate the actions of another person, for this is
when you are withdrawing your will to love from them.

Understand that this psychological action alerts your
conscious-mind to *beliefs you hold about their* **actions** *– not the
person.* Non-appreciation tells you to look to your beliefs *first* to
see if they need adjustment in order that you can return to acceptance and appreciation; or, if their actions are truly *unacceptable –
to you* – then you need to make this clear to the other person if
they are a key figure in your co-creations – your partner, for
example.

This course of action is easier to understand and implement
when you consider the actions of a child running across a road,
less so when the actions of an adult or group of people are at
issue. This is because where children are concerned; your own
beliefs are less able to interfere with your will to love them, as a
subconscious hardwiring exists to re-establish appreciation and
acceptance of a child as soon as possible. In addition, children
have yet to layout their own definitive belief beds, or concern
themselves with defending the beliefs they are currently cultivating. Whereas, unacceptable actions by adults invariably
involve complex belief systems (religious doctrine under the core
system of *Spirituality,* for example) and judgmental attitudes
born of the belief system of *Duplicity* (refer to *Chapter 12.*)

Human love and sexuality

Because sexuality is, along with emotions, a primary aspect of
the expression of human consciousness in the physical realm –
and we have (overlapping) belief systems that attempt to
translate these drives into a semblance of understanding – our
interpretations of Divine Love get into a right old mess.

Out of this mess comes human love.

Our conventional definition of love relies upon "deep

affection" and "attraction" as its mainstays. Certainly, we can equate attraction with that magnet of our will to love that Divine Love implants within us. You can think of this as the natural power of Attraction sown into the fabric of your being by the natural power of Divine Love.

Affection, on the other hand, is a confusion arising from our lack of understanding on the actual nature of emotions. Psychology highlights this confusion by continuing to use the term "affect" when referring to feelings and emotion.

Affection *is* a feeling; in that, *it is an emotional-signal type of feeling* that alerts you to the fact that emotional energy is available to you should you wish to stimulate your will to love – should you wish to express genuine appreciation. You can call the emotion that brings this energy "love" if you like; however, keep in mind that it is natural for feelings to ebb and flow and for emotions to subside quickly.

This is why the "love" in a relationship appears to dissolve rather alarmingly once shared actions become routine. It also explains why **continued acts of affection can literally re-energize a relationship** – when they are ebbing, get them to flow into appreciation.

Furthermore, we can regard "deep affection," often felt for offspring, at times for another adult, as an innate ability to sustain acts of affection towards them. This is indeed an approximation of Divine Love, or one way we are able to express Divine Love in a manner disentangled from sexuality and its belief system – it is a pure, nurturing, unconditional, motherly love.

A loving relationship

Affection and attraction are then very much to do with how we translate Divine Love into human love. They are reasonably honest expressions of love, which we then relentlessly entrap within actions we generate from our core belief systems. The belief systems of *Emotions*, *Sexuality*, and *Relationships* enter the melee of our attempts to express our will to love, not to mention the refereeing system of *Duplicity*.

When it comes to expressing love in a relationship, our belief systems set up a series of expectations (see *Chapter 16* and refer to *Figure 4*). We produce expectations concerning the other person; we place expectations upon ourselves; we have expectations about how relationships should be enacted – all mixed in with the underlying desire to express ourselves honestly, *without* all of these expectations!

In all of this, *a genuine expression of love between individuals reflects a mutual allowance of each to generate and create that which they desire without restriction.*

Sexuality represents an important way in which Divine Love can express itself in the physical realm; however, our beliefs have put enormous restrictions upon this route for expression. Our beliefs on *gender* and *sexual preference* are typical examples of such restrictions.

You may be surprised to learn that the expression of Divine Love has no concern for gender. As Divine Love is a *natural principle* of the Universe, it is *natural* for an individual to love another, *regardless* of their gender.

Furthermore – and this refers to Divine Love's "attraction magnet" mentioned earlier – when it comes to sexual preference, this magnet, along with our *family of alignment*, is determined (by your Essence) pre-birth. It is subconsciously set for you to be attracted to the opposite sex, the same sex, or both when your physical body reaches sexual maturity. It may come as a bit of a shock to you, but from the greater perspective of your *Essence* self – you have a bisexual *Identity*. Your outer self has bisexuality at its core as it explores sexuality through choices made at the Essence level as to gender and sexual preference for the current lifetime.

Sexuality is a primary mode of expression for our consciousness to explore in the physical realm. Seth reminds us that too many of us equate sex with love.[148] In the West, we have compounded this erroneous equation by imagining that apart from the aforementioned "motherly" love, sexual acts, physical intimacy, are the *only* natural way to express love. This has led us into further restriction over the use of any form of physical intimacy as we are now apt to construe this as a prelude to sexual acts. Think of the father's angst in stroking the neck of his daughter, or the "get off" cries of many a female who just wants a cuddle.

The more we equate love and sex, the more conflicts arise, and the more creativity suffers. Our natural bisexuality, given acceptance and an opportunity to express itself fully, would actually go a long way in clearing the entangled problems we face due to our abject confusion over the expression of love.

To love someone is to *allow* for and *appreciate* his or her differences from you. Genuine love is creative and seeks to explore – and not just the fascinating physical bits and pieces. It seeks to explore all aspects of the beloved one, including the characteristics and actions that appear to be in contrast to your own. Genuine love sees and accepts these contrasts for what they are – idiosyncrasies that make the beloved special, that give them their unique identity.

Consciousness, through Divine Love, delights in the differences and contrasts of all of its expressions – because It *knows that all such expressions are of Itself and contributing to Its desire to know Itself.*

 Human love brings us as close as we can to Divine Love and thus the nature of Consciousness. We can get closer still by adopting the same attitude toward others as expressed above. There is also one important person we need to love in order to love others, as Seth remarks in *The Nature of the Psyche: Its Human Expression*:

Love incites dedication, commitment. It specifies. You cannot, therefore, honestly insist that you love humanity and all people equally if you do not love one other person. If you do not love yourself, it is quite difficult to love another.[149]

Love your self

The final sentence of the above quotation is a topic taken up by most channeled guides. If you cannot seem to find your will to love your Self, if you are unable to appreciate your own uniqueness, then it is unlikely you will be able to genuinely love another.

When you know that Divine Love, the vitality of Consciousness, is to do with experience through actions, *you can experience it for your Self* through *acts* of acceptance, compassion, gratitude, forgiveness and appreciation. This is the only way you can connect with it.

As you connect with it through such acts, you begin to realize that your uniqueness *is* your connection to the Oneness of Consciousness. You therefore owe it to your Self, and Consciousness, that you express your uniqueness to the best of your ability.

You also begin to realize that as all selves are individuations of Consciousness there can be no separation from this Oneness. As you are part of this Oneness, and take up your place within this greatest of Selves, you will be able to see that to denigrate or disparage any self within this Self, can only be an act of *self-condemnation.*

By not being appreciative and compassionate toward your Self, even that pesky ego part of your Self, you cannot experience Divine Love, or express human love – our best translation of its action.

Abraham (Esther Hicks) has this to add:

It is absolutely imperative that you come to a place of positive vibration, which means you must adore you... The balance that you are wanting to bring into your life experience is the balance of appreciating you...

And you appreciate you – not all at once on the big things – you appreciate yourself one thought by one thought, one segment by one segment, one moment by one moment, by looking for reasons to appreciate yourself.

If you are having trouble in your relationship, it is because you are not liking yourself. Much as you would like to give the blame to the other for what is happening, it is your lack of appreciation for self that is responsible *for every area of lack* in your experience.

When you are condemning the World, whether it is the political world or the religious world, or the economic world or the ecological world – when you are looking at the flaws in the world, it is not about the world, *it is about you!* It is about the way you feel about you.

And so we say friends, nothing is more important than that you establish your own relationship with you. It our promise to you that your Inner Being adores you, but you close the door when you think thoughts of lack about yourself.[150]

Anita Moorjani's NDE taught her the importance of self-love.

You may frown or cringe at the thought, but I can't stress enough how important it is to cultivate a deep love affair with yourself... But my NDE allowed me to realize that this was the key to my healing.[151]

Moorjani goes on to say that when you realize that you are love, because you are, *in Essence*, the Divine Love of Consciousness, you don't have to work at exercising your will to love others – "we just have to be true to ourselves, and we become instruments of loving energy, which touches everyone we come into contact with."

Self-love and self-appreciation have nothing to do with selfishness in the classical sense of the word. Metaphysical literature concurs with Moorjani when she says, "Selfishness comes from lack of self-love."

Selfishness is the result of beliefs that generate fears (the other end of the Love/Fear continuum) that drive your actions.

Moreover, Omni makes the point that if you have issues to do with lack of *money* – defined as the "physical manifestation of the energies of love and power"[152] – you will inevitably be experiencing issues to do with lack of self-appreciation and self-worth, which fire feelings concerned with fears of powerlessness.

Science on love

The "psycho-evolutionary theory" of emotion proposed by Robert Plutchik, Ph.D., describes love as a combination of the primary emotions of joy and trust. This is perhaps our best "scientific" translation of Divine Love.

Metaphysical literature suggests that joy begins as a feeling that can escalate in intensity to an emotion. The feeling signals that in this moment you are validating and appreciating yourself. The emotion communicates that you are exercising a *trust* in yourself, an acknowledgement that you are expressing yourself freely in your choices and in accordance with Divine Love.

Abraham states that while the basis of life is freedom, joy is the true "objective" of life. Joy is the feeling and emotion that informs you that you are freely expressing your personality in alignment with your intent and purpose – the objective of your life. Omni (John L Payne) offers this on joy:

Many of you have for so long held to the belief that the path to God or to enlightenment is the path of suffering. Suffering has served you in teaching you all about who you are not and what you do not want. The new teacher is joy. It is not that joy is new, but that you are only now awakening to it, for your evolution has taken you to the stage where you can feel the true essence of your soul. This is truly a new dawn, this is the return of the Christ, this is the awakening of the God/Goddess within, this is the dawning of a new age.[153]

According to Plutchik, the other primary emotion involved with love is trust. According to metaphysical teaching, the communication of joy indicates this to be the case, although trust isn't strictly an emotion, more a state of being. Trust is an expression of freedom – "the basis of life" – a psychological state, which is allowing energy to flow freely through your Self in its "natural manner." That natural manner is in accordance with your intent and purpose.

An example of when we freely allow this trust in our Self to come through (albeit without conscious awareness) is the act of driving a car when engaged in conversation with other passengers. At the end of the journey, it is difficult to recall the specifics of how you got there! What you did was move your energy from one location to another in the physical realm without concentrating your thoughts, but *trusting* that you would get to where you wanted to be without anything getting in your way.

Omni's mention of issues to do with lack of money a little earlier illustrates when this trust of the Self flies out the car window. Moving your energy to a place of financial freedom involves a complex series of beliefs getting in your way, beliefs that revolve around a lack of trust in yourself. Money issues and the beliefs that get in your way are all about the subject of how deeply you trust your Self.

When you are enjoying the *state* of trust, you should realize that any desires you have set in motion do not require any great effort on your part to bring them into reality. You simply need to remain for as much as possible within the state of trust – trusting

[handwritten margin note: disagree doubtful]

in the natural flow of energies and allowing them to bring about manifestation in *natural time*.

The humanistic psychologist Eric Fromm (1900–1980) suggests in his book *The Art of Loving* that love is the antidote to our perpetual anxiety brought about by the ego's perceived separation from other things. According to Fromm, our greatest need is to overcome this separation by reuniting through love. It may well be that when he wrote the book in the mid-1950s he was intuitively recognizing that our biggest separation in becoming consciously self-aware was from Divine Love and the Oneness of Consciousness. He suggests a *reconnection* is required for us to overcome our fears of separation.

Fromm, Carl Jung and Humberto Maturana are notable psychologists that have their own variant definitions of the principle that genuine love between two people includes a mutual regard for the unique identity of the other, and their right to express themselves fully without imposing restrictions.

The field of Biological Science is beginning to make significant progress in identifying the effects of emotions on human physiology. It is also beginning to reveal how Divine Love, albeit thought to be a combination of emotions, translates its energy into chemical expressions in the physical body.

For example, oxytocin is a hormone produced in a part of the brain known as the hypothalamus. First recognized as a peptide influencing uterine contractions during childbirth and milk production during suckling (think "motherly love" here); research is now linking it in humans with the state of trust just mentioned, along with feelings of *commitment*. Stored and released by the pituitary gland, we might consider oxytocin to be the chemical constituent required in any loving *reconnection* talked of by Fromm.

Now referred to as "the hormone of love," research begun in

[handwritten margin note: not denying science/brain bcos of love]

the late 1990s reveals oxytocin to be affecting synaptic strengths in the brain, producing, it appears, a "special" type of neural bonding, which is reflected psychologically by less selfish considerations and more of a recognition of mutual intent.

In *The Nature of the Psyche: Its Human Expression*, Seth tells us that,

[Divine] Love is a biological necessity, a force operating to one degree or another in all biological life. Without love there is no physical commitment to life—no psychic hold.

Love exists whether or not it is sexually expressed, though it is natural for love to seek expression. Love implies loyalty. It implies *commitment* [my emphasis].[154]

To round off our talk of love and its biological translations, Seth makes the point in *Book 4* of *The Early Sessions*, that Divine Love is *"always* a protection" – protecting, quite literally, the integrity of all of the systems of your Self – the biological, the chemical, the electromagnetic and the psychological systems.

CHAPTER 18:

SO WHAT OF FEAR?

Fear concentrates the mind.

Fear tells your conscious-mind to *focus* on what you are creating. It does this to have you *act* on what you are creating.

Fear can take two forms of expression. One is a direct communication from your Essence self, an impulse to act immediately to protect the integrity of your physical self – a "natural" bypassing of the thought processes – that relays the energies behind the primal survival mechanism of Consciousness. You have a lion running toward you, no need to think, just act!

Most creatures engage "fight or flight" as a suitable action; however, fear is also *immobilizing* – which is why animals can physically freeze as a survival strategy. In the case of the human animal, this survival strategy now often translates into a potent and toxic psychological immobilization.

The other type of expression takes the form of an emotional-signal, alerting your conscious-mind to the psychological factors behind what you are creating for yourself. This emotional-signal can invoke various emotions, each with a more specific communication on what thoughts and beliefs are at play in your creation. This is why fear is at the core of all "negative" emotions.

Fear and lack of trust

Elias explains that part of the message relayed by fear is to wake up to the fact that what you are creating for yourself is a result of a *lack of trust* within you.

Fear therefore brings you the opportunity, like any negative emotion, to examine thoroughly the physical and psychological elements involved in the situation. If you sense fear, and there is no immediate need to act, then you know that something is triggering a lack of trust within you, and trust, as we know, is to do with how freely you are allowing energy to flow through you on its way to physical manifestation.

Trust is the "state" you require for joyful emotions to come through. When your state of trust is waning, you are moving away from the power of Divine Love, deviating from its guiding influence upon your intentional path. Rather than trusting in Divine Love to steer the streams of energies going through your garden of beliefs, you are directing them toward belief beds that heartily quaff their waters to produce a torrent of thoughts attracting fearful emotional-signals.

Your state of trust enters a state of fear, which drains your energies (remember emotional-signals, like all feelings, *consume* energy), demotivates you, immobilizes you, and keeps you from your path of intent.

The longer you remain off your path of intent, the more you will draw contrast and conflict into your creations. The more you maintain the state of trust, the easier your desires come to fruition, and the less conflict is experienced.

You are so blinded to your probabilities that you believe that the pay-off that you receive presently is the most pay-off that you may receive! What you do not realize is that as you move effortlessly in trusting of yourself, and listening to yourself, and letting go of fear, your pay-off increases![155]

For someone like Anita Moorjani, a person who has dallied with the *Transitional Area within Consciousness,* who has reconnected with the all-encompassing state of Divine Love and can recall the experience, a *knowing* prevails:

Even with this inner excitement, however, with this feeling that I was on the precipice of some great adventure, I still didn't feel that I had to *do* or *pursue* anything for it to happen. *I just had to be myself fearlessly!* In that way, I'd be allowing myself to be an instrument of love. I understood that this was the best thing that any of us could possibly do or be, for both the planet and ourselves.[156]

Our greatest fear

Our greatest fear, according to our channeled teachers, is perhaps the greatest paradox. We are afraid of the physical dimension of existence. This fear sits at the core of our collective consciousness.

Physical reality, the Objective Area within Consciousness, is ultimately a place of experimentation – an experiment in experience for Consciousness. The "normal" place or state of Consciousness – where *our* consciousness does not have its attention glued to experimenting with experience – is the Subjective Area within Consciousness.

All physical dimensions exist for Consciousness to explore Itself. Humanity's consciousness is helping out in this regard, although at present we are somewhat hampered by an ego-self that believes it is separate from its Source and has no understanding of its role in this greater scheme of Consciousness. Fear is always a result of a lack of understanding.

Intent drives human consciousness, along with other individuations of Consciousness in the physical world of exploration. We have our personal intent, and underlying this is the intent of Consciousness to explore through experience. The problem for us is that exploration involves going where no one has gone before, seeking out the unknown, experiencing new and unfamiliar experiences, embracing that which is not understood – which generates fear.

As you have read, emotions are the primary energy resource for your creational use. Fear directly connects with emotions. Therefore, fear becomes a primary element of our experiences in our physical realm but does not exist outside of physical dimensions.

As with any *thing*, there is good reason for its existence. Fear *can be* motivating, when received as the impulse to act immediately, for instance. It is also beneficial in the sense that its emotional form advises your conscious-mind of the psychological reasons for its being. Of course, it can also distort the flow of energy through you, drain your energy, and thereby immobilize you.

However, you can reverse these debilitating effects when you understand that you are dealing with energy, and this understanding, along with that of its reason for being (belief patterns), allows you to manipulate its energy and the energies it attracts (emotions) to your benefit.

Just as important to the exploration of the physical dimension is the exploration of your Self. New experiences and routes of exploration come with each lifetime in the physical realm. These routes may be unfamiliar to your overall Self, but the important thing to remember is that they are paths of exploration *within* your Self. You are therefore, *safe*, protected by Divine Love. You have nothing to be afraid of *within* your Self.

Fear of loving

One channeled character that has not had a significant mention until now is that of Kris (through Serge Grandbois).[157] Amongst Kris's teachings is a significant contribution relating to fear – the fear of loving.

In coming to terms with our greatest fear of what the physical realm has in store for us, we have learnt to suppress our feelings and emotions. This suppression includes the feelings and emotions related to the expression of Divine Love. Kris suggests that suppression of "Love" comes about through a subconscious awareness that here is the driving force behind physical creation – this energy is therefore something to be truly afraid of – despite the fact that it is our salvation.

One of the main reasons for fearing Love, or *acting in a loving way*, is that we believe (the belief generating the fear) that to do so will put us in a vulnerable position.

Our collective beliefs about *vulnerability*, such as "an openness to attack," which would compromise our existence, stems, once again, from our misinterpretation of the "survival instinct" of Consciousness. To act in a loving manner is therefore dangerous.

We have learnt that human love often leads to heartache and pain. It therefore *makes sense* to the ego-self to suppress our will to love, to suppress our sexuality in the expression of love, and to generally suppress our desires, which come out of our natural affinity for love.

We have come to a stage where we fear loving and consequently dislike or even loathe our Selves for having the will to love.

As we cannot appear to be seen acting in a loving manner, we assume it to be far "safer" to hate. Hating war is what we need to do to end it, rather than love peace. We justify hate by fearing Love, which leads us to hate everything rather than Love everything.

Your greatest limitation

The greatest limiting fear we all have is to do with Self-examination; we are afraid of what we might find within our Selves and afraid of what we might create for our outer selves to have to deal with.

We fear a deep black hole within us that contains all manner of horrendous traits and behaviors waiting for us to bring them into the physical world. So frightful are the contents of this Freudian fragment of ourselves that we never consciously go anywhere near it.

Which is a shame, because all there is in anyone's deepest

black hole is a collection of dubious beliefs. They are the dodgy beliefs you have acquired over your formative years, together with perhaps a few reinforcing beliefs gleaned from your "other selves" (a subject covered in *Book II*), and other lifetimes. Your black hole contains only the beliefs that are the most skillful at getting you to disparage yourself in some way. They are the ones you have invested a great deal of energy in, beliefs that suggest that you are not worthy, not powerful, not able, not as accomplished, not as good as someone else.

Unhappiness with life stems from this fear of Self-examination – which means, that without any form of regular Self-checkup, unhappiness reigns because of the beliefs in your black hole going unchecked. It is therefore your *beliefs* that generate fear and unhappiness. To dissolve either, you need to examine your beliefs, and before this you simply need to be aware that *all* beliefs, however entrenched, are malleable and not set in stone.

In becoming aware that your beliefs are at the heart of your personality's emotional climate, and that even though a few may establish themselves as truths for you – yet are *still open to adjustment* – you liberate your thinking. Strong beliefs are thoughts you keep thinking about, and thus invest energy in, but that energy is the malleable constituent of any belief or system of beliefs.

Your beliefs form a membrane around your outer self that has the final say on the "tonal frequency" you send out to the universe, as well as filtering the information and the probabilities you draw to yourself. Acting upon this awareness will free you to look beyond beliefs in your personal explorations and enjoyment of the physical realm.

As you broaden your awareness and begin to accept the nature of beliefs, also be aware of your ego's arrogance!

Albeit your ego-self would like to think so, the widening of your awareness is not creating a "better" you, which is an assumption made by the ego's adherence to the belief system of

Duplicity (see *Chapter 12*) – seeking to make judgments.

In actuality, by widening your awareness you are creating a platform of *acceptance* (a facet of Divine Love) of the entirety of your Self and the primary medium through which you create your reality – beliefs. Your ego might think this makes for a better you, but it is more of a remembering, a reconnecting, to the breadth of who you are.

Of course, acceptance of "unacceptable" beliefs can be tricky! The trick is to recognize these types of beliefs as elements within you that supply the contrast required to truly define what your preferences are, elements that steer you on your path of intent and purpose. Elias:

Therefore, the key to acceptance is to be accepting of *all* of your reality, be it in your belief systems, good or bad, *all* of which is your creation, which is *You*; and as you are not accepting of certain elements of your creations, your belief systems – *You* – you reinforce your element of fearfulness.[158]

Your wider awareness lessens the hold of your belief systems as well as lessening your fears about what your Self has to offer the world.

Eliminating fear

You cannot eliminate beliefs from your psychological structuring. They are the medium through which you create your reality. You can, however, manipulate their energies and the energies of emotions in order to quell, if not eliminate, your fears.

All "negative" experiences are associated with a fear of some description. They bring out our fears ready for examination and remedy. This is why negative experiences fascinate us rather than positive experiences – think of the news media. At present, our collective awareness is not broad enough to realize that this is what negative experiences are all about, we play with them like a cat with a mouse, until the mouse bores us and we catch another interesting plaything.

We are not yet able to allow and accept negative experience as the most illuminating method of self-reflection. It is, nonetheless, the most objective and succinct guide to Self-knowledge.

Your inner self though, is aware of this. Your Essence self does not operate under the confines of beliefs. Duplicity (judgment upon duality), the most pervasive of belief systems, doesn't exist in the Subjective Area within Consciousness. There is no positive or negative, right or wrong, good and bad where your Essence is concerned. You exist, you are, and that's it; judgments don't mean anything. You experience duality and judgment, as they are part of a system of beliefs. This experience generates emotions, negative or positive ones, *for* the experience of them! *For* the reasons described above.

Abraham (Esther Hicks) reminds us that fear tells of a resistance within you, a resistance that affects the natural flow of energy relating to your desire. The thing that sets up the resistance is a contradicting belief you hold. In other words, all that fear means is that you have a belief that does not marry with your desire. So once again, dealing with the belief, by adjusting the thoughts it throws up, will nullify the fear.

You, the outer you, the part of your Self that focuses on the physical plane, cannot reach a place that does not contain the contrast of "negativity." Therefore, fear, the source of negativity is always with you, just as Divine Love, the source of positivity, is always with you. Fear can only leave you when your outer self leaves the physical dimension.

Rose (Joanne Helfrich) adds this on eliminating your fears:

… and that is most of what suffering is: fear. When you lose your fears, you find less suffering, and may end it. For when you fear, you only perfect your ways of suffering, and there's no reason for this. In spite of what your religions have spoken about suffering, suffering is not a sacred thing. Indeed, there is no need for suffering in any way except to end it. So do so.[159]

To eliminate fear, to avoid the fearful end of the emotional continuum stick of Divine Love and Fear, you must trust and accept your Self – beliefs and all.

When you *assimilate* this awareness, when you begin to *live* these words rather than superficially understand them, you diminish your capacity for generating fear. You will still have beliefs that are capable of generating fear, but you will know how to deal with them and it. You cannot ignore fear. You must face up to it and determine to conquer it when it arises. If you ignore it, it *will* come back to haunt your enjoyment of life.

Moreover, as you practice dealing with fear it will become a rare experience. Perhaps, ideally, to a rarity confined to an *impulse* concerned with self-preservation.

Ten Principles for Conscious Living

Love is expansive, it encourages you to be all that you can be, it empowers you, and it removes limitation. Love is not jealous, angry, or afraid, it does not question, it is simply accepting of all that is. Fear, on the other hand, is limiting. It drains you of the energies of Divine Love, the vitality of life.

You can utilize the energy of the emotions you accept into your Garden of Beliefs to nurture the thoughts and beliefs that support your intent and purpose in life, or you can assign their energies to the thoughts and beliefs that perpetuate your fears of applying your outer self to this spiritual path.

With such thoughts in mind, the following principles for living a Love filled, fear free, joyous life may come in handy. From close examination of the numerous metaphysical messages on the natural principles *(Chapter 3)* and the natural powers of Divine Love and Attraction *(Chapter 4)*, it has been possible to deduce this set of tenets to live by.

Certain channeled sources focus on particular principles; Abraham, for example, focuses on the "Law of Attraction" and principles derived from this natural power. The term "principle" suggests a moral code, which implies "good and bad" or "right and wrong behavior" – ideas generated by the belief system of Duplicity. Remember that the list below offers *guidance* on behavior; it is not a set of commandments designed to stimulate your propensity for judgment. Indeed, some suggestions attempt to guide you away from being judgmental, as in doing so you undermine your own ability to express the natural principle of creation.

Not wishing to undermine the desire to produce a set of *principles* rather than *commandments* to live by, there are ten of them! Actually, if we include "Don't take life too seriously – laugh whenever you get the chance," we have eleven.

Remember that a principle "tells of the nature of things… more of a state of being," which infers that these principles do not govern you, Consciousness does not decide that you must adhere to them; they are *universal* principles that describe the *nature* of the universe and how things work.

These principles are another human translation of how you, your consciousness, can gain the most from knowing how your Self works, and how the universe works – according to the metaphysical literature. If you can observe the majority of them, the majority of the time, then you are primed for a life enriched by joy, abundance and fulfillment.

Don't take life too seriously – laugh whenever you get the chance. Then,

- **Accept and Allow.** *This is the key to living a life full of Love.*

    Acceptance is about *eliminating judgment* of your Self,

others or situations.

Eliminating judgment does not mean you will lose your ability to choose what is desirable to you, what you prefer.

To *allow* is to invoke the natural power of Divine Love.

We should allow ourselves a complete and total acceptance of all that is because all that we observe – our Selves, all others and all creations – are expressions of Consciousness.

Because Divine Love is an absolute of Consciousness, and you are an individuated expression of Consciousness, you are therefore an expression of Love.

You may be an individuated "portion" of Consciousness, but you are not separate from It. You are therefore never alone.

To fully accept and *appreciate (see below)* the *truth* of Divine Love – which means you are an expression of Love – is a prerequisite for mastery of the natural principles and powers.

This appreciation initiates *the creation of your desires* – in accordance with your intent and purpose, and under the guidance of Divine Love.

- **Be Compassionate.** "… [At] its essence is a basic kindness, with a deep awareness of the suffering of oneself and of other living things, coupled with the wish and effort to relieve it."[160]

  This awareness involves the recognition of a responsibility to your Self and to your creations. Therefore, you do not deliberately attempt to hurt (violate) another expression of consciousness – while at the same time you do honor the choices you have made. Suffering and pain exists as a contrast to well-being and bliss. They are intended to remind us of what we don't want to create in our lives.

what about suffering from loss/death?

The extent to which we experience suffering, either individually or en masse, is reliant upon the frequency of compassion we exhibit personally and collectively.

Compassion is the ultimate gift you can give. You can awaken this facet of your personality and exercise it through simple acts of kindness. Love and compassion are integrated emotions, as genuinely loving and accepting your Self and others includes compassion.

By being open to *receiving* as well as providing compassion, you encourage growth for all concerned. Compassion exercises your *empathic inner senses,* allowing you to change places with another. Remember that people who are "suffering" in some way are reflecting pains, discomforts or irritations within your Self – albeit to a different degree and/or on a contrasting timescale to your Self.

We are vessels for the carrier wave of compassion and we set its frequency.

- **Be forgiving.** *However, we do need to be very clear on what forgiveness is actually all about.*

  Forgiveness is **not** about saying that what we or another person said or did is okay now – we were hurt, but let's forget about it.

  What we forget in approaching forgiveness in this way is that we create **all** of our reality and that *we draw our experiences to us.* You attract "hurtful" events to you by subconsciously focusing your attention on discomforts and irritations within your Self.

  There is nothing "outside" of you that can hurt you – you can only bring hurt upon your Self.

  This is something your inner self "arranges" for you so that you become consciously aware of any internal discord; you draw such events to you for *learning purposes.*

[handwritten margin note: Disagree above?]

If you are unable to forgive your Self, you are denying your own power of creation and free will. An inability to forgive another means you hand your power of creation over to them. In either case, you are not recognizing your creative gifts or the fact that you create your own reality.

Complaining is a behavior related to the action of forgiveness. It is a subtle way your ego-self has you to deny your creative abilities by apportioning *blame* (handing over your power to someone else) for the complaint you have created.

Recognizing, accepting and appreciating the truly powerful being that you are bring forgiveness back into its true context, and it can thus become second nature to you. You can forgive yourself for your shortcomings, knowing that you should work on resolving them. You can forgive others for the co-created events that also bring you awareness of the issues you need to look into.

Non-forgiveness is to forget that you are loved beyond measure.

- **Express Gratitude.** *Be grateful for **everything** you create for your Self.*

  Be extra grateful for those seemingly "negative" or painful experiences – if your ego-self can bear it! Negative events teach you about your Self; they are lessons that reveal more about your Self than positive events – that's why they grab your attention! Life's lessons induce a more defined spiritual awareness and they steer you back onto the path of your life's intent and purpose – your *"Way of Spirit"* nurtured by Divine Love.

  Genuine gratitude is a reflection of your knowledge and appreciation of all that you are and can be. Just as you create experiences to remind you of your shortcomings, you also create moments of *appreciation* of your Self. These moments may be in the form of gifts from others – be they physical items or self-affirming acts of compassion. By receiving and being genuinely grateful for the smallest gift you have created for your Self, you invite into your life further acts of self-appreciation.

Gratitude is thus the attractor of abundance in all its forms.

- **Be Appreciative.** Genuine appreciation is an expression of Divine Love – it is the ultimate expression of *Acceptance*. Genuine appreciation does not have an expectation attached.

  *You need to appreciate **all** that reality is echoing of your Self.* In so doing, you are recognizing the *value* in all of what you are creating for yourself.

  To *know the value* of your creations, without the interference of fear and resistance, resigns you to the power of Divine Love, taking you beyond mere thankfulness.

  Heartfelt appreciation can surprise you. This is because every time you offer it you expend energy, you give your energy to the universe, which will replace this energy, reflect it back to you, in the form of abundance.

  You can appreciate your Self more by spending quality time, or "natural time" (see below), on both inner and outer expressions of your Self. A balance can be achieved through spending equal measures of time on nurturing and appreciating your inner self and inner senses (through meditation for example) and on nurturing and appreciating your physical expressions of Self (your body and its outer senses). Such appreciation and acknowledgement of all of your faculties, whether inner or outer in expression, enhances your creativity.

- **Be creative.** *Creation is a quality of all existence, a natural principle of Consciousness.*

The physical experience is a highly creative one, which is why you are here. Your inner self expects your outer self to be as creative as possible in your exploration of your intent and purpose.

Creation is about experiencing your Self – as what you create is a reflection of where your Self has its attention. Intent drives you to create experiences; and your experiences service a learning need not only for your Self but also for the greater whole – the consciousness of humanity, and Consciousness Itself. All experience is valid; it is your interpretation of the experience that makes for happiness or otherwise.

You can choose to see yourself as a victim of an experience you have created or you can choose to reframe the seemingly "negative" experience into a positive, though perhaps painful, learning experience. Painful experiences provide you with extremely valuable information on what you truly desire from your life.

- **Be spontaneous.** This complies with the *natural principle of spontaneity* – would you believe! *Expressing spontaneity instills a **trust** of your creative abilities.*

  Spontaneity recognizes that the only "time" that actually exists in the broader reality of the Subconscious Area within Consciousness is the *"spacious present"* – which implies that the point of creative power is always in the "now."

- **Be patient.** Being patient does not contradict being spontaneous. *Patience allows for your natural flow of creative energy.*

  Patience is not to do with simply waiting and doing nothing. It is an *action* in itself, one that associates with a deeply felt *trust of your creative abilities*. This trust comes about through knowing your Self and when your inner self is driving your actions – **not** *your ego-self.* You are trusting that the probable realities you have already created for yourself in accordance with your desires, will be materialized in accordance with natural timings.

If you feel impatient, you are allowing your ego-self to interfere with the natural flow of your creative energies working in *natural time.* Impatience is a symptom of your ego-self's attempts to force an event outside of its natural timing.

- **Spend more time in natural time.** Our culture's strict adherence to linear time (using our time wisely) can result in the creative energy flows within us being restricted or impeded. Generalized anxiety or feeling drained of energy are symptoms of such occurrences. We squeeze our energies into time-confined channels rather than allow them to flow naturally through us in their own natural time.

  Utilizing the time-based inner senses can alleviate matters for you. Applying the principles of *spontaneity* and *patience* will also allow your creative juices to flow more readily.

- **Be Open and Vulnerable.** *To be vulnerable is not an invitation to be hurt.*

  Being vulnerable is about being open to receive – open to receive the gifts you bring to your Self through being *grateful* and *appreciative.*

  Receiving is just as important as giving. It is another act of *allowing,* of *loving* your Self. Receiving allows you to participate in the magnificent richness of the physical world. It is an action that enables you to draw-in and connect with the outer reality *you are creating for your Self.*

  The way you can receive what you need is to appreciate

your Self and to feel your vulnerability. *Vulnerability is the softness through which your Essence (inner self) can enter your ego's guarded world.*

You don't create your reality in isolation. You interconnect and interact with others – which affects the personal reality you create. Interactions with others trigger fears within us as we imagine that some may wish to harm or take advantage of us. *This fear has us construct a shell of invulnerability around us.*

However, for you to realize the divinity of your being, you can't have barriers erected between your Self and your environment. No one can be intrusive, hurtful or take advantage of you unless you allow them to do so. To do so, indicates that *you are denigrating your Self* – you draw the hurtful probability to you to reveal this fact. You project your Self-disparaging "victim" mentality into the world and the natural power of Attraction does the rest.

Once you become confident ~~in your Self,~~ trusting in your creative powers, you can afford to be ~~open~~ and vulnerable as you will no longer be generating this fear. Genuine openness and vulnerability does not include the threat of being hurt or harmed. There can be no threat when you are very aware that if hurt or harm befalls you — *you have created it*—not some other person.

You may wish to know how we might survive our turbulent times. Your survival rests on your ability to *appreciate* and work with your environment—the reality we have created for our Selves. It is dependent on the free flow of your creative energies and by each of us becoming a vulnerable expression of Consciousness. Your vulnerability allows your *Essence* to flow to every part of your being. Your openness and vulnerability will allow others to recognize their personal vulnerability.

Yes, on the surface, embracing your vulnerability

[handwritten margin note: Disagree—how can we not be bothered at all?]

appears risky. However, you will find that genuine vulnerability opens you up to the majesty of your Self. Taking the risk opens your outer self to the totality of your Self and it opens your heart to others. In order to survive, you must raise your level of consciousness closer to that of Consciousness Itself – and vulnerability is the elevator. So drop your shell of invulnerability; it is an illusory form of safety. Welcome your vulnerability and express your spirituality.

EPILOGUE

According to our metaphysical friends, you are currently experiencing a set of actions (a period within linear time) that relate to a highly significant evolutionary development of the consciousness of our species.

These channeled guides, existing as they do in a dimension where all actions happen in the one "spacious present," have an exclusive view of the probable futures available to us in the next few decades of linear time. Apparently, the most probable of our probable futures is certainly a dramatic one, and may be, on occasion, traumatic – no change there then.

After reading this book, you will think. Now there's a prediction!

Thinking is what we do a lot of the time. We like to think that thinking is the best way to assimilate information. You are likely to think, as I have done repeatedly, "Why should I take the word of a bunch of dead guys seriously? And, even if there is some truth in what they're saying, what's it got to do with me?"

I would ask you to not think for a moment. Don't think about these issues, but instead see how you *feel* about them. Feelings, after all, are the means by which your inner self talks to you, and your inner self is far more adept at guiding your thinking.

You may find that as you tune into your feelings, you sense a "knowing" that brings some validation, as well as a little fearful emotional-signal.

What's that emotional-signal to do with?

It is sent to your conscious-mind to inform you that your ego-self is generating some fear over the statements. Trauma was mentioned, egos don't like trauma. Furthermore, dramatic probable futures and evolutionary developments smack at "change" – egos definitely don't like change. Ask your inner self, "How scared am I if these statements are perfectly true?"

Pretty scared? That's okay. As we have learned in this book, fear is essentially mistranslating and misdirecting Source energy meant not only to sustain your existence in the physical realm, but also to *invigorate* your participation within it.

Your ego is the agent that misinterprets these surges of Source energy – turning excitement into fear, which *produces* traumatic events! This book and those that follow, aim to have you understand fear and conquer it, so that you can freely express yourself in the dramatic times ahead. Excitement is the new fear, as it were.

To appease your nervous ego, and return your conscious-mind to the thinking process it adores, take a moment to review the physical evidence-based observations of your outer senses. Are you noticing any mass events that might confirm that the oft mentioned *Shift, or shift in consciousness,* may just contain a smidgen of validity? Think about fundamentalism in religious belief systems; think about the stability of dictatorial political systems; think about the greed endemic within our corporate and financial institutions; and bearing in mind Omni's words on the definition of money, the "physical manifestation of the energies of love and power"[161]... think about the distribution of wealth across our global society.

As may be apparent from this first book of the trilogy of *It's About You!,* I for one prefer to take the word of these "energy personality essence[s] no longer focused in physical form" because I feel a trust in what they generally have to say. It's taken me many years of intense study of the works of a good few channeled guides to be able to say that I not only *believe* a great deal of what they have to say, but trust it to be of genuine benefit to my existence, your existence, and that of humanity.

It has taken this length of study to appease my own ego; contrasting and comparing the material with other "bona fide" philosophical works before facing the fear of putting my voice on the subject out into a world that is frantic with derision. I have turned my fear back into its original energetic form – excitement!

My studies began with the *Seth Material*, and it was this broad and profound body of work that set me on a path with a purpose; the same purpose behind the appearance of many channeled entities before and since Seth. That purpose is to convey knowledge on the nature of our reality and how we go about forming it – in as pure a form as possible. That is, untainted by the belief systems to which we currently adhere.

Seth made a point in his work that we should *not believe* what he was saying.

It took me quite some time to understand what he meant by this.

He knew that *belief systems* are the governing means by which we express our outer selves in the physical plane. We can't get away from them while we're here.

This means they are the unavoidable filtering system, the membrane around us, through which all knowledge, all information, must pass in our mental processing of it.

As it passes through, the ego inevitably compromises the purity of the data as it seeks to graft it onto an already established tree within our garden of beliefs. Seth knew that the genetic makeup of the knowledge he was relaying doesn't take to being grafted – or genetically modified for that matter! The thoughts and ideas require a fresh patch of their own, free of the choking weeds and creepers of ancient outmoded beliefs. A new belief bed, carefully and mindfully attended, is required for the thoughts and ideas to propagate into a system of beliefs that will in turn establish a hold upon the overall appearance and design of our belief gardens.

Seth wasn't concerned with us believing him, or turning him into the next guru to follow. He, along with the majority of other channeled guides, simply wants us to know of the nature of thoughts, beliefs and emotions, so that we can begin to prune, grow, manage and design a garden that would reflect the beauty of our Selves as an individuation of Consciousness.

He was very aware of the dangers of distortion of his ideas if we were to assign them immediately to our currently held belief systems. By saying he didn't want us to believe him, he was alerting us to the importance of examining *our* beliefs, *anyone's* beliefs, as *all* beliefs should be examined constantly for their appropriateness in the formation of our personal and collective realities.

Having said this, the purpose of this book is to make this metaphysical material more believable! Its aim is to provide you with a broad yet sturdy platform of knowledge that relates to your unique multifaceted Self and the key forces by which you create your reality.

This knowledge base will not only prepare you, but also bolster your confidence, for taking the next step in attaining a fulfilling, purpose driven life. It's a step that the majority of us aren't even aware needs to be taken, but it is a step that the majority of us need to take. It involves coming to terms with, facing and resolving, any fears born of debilitating belief structures you hold. It is the work you need to do to free yourself from the habitual actions that deflect you from your path of intent.

Free Your Self, the next book in the *It's About You!* trilogy, focuses on your current state of being in the physical realm. The book deals with healing and balancing the psychological and emotional energies that shape your personality. It's concerned with clearing away the weeds and creepers of your garden of beliefs, taking stock of the beliefs you hold dear, and uprooting those beliefs that obscure your personality's original design intent-ions.

Feeling nervous again? Good. That's as it should be. Feel the fear and see if there's a crumb of excitement mixed in.

Free Your Self is about liberating your outer self so that it can fully express its creational abilities. This cathartic action will reverberate through the entirety of your Essence self and, as you are now aware, through the many interconnected layers of the Oneness of Consciousness.

Free Your Self, and the final book in the trilogy *Live Your Purpose*, take the exercises and practices introduced in this book a few steps up the ladder of *living* the ideas and principles, rather than simply understanding them intellectually. They form the psychological and physical processes you need to commit to as you consciously commit to living your life's path of intent and purpose – as Rose (Joanne Helfrich) would say, living your *Way of Spirit*.

Completion of the trilogy will awaken a trust, an appreciation, and an allowance of your Self that will reconnect you with Divine Love and the principles for living that it marks out for a life of ultimate fulfillment. Practicing and maintaining the processes will eventually provide you with a profound awareness of the intent and purpose of your life.

A message from Elias, delivered in session 165, April 19, 1997:

(The script in italics is my abbreviation of some of the text.)

... You, once again, shall not betray you. You are your highest expression, and you shall always look for your highest value fulfillment, and you shall accomplish this.

You might complain that life is all too difficult, plagued by conflict, and however much you strive to accomplish something, you never seem to attain it.

... and you may even express that you do not understand your purpose or your point. If you are allowing yourself the freedom to accept self, and to know that you have manifest to experience, and that no experience is worse or better, and that you are perfectly creating within every moment of your focus, you shall eliminate much of your conflict.

I have expressed this many times, although to this present now within your physical focus, you do not understand. You wish to be seeking out individuals that shall map your road for you, that shall express to you, "Move this way. Accomplish this. Occupy yourself with this job. Be creative within this area, and you shall be successful."

You shall be successful when you are believing in you.

When you loosen the grip of your belief systems, particularly the belief system of Duplicity that constantly has you judging yourself, then you will accomplish far more. But if you continue along a judgmental path, striving rather than accomplishing, and not addressing to the belief systems that you hold, you shall continue within your conflict.

Do you not think that if this were not so, that throughout your ages individuals upon your planet would not have already formulated the method for complete, ultimate successfulness in every area?

You are inventive creatures. You are extremely creative. You may build machinery to explore your physical space, but you may not solve these tiny individual problems of successfulness within individuals; for no prophet or psychic may express to you a method for accomplishment, if you are not trusting of you.

APPENDIX I:

Catalog of SAY THAT AGAIN boxes

(1) Consciousness. The three forms of Consciousness...   27

(2) Worldviews. Defining personal and collective
worldviews...   31

(3) Intent and Purpose. A concise definition of intent and
personal intent...   40

(4) The Individuation of Consciousness. The path to
Self expression...   43

(5) Areas within Consciousness. Concisely defining the
Areas within Consciousness – *Objective Area, Subjective
Area, Subconscious Area, and Transitional Area*...   48

(6) CUs and EEs. A concise definition of *Consciousness
Units* (CUs) and *Electromagnetic Energy Units* (EEs)...   51

(7) The Natural Principles. Highly difficult to explain
concisely, a re-reading of *Chapter 3* is recommended...   68

(8) The Inner Senses. A brief synopsis of their
importance...   76

(9) The Natural Power of Divine Love. The briefest of
descriptions of this primary natural principle...   84

(10) The Natural Power of Attraction. A concise definition
of this natural principle that is popularly called the
"Law of Attraction" (LOA)...   87

(11) The nine basic expressions of human intent.
Explaining the subtle divisions between the differing
genera of intent of human consciousness...   95

(12) Your outer self. The three central psychological
aspects that deal with the objective reality of the
physical plane...   121

(13) Your ego/ego-self. Your ego's function and purpose...   126

(14) **Mind, conscious-mind and personality.** Concise definitions of the collection of psychological structures that we term "the mind" and the personality...   133

(15) **Thought as a mechanism.** A metaphysical definition of the thought process...   163

(16) **Truths.** Defining truth – absolute truth, relative truths, personal and societal truths...   189

(17) **Feelings.** The different forms of feelings, and the special type of feeling – "emotional-signals"...   211

(18) **Emotions.** A precise description of these independent energy forms that supply your outer self with energy and information...   237

(19) **The ego's attempts to rebuff an emotion.** Summarizing the ego's futile attempts to deny, reject, or repress an emotion...   259

A basic "shortcut" version of EFT

Have pen and paper to hand for making notes.

Step I.

Identify, *as specifically as possible*, the problem you wish to address.

Example: "This feeling of panic that's making my heart race, and my thoughts are all over the place, and it's making me thirsty, and I have a slight headache as well, and I'm scared."

Get the point? Really focus in on whatever it is that's troubling you, whether mental or physical, and thoroughly describe it to yourself. If you haven't come up with one in your description, sense an emotion that best fits the symptoms you've described –anxiety or "non-specific fear" would fit with the above example.

When you have tuned into the problem, particularly the emotion, assess the level of distress you are experiencing, **right now**, as you contemplate the problem. On a scale where zero is no intensity of feeling whatsoever, to ten, which is unbearable – rate your level of distress. **Write it down.**

Remember, if you are contemplating a problem from the past, or envisioning a coming event, it is not a rating of the distress you **once** felt or **will** feel – but what you feel **now – at this moment**.

Now insert your statement of the problem – remember to be as specific as possible – into the following statement – and right it down:

"Even though I have this... (statement of the problem)... I deeply and completely love, trust, and accept myself, without judgment, anyway."

Example: "Even though I have this feeling of panic, which is making my heart race and my thoughts are all over the place, and I need some water, and I'm getting a headache, all because of this anxiety – I deeply and completely love, trust and accept myself, without judgment, anyway."

Step 2.

When you have written your statement down, put it somewhere you can read it and locate your "sore spot." That is, go to the u-shaped notch at the top of the sternum – about where the knot of a tie would be. Come down 3 inches (7.5 cms), then over to the left about 3 inches. Press and rub around this area until you find a slight tenderness under the skin. The sore spot is where you find this tenderness. Don't press too hard, as this is where lymph glands are situated. If this spot is too tender, try the other side (3 inches to the right of center). If neither is suitable, then use the side-of-the-hand spot (karate spot), on either hand, as instructed below:

Preferably using the sore spot, rub the area gently in a circular motion with the tips of your fingers. If using the karate spot, tap this spot (not too hard, just firm tapping) continuously with a couple of fingers.

Do this whilst reciting the following statement, with conviction, 3 times:

"I deeply and completely love, trust and accept myself, without judgment, even with all my challenges and seeming limitations."

Step 3.

After step 2, take a deep breath in through the nose and release it slowly through the mouth. Now focus in on the issue you want to resolve. Go over what you have written down from step 1 a few times and then while you slowly read out your statement, continually tap the karate spot. You can read it a second time or embellish what you are saying if it feels right to do so – but take your time and keep tapping the karate spot while you speak everything that comes up aloud.

Example: "Even though I have this feeling of panic, which is making my heart race and my thoughts are all over the place, and I need some water, and I'm getting a headache, all because of this anxiety, and I hate it when I get like this, and it reminds me of when my Mom shouted at me in the garden, and she didn't realize it wasn't me, and I hate to be shouted at – I deeply and completely love trust and accept myself, without judgment, anyway."

Step 4.

When you have finished talking it out whilst tapping the karate spot, follow the short sequence below of places to tap. Just firmly tap each spot (about seven or eight taps) as you remind yourself of your statement by shortening it to the primary issue – **the emotion you have assigned to it**. If you have not got a specific emotion, take a guess at which one might best suit the issue – fear, anger, sadness, guilt, grief, frustration, whatever – just put an appropriate emotion to it – and as you tap each of the spots in the sequence below, repeat your emotional word or phrase at least once.

Example (from the above example): "This anxiety" or, "This fear of being shouted at" or, "This guilt I'm feeling."

Begin at the **eyebrow spot** – tap both if you want – where the eyebrow ends at the bridge of the nose. Tap and repeat the reminder term.

Next, the **side-of-eye spot** – both sides if you want to – on the bony orbit, next to the eye. Tap and repeat the reminder.

Then **under the eye** – on the bony orbit directly under the pupil. Both spots if you like. Tap and repeat the reminder term.

Then **under the nose** – between the top lip and bottom of the nose. Tap and repeat the reminder.

Then the **chin spot** – between the bottom lip and chin. Tap and repeat.

Then the **collarbone spot** – both sides if you can, just under the ridge of the bone, about 1 inch (2.5cms) down and to the side of the u-shaped notch at the junction of the sternum. Tap and repeat the reminder term.

Then **under the arm** – about 3 inches (7.5cms) down from the arm pit – where the side bra strap would come for women. Don't tap too hard as there are lymph glands here. Tap and repeat the reminder term.

Finally – tap the **crown of your head** seven or eight times as you repeat the reminder term again.

Then take a deep breath in through your nose, and release through the mouth.

Tune into your "issue" and rate how you now feel on the zero to ten scale.

If your score has dropped by two points or more from when you wrote it down on Step 1, repeat the tapping sequence above again, but begin with tapping the karate spot and repeating this revised statement three times:

"Even though I **still** have some of this… (emotion – e.g., fear, anger, whatever, as in the reminder term)… I deeply and completely love, trust and accept myself anyway."

As you progress around the spots above, now say: "This **remaining**… (emotion term)… "

Keep repeating the tapping sequence with this statement to start and the "remaining (emotion)" reminder phrase as you go around the spots until the rate of distress you feel falls to zero or one. Then take a deep breath in through your nose and breathe out through your mouth.

If you are not able to drop your rating to zero or one, make a note of the issue you are dealing with and consult an EFT practitioner.

Resources:

Go to www.newworldview.com or www.counsellingfory-
ourself.co.uk for a printable PDF version of this EFT shortcut
procedure.

www.garythink.com is the website of the EFT founder, Gary
Craig.

Go to www.eftuniverse.com for a practitioner listing and
more information on EFT.

Other important Energy Psychology and Energy Medicine
websites:

www.energypsych.org (Association for Comprehensive
Energy Psychology).

www.issseem.org (International Society for the Study of
Subtle Energy and Energy Medicine).

www.innersource.net (Energy Medicine practitioners Donna
Eden and David Feinstein Ph.D.)

APPENDIX III:

THE NINE GENERA OF THE INTENT OF HUMAN CONSCIOUSNESS

The human articulation of intent loosely conforms to nine distinguishable types of expression – first referred to metaphorically by Seth and then by other channeled guides as the *"families of consciousness."* Essentially, they are differing developmental paths of activity peculiar to humankind, involved with the growth, learning and evolution of each individual and humanity itself. Although your personality encapsulates all types of intentional drives, it chooses to experience the physical dimension with particular expressions of intent to the fore.

Seth, perhaps deliberately, only gave a brief outline on how each of his "families" of intent translates to human activity – through psychological leanings or personality traits, to preferred physical pursuits. Perhaps deliberately, as at the time of delivery there was, and still is according to Elias (Mary Ennis), an acute possibility that the casual reader can misunderstand the metaphor's premise, overplay the differentiating factors, and under emphasize the subtleties of this insight on the expression of our consciousness.

A deep understanding of this material is required before using it when attempting to help others. A precaution that will prevent the information from being co-opted into yet another distorted belief system.

This said, your Essence self "belongs to," and your current personality "aligns with," a particular family or genus of human intent. We rarely overtly express the characteristics of our family of belonging during our lifetime; instead, they bring an underlying subtlety to the qualities expressed by our personality's family of alignment (see *Chapter 5*). Your primary, overtly expressed, intentional characteristics fall within the spectrum of activities and issues explored by your family of alignment.

The Elias transcripts, and more recently the teachings of Rose (Joanne Helfrich), give us a clearer picture as to what actions we can expect of individuals *aligning with* a certain family of intent. Remember though, that the demarcation lines between the families are as undefined as the overlapping colors of a rainbow. You can *align* with more than one genus, or form a mix, a sub-family – although one family of alignment is the norm. Furthermore, *your personality always encapsulates all of the differing intentional leanings of the nine genera.* You hold the potential to express any of their intentional idiosyncrasies, particularly in relation to the circumstances of the moment.

Essentially, the genera or families of human intent provide a fluid, yet significant guide to the subtleties of intent as expressed through human experience. As such, and in view of a person's allegiance to the expressions of certain families rather than others, they give indication as to person's personal intent, and thereby purpose, for the current lifetime.

The colors in parentheses are those associated with the family's tonal frequency. That is, each family has a particular vibrational tone that can be reasonably well associated with the wave frequencies of certain colors. There is a resonance in vibrational quality. Tone and Color are *relative truths* (see *Chapter 11*) – they are qualities of existence that transfer between dimensions other than the physical realm – the vibrational movement they embody is a quality of Consciousness. A family's tonal frequency is an *intentional* tone that, from the physical perspective, can be associated with certain colors, and translated into sound – as representations of the actual tonal quality.

TEACHERS (BLACK) also referred to as SEERS

This intent involves the act of teaching, the relaying of knowledge to others in its purest form. There is an aim to encourage originality through teaching and promote learning through experience. Along with the action of teaching others comes a concern for accuracy when conveying information in order to maintain the integrity of the information. This may translate to a pedantic trait of the personality, an obsessiveness to detail.

Even though this family of intent includes accuracy of information transfer, there is no adherence to any particular "truth" as there is an appreciation within this intent of the futility of imagining there to be one philosophical outlook that can convey or describe the only absolute Truth – that of Consciousness.

Personalities aligned with this family of intent are generally playful, flexible, and humorous, although they can also be stern and critical. High amongst their values is an aesthetic sensibility. This aesthetic appreciation is one of many links and involvements with the intent of the family of Artists.

SPIRITUALISTS (RED) also referred to as the REMEMBERERS

The title "spiritualists" should not be confused with the term's popular use to describe those people who practice spiritualism – communicating with the dead. The *intent* of this family is far more subtle in meaning, emphasizing the spiritual nature of existence and very much concerned with keeping us aware of the natural rhythms of life, such as "natural time" (see the *Ten Principles for Conscious Living* at the end of *Chapter 18*). Perhaps a better expression to personify the intent would be "spiritual counselors."

This intentional drive is of particular importance to us at present as we see our "forgetting" or suppression of it reflected in many environmental issues. This family of intent is involved with true spiritual (Essence) connection, directing our energies inwardly to review the *natural principles* of Consciousness.

Personalities aligned with this intent tend to manifest within primal cultures – Native American Indian tribes and Australian aborigines, for example. They keep their *selves* to themselves!

They are deeply involved in the Divinity of Nature, having an extraordinary connection with all living things – on telepathic and empathic levels. They attune themselves to their *empathic inner senses* (see *Chapter 3*), able to bring to awareness the energy potentials of inorganic matter such as crystals and mineral compounds.

This genus of intent nourishes humanity's collective psyche – reminding us of our own Divinity.

INNOVATORS (ORANGE) also referred to as FORMERS

This family of intent is involved with creating, initiating, inventing and innovating. Personalities aligned with this type of human intent are in touch with and attuned to their *conceptual inner senses* (see *Chapter 3*) – ideal for exploiting the natural principle of creation. They are truly inspired, able to connect to concepts forming *worldviews* at the Essence level of our consciousness in order to offer originality of ideas to the physical realm.

Innovators spread themselves across all occupations, they tend not to take the spotlight but allow others to take on and develop their originating ideas. They are particularly adept at inventing physical *things* as well as efficient *systems* for the benefit of society, business, and politics.

REFORMERS (YELLOW) also referred to as the HEARERS

This family of intent is involved with reform through revolution. The intent originates as a peaceful desire to change the status quo, but core belief systems can distort energies associated with this intentional drive by misinterpreting the *natural aggression* (see *Glossary of Terms*) that is closely bound to the expression of this genus of intent. In other words, a personality aligned with this intent may attempt to justify violence as a means to an end – which it can never be.

The intent activates reform at all levels, from personal belief systems to collective belief systems reflected in world institutions – political, religious, financial and educational – to family values and societal mores.

Such aligned personalities change themselves, their location, and their environment. They are restless, passionate, *compassionate*, understanding, and very much attuned to their emotions. These personalities have excellent precognitive abilities, indicative of an affinity with the *time-based inner senses* (see *Chapter 3*). They have a *feeling* for probabilities.

EXCHANGERS (GREEN) also referred to as the TELLERS

This family of intent is to do with communication and the exchange of information and knowledge. We require this intent in order that we spread ideas, attitudes and concepts across differing cultures. It is an intent that brings an individual the ability to see and form connections – join the dots, as Rose (Joanne Helfrich) might say.

Personalities aligned with this intent enjoy traveling and trading, often satisfying such pleasures as merchants and seamen pursuing a nomadic lifestyle. They are colorful characters, extremely vocal, keen to express humor whenever possible as a device for leveling communication between peoples of contrasting belief systems.

In the medieval period a Court Jester would have been an example personality with the Exchangers intent to the fore – exchanging and communicating the beliefs of the "commoner" with those of the aristocracy.

ARTISTS (BLUE) also referred to as SPEAKERS

This family of intent, like the Reformers, is involved with changing the status quo. It is an intent, like the Teachers, that appreciates the aesthetics of physical expression and therefore encourages actions of change by way of artistic endeavors. This family displays a creativity born of spiritually driven action – interpreted by us when seen in others as a "doer."

Personalities aligned with this genus of intent are extroverts, naturally playful, and like the Exchangers, keen to use humor. They are independent and nonconformist, thus championing individuality and shunning group activities. They revel in thought, initiating new thoughts on a subject, and thoroughly enjoy the spotlight. Personalities of this intent find fulfillment across the breadth of the arts – and in the "less conventional" sciences.

Seth mentions that this "family of consciousness" came to the fore in our collective psyche to "stir the pot" in order to initiate our *shift in consciousness.*

HEALERS (INDIGO) also referred to as the READERS

This family of intent is involved with healing and helping others. It is an intent aimed at both individual and cultural healing. Its drive, like that of the Spiritualists, recognizes natural principles and natural states of being – not least our natural state of health – which is dependent upon our ability to align with and express the natural power of Divine Love.

Personalities with this alignment express healing from a spiritual perspective. That is, they are able to channel their energies to assist healing on the differing levels of spiritual (Consciousness) expression in the physical world. They are thus adept at societal and planetary healing as well as healing the psychological, emotional and physical states of an individual. This family of human intent promotes *self-healing*, in the knowledge that it is only the individual's Self that can facilitate true healing.

Our current belief systems concerning health issues can confuse some personalities aligned with this intent as they imagine that "fixing and preventing" define the requisites of healing. In actuality, "dis-eased" expressions of Consciousness simply require *assistance* in returning to their *natural state of well-being*.

Some personalities, when in full alignment with this intent, can "read" the "vibrational signature" (see *Glossary of Terms*) of another individual or life form and use it to assist healing simply by being in their presence. In assisting other people, aligning with this intent can at least facilitate a feeling for the "tonal frequency" (see *Glossary of Terms*) of the dis-eased other.

IMAGERS (VIOLET)

This family of intent focuses upon the expression of physical forms. This is primarily to do with the human form, but also the design of other living forms and all physical structures. It is an intent dedicated to perfecting the beauty, elegance, and performance of a physical body. Like the Teachers and Artists, it comes with a deep appreciation of beauty.

Personalities with this alignment of intent tend to manifest as athletes and artistic performers, such as ballet dancers. They have inspired design capabilities, being excellent manipulators of the physical form, so can enjoy being involved in the broad spectrum of artistic design, from graphic design to architecture to choreography.

According to Rose, this family of intent is under-utilized at present in the design of our physical constructions. We often neglect the spiritual *desire* for beauty for the secular *want* of functionality.

NURTURERS (PINK) also referred to as the BEARERS

A genus of intent concerned with nurturing. This drive to nurture includes all creatures of the Earth, but in relation to the human creature, it promotes a complete and spiritually astute nurturing of children. There is an underpinning interest in manifesting a healthy, balanced, human "Earth stock" – a bank of physically healthy, psychologically well-adjusted, emotionally aware, "quality" individuals.

Personalities aligned with this intent often belong to, or produce large families, but the intent focuses on nurturing, so it is not incumbent upon such a personality to produce many children, if any at all. They are though, family oriented, with excellent parenting skills.

Nurturers demonstrate great affection, patience, fairness, and understanding, whilst directing without being intrusive. The intent brings awareness of the importance of learning through experience, so they don't block or admonish impulsive or spontaneous behaviors in children as there is a subconscious understanding of these important inner energies seeking expression.

The expression of this genus of human intent helps to diminish the judgmental attitude within us that we all struggle to control.

APPENDIX IV:

FEELINGS, EMOTIONAL – SIGNALS AND EMOTIONS

We have a great number of terms for feelings and emotions. This is not altogether surprising as we come to realize that feelings and emotions are the fundamental method by which our inner self translates and transfers the gradations of energies and information to our outer self. We confuse feelings with emotions not least because we don't realize that they are different forms of energy with different communicational intent.

Feelings are signals such as impressions, intuitions, inspirations, or "direct knowing" that precede a direct transfer of information. A peculiar type of feeling signals the imminent arrival of an emotion that provides both energy for action and important information concerning, amongst other things, our psychological constructions. We are calling this type of feeling an *"emotional-signal."*

One thing we need to remember when dealing with our "negative" emotions is to be mindful of the information it contains and act upon it. Presently, we tend only to administer to the *emotional-signal* that *precedes* the emotion – which may bring temporary relief from the following emotion's effects, but will not normally provide a permanent solution to a recurring emotional issue.

The communication encapsulated in emotions is there to help us utilize their energy in a consciously controlled fashion. Practice in heeding the message behind emotional energy will eventually allow you to manage your actions and interactions more easily – through freedom of choice, not through fearful habitual *re*-actions.

The following list contains a mixture of terms we use to describe either a feeling or an emotion, or both. The framework of its construction comes from blending psychological research with metaphysical contributions. It is an attempt to clarify what you are experiencing, and what you might be doing to yourself psychologically and physically when you experience the energy form.

Research, originally based on facial expressions, identifies six to eight *primary emotions*. The eight primary emotions (marked with an asterisk) put forward by Professor Robert Plutchik (1927–2006) in his "Wheel of Emotions" model form the foundation of the list.

Primary emotions are described as having a subjective component (inner recognition); a physiological component (effects on the nervous system and endocrine system, producing sweating, gooseflesh, etcetera); and a behavioral component (smiling, crying, running away, etcetera).

Science recognizes that primary emotions exist within other animals, apply to all evolutionary levels, and are key survival tools. In the main, metaphysical literature agrees with these findings, but we have a lot more to learn about emotions – they are far more than survival tools, they are integral to our expression and a key energy resource in the creation of our reality.

In the interests of brevity, I have confined the list to the primary emotions and a number of offshoot feelings and emotions that are most familiar to us.

Terms headed by a capital letter in explanations signify that they are included in the list. The three categories of definition attributed to the terms are:

1 **Feeling** – A signal that precedes direct transfer of infor-mation and/or energy to the conscious-mind and physio-logical systems.

2 **Emotional-signal** – The feeling that acts as a precursor to the potential onset of an emotion.

3 **Emotion** – The independent energy form that, as a bare minimum, provides your outer self with additional energy for action and information on your inner state of being. It invariably includes with its dispatch important information on your psychological structuring – usually concerning your beliefs.

Some additional terms are included because the channeled material refers to them with regard to confusion, or they hold a particular significance for us.

- **Acceptance:** A feeling that is an expression of the natural power of Divine Love. It is the basis for combating the belief system of "duplicity" and a judgmental attitude. (*See Chapter 18, Ten Principles for Conscious Living, for more on acceptance.*)
- **Aggression**: A feeling that is thought to be a combination of the primary emotions of Anger* and Anticipation*. Aggression is a signal generated by your body-consciousness, a surge of energy. Feelings of aggression stem from natural impulses to do with the expression of intent through creative actions. Nature displays "natural aggression" through acts such as a flower bursting from its bud, a butterfly emerging from its cocoon, and any birth process where new life comes into the physical realm.

  Seth advises that we should handle feelings of aggression very quickly by turning their energy into beneficial actions, such as physical activity for the body. The problem with aggression lies in not acting in this way, thus allowing the energies to build before we release them uncontrollably through malevolent actions.
- **Anger*:** A scientifically recognized expression of an emotion. It begins as an emotional-signal that can rapidly escalate into an emotion of the same name. The principle

message conveyed with the emotion is that you are confining your choice of action. A belief or set of beliefs you hold with considerable electrical (emotional) charge is confining your ability to choose how to act. You are placing blinders on your conscious-mind.

Anger is an extreme of the emotional-signal of Frustration, which arises as you mentally begin to shut down your freedom of choice. When your options are restricted to seemingly only one course of action the emotional-signal of Rage appears.

Extreme anger automatically focuses all of your conscious-mind's attention on solely the outer five-senses information (physical data) for working out how to act. Invariably, the outer senses do not contain enough information for the conscious-mind to come to a sound decision on how to act.

As the sensible (inner and outer) solution on how to act comes through information that is within, not outside of you, your ego perceives itself to be a *victim of the circumstances*. Being a victim relinquishes all responsibility for its, and thereby your, creations. Thus if you create a release of the energies of anger through violence, you may have subsequent emotional-signals *(such as "artificial guilt," see Guilt)* that appear to absolve you (your ego) from your actions. Of course, allowing such emotional-signals to persist does nothing of the kind. It will however, likely mask the direct *feeling* of *natural guilt*, which follows a violation. Anger is not the same as Irritation.

- **Anticipation***: Anticipation is a scientifically recognized expression of an emotion. It is an emotion that can be preceded by the positive emotional-signal of Excitement, or a negative emotional-signal of nervousness *(Anxiety – see below)*.

Excitement is a positive, empowering energy that helps

drive the creation process in accordance with your intent and purpose. Anxiety's energy also steers your creations, but with a contrasting outcome in Expectation.

With this information in mind, it is not surprising that Abraham (Esther Hicks) suggests we foster the former emotional-signal in combination with the emotion of anticipation.

- **Anxiety:** Anxiety is an emotional-signal that announces a doubt that can escalate in intensity into the emotion of Fear*.

  Fearful anxiety's communication is that you are presently unable to see the choices you have available to you in working out your next actions.

  We physically express anxiety in accordance with the degree of emotional energy involved. Crying and shaking, for example, are the physical expressions of anxiety that signify a release of energy by your body-consciousness. Your body-consciousness does this because you are holding energy tightly within you, binding it to you and creating a physical tension. Your body-consciousness is saying, "You need to relax!"

  Anxiety indicates that you are creating a *fog* in your conscious-mind that makes it more and more difficult for you to see the choices you have available to you.

  Whereas Anger *confines* your view of the choices available, anxiety produces an obscuring mist. *You know you have choices available, you simply cannot see them clearly enough to make a decision.*

- **Appreciation:** Appreciation is a feeling that is an expression of the natural power of Divine Love. It is the basis for instilling a Love for your Self – not simply the ego-self. (*See Chapter 18, Ten Principles for Conscious Living.*) As Jean Houston says, "What you appreciate, appreciates."

- **Compassion:** A feeling that is derived from the natural power of Divine Love and the exercising of your empathic set of inner senses. *(See Chapter 18, Ten Principles for Conscious Living.)*

- **Depression**: Depression begins as an emotional-signal that heralds the discounting of your creative abilities. It can escalate to an intensity of emotion that comes with the communication that you perceive yourself to be completely powerless to create and are thus a *victim* of circumstances.

  Depression is a condition that indicates anxiety levels are so great as to block the blue energy center, the Throat chakra *(see Chapter 9)*.

- **Desire**: Desire is a feeling that emanates from your inner self in accordance with the needs of your overall Self and its determination to fully express your Self in harmony with your intent and purpose.

  Desire is the human expression of intent, if you will. Want, on the other hand, is a distortion of this expression of intent, brought about by the influence of beliefs.

- **Disgust***: This is a scientifically recognized expression of an emotion. The *feeling* of disgust informs your conscious-mind that the perceived action or event is in high contrast to your beliefs and values. If the feeling persists, after the event, it turns into an emotional-signal, and from here can gain further energy reaching the status of an emotion.

  The emotional message of disgust suggests that you look to your beliefs as to which of them may be in contradiction with the values highlighted by the action or event.

- **Disappointment**: Disappointment is an emotional-signal that resembles a combination of the emotions of Surprise* and Sadness*.

  Elias suggests that disappointment is an energy that quickly gathers into an emotion if we do not notice the initial signal. The signal informs your conscious-mind that a perceived event is not in line with your desires. If your thoughts dwell on this, thus building energy, disappointment becomes an emotion with a message. The message infers that you are discounting your ability to create that which you Desire.

Disappointment arises as an automatic response to an Expectation (*see below*) that has taken an Anxiety plus Anticipation* path to manifestation. Your concentration of thought has been upon the lack of that which you Desire or upon the possible negative outcomes. Our ignorance of how we build our expectations (*refer to **Emotions and expectations**, Chapter 16)* and how they become manifest in the physical realm results in many disappointments. This in itself can easily lead to the emotional-signal of Frustration.

- **Doubt:** The feeling of doubt signals a lack of Trust* in your outer self. This may stem from beliefs about your abilities or your Worthiness. The feeling of doubt precedes emotions that can quickly escalate in intensity and produce extremely debilitating conditions such as Depression. See also, Fear* and Trust*.

- **Excitement:** The *feeling* of excitement is a direct sensing that indicates to you that what you are focusing your attention upon is in agreement with your path of intent and purpose. As Bashar (Darryl Anka) suggests, if you feel excited in any given moment then you can trust that what you are doing is in alignment with your intent; you cannot but draw to you physical events and experiences that are also in line with your intent and purpose. Excitement in combination with the emotion of Anticipation* provides the momentum to project your desires into physicality.

Excitement tells you which experiences, however diverse they may be, link to your path of intent. Don't be afraid to follow your excitement. If it shifts from something you are doing to something else, go where the excitement takes you. It will lead you to the places, the people, and the situations that are in harmony with your desires.

- **Expectation**: An expectation is a feeling that describes a potent combination of emotional energies. We cannot classify expectation as an independent emotion as it is often an amalgamation of energies constructed from various emotions.

  Here are some example combinations we easily recognize:

  Excitement plus Anticipation* produces a positive expectation of an event that is in line with our intent.

  Anxiety plus Anticipation* produces Worry – an expectation of a negative creation.

  As a combination of the energies of Anticipation* with Anger* (see Aggression above) would suggest, this driving energetic potency of expectation requires direction. Turning your expectations into preferred outcomes is all about learning how to consciously manipulate and direct your emotional energies. You manifest your desires (and other psychic constructions) through the force of expectation.

  Your conscious-mind's concentration on thoughts alone will not bring about an expectation's materialization – at least, not until you spend some considerable time sustaining a purity of thought. If you wish for a Desire to become real, you need to be fully conversant with the nature of your beliefs, for it is your beliefs that affect an expectation's likelihood of coming to fruition.

- **Fear***: Fear is a scientifically recognized expression of an emotion.

  Like Love, fear expresses itself through all forms of information transfer. It can come as a direct *Impulse* to act, or express itself through an emotional-signal leading to an emotion. This spectrum of expression indicates that fear is actually a state of being rather than a feeling or emotion.

Fear as an Impulse, a direct sensing and information transfer, happens in conjunction with our will to survive. As an emotional-signal, it alerts you to self-doubt arising within you (see Anxiety); and the full-blown emotion produces all manner of debilitating symptoms across the physiological and psychological systems of your Self.

It is important to realize that fear is not part of our psychological structuring.[160] Fear is something we *generate* from our psychological structures – namely the beliefs we hold, and the thoughts we nurture.

Fears can arise from our misinterpretation of what *is* a basic psychological structure guiding our actions – the survival of Consciousness. *Your* consciousness translates this quality of Consciousness into basic physical terms – forming a psychological structure that ensures your survival within the physical plane of existence. When energy associated with this primordial drive channels through you as an *impulse*, you act immediately, *un-consciously, and without thinking. Thank goodness!

However, when energy traverses through you as an emotional-signal and then emotion, you are, in the moment, consciously accessing a distortionary element in your psychological structure that translates this funda-mental drive. Fear and Hatred come about through an inability to decipher correctly the nuances of inner data constructing this important psychological system for survival.

The overall problem of fear has much to do with the ego's refusal to incorporate subconscious information and experiences supplied by the inner self. Thus, *lack of under-standing causes fear,* which is a condition that diminishes our connection to the natural power of Divine Love (*see*

Chapters 4, 17 and 18).

The experience of fearfulness comes with the basic message that you are generating a *lack of Trust** within you.

- **Forgiveness**: This feeling originates as an *Impulse* (direct communication from your Essence self) to act in a *compassionate* way. Feelings of hurt generate the impulse of forgiveness – you, or most likely someone else, has literally hurt your feelings (psychological structure) or your physical creations (your body, or another physical construct of your own creation).

The impulse directs you to act compassionately, *in the first instance,* toward your Self. This is because it relates to your own creative abilities and the natural principle of Creation.

The original impulse to act is an attempt to remind you that you create *all* of your reality, even the hurtful, negative events. If you perceive another party to be the perpetrator of any hurt to you, realize that they have co-opted with you in *your* creation. They are reflecting back to you a need for you to examine your feelings and beliefs that associate with the hurtful event and attend to them.

To **blame** others for *any* experience that is not to your liking, puts your creative power outside of yourself, denigrates the other party's co-creative abilities, and proclaims you as a *victim*. As with Anger, being a victim relinquishes all responsibility for your creations. Blaming yourself thus denigrates your own creative abilities and is an admission that you do not belief you have the ability to create the reality you prefer.

Forgiveness is not about "correcting" a hurt in the manner we are used to. When you understand the impulse for what it is, directing you to be compassionate – be so, in your forgiveness of yourself and others.

Forgiveness should also exercise your power of

Appreciation. Learn to appreciate a seemingly "negative" co-creation for what it brings to you. Compassion and Appreciation then combine in a genuine expression of forgiveness.

Appreciate that the other party helped bring this feeling to you for the purposes of your own learning – the craft of conscious creating – and growth. *(See Chapter 18, Ten Principles for Conscious Living.)*

- **Freedom:** A feeling of freedom indicates a psychological state that is allowing energy to flow freely through your Self in its "natural manner." That natural manner is in accordance with your intent and purpose.

- **Frustration:** Frustration begins as an emotional-signal that brings your attention to an element within your awareness that you perceive to be reflecting some form of lack in your outer self and your creative abilities.

This signal of lack can relate to many different ways of discounting yourself – that you lack the ability to choose or make a decision, are not good enough, not wealthy enough, not strong enough, not quick enough, not *enough* in some way.

If the signal grows, through thought, into the emotion of frustration it can result in a considerable belittling of your outer self.

The communication with any emotional energy attracted by your thinking indicates that your conscious-mind is confused as to the nature of its choices for action; which, as energy builds, can attract both the emotional-signal of Anxiety, and the emotion of Anger*.

We often view frustration as a "normal" state because we experience it so often.

Anger* is the extreme of frustration, an emotion that indicates the perceived confusion over choices has turned into a perception of no choice at all.

- **Guilt**: It is important to remember that guilt takes two forms – *artificial guilt* and *natural guilt.*

  Artificial guilt stems from the transgression of laws and ethical codes constructed as part of a particular belief system. For example, feeling guilty about a sexual act (that is consensual and enjoyed by the parties involved) you have performed because you believe it to be "sinful" produces artificial guilt.

  Natural guilt is an instinctive psychological mechanism to protect against your outer self continually committing acts of violation. The *feeling* is a direct sensing from your inner self to your conscious-mind that you are about to, are in the process of, or have just, violated the principles of Divine Love.

  The *emotion* of natural guilt is the result of transgressing the natural power of Divine Love. It provides you with the energy to make amends if possible and the message to closely exam your beliefs regarding the act in question. Natural guilt will occur if your actions violate your outer self or another Self (expression of Consciousness).

  Rape, for example, is a violating action producing natural guilt. If the perpetrator of this action does not experience the feeling or the emotion of natural guilt (which invokes feelings of Remorse – *see below*), or their energies are repressed, a psychotic disorder either exists or can develop.

- **Happiness**: The feeling of happiness is entirely reliant upon your interpretation of an experience. You generate happiness when you create an experience that is in accordance with your Desire and intent. The intensity of happiness is proportional to the degree to which the experience reflects the detail of your Desire and synchronizes with your intent and purpose.

The durability (we see it as continuity) of your happiness is indicative of whether the positive experience is *actually* in harmony with your overall intent and purpose.

For example, imagining that great financial abundance will make you happy, and on its appearance, it does so only fleetingly, indicates that your imagination generated a *"Want"* for financial abundance rather than a *"Desire"* for what financial abundance would bring you.

To many of us happiness is an illusory experience. Elias remarks that this is because we know happiness to be pleasurable, and we have many beliefs that block the experience simply because of this knowledge.

Any feeling of pleasure is actually a natural expression of your Essence.

Disappointment (*see above*) is a feeling closely related to happiness as it gives indication of when an experience is not in line with your Desire.

- **Hatred**: Hatred begins as a feeling before exploiting an emotion for its energy. It is the result of a psychological manipulation of the emotion of Fear*.

As with Fear*, hatred is to do with our misinterpretation of the quality or drive within Consciousness to maintain existence (we translate this as "survive"). Misconceptions plague our attempts to translate this quality of Consciousness into a cohesive psychological structure within our own consciousness.

Depending on the degree of distortion or errors in our own psychological construction, this structure then affects, detrimentally, our physical creations. Errors in translation may become habitual and the distortions can influence other psychological structures. We integrate the errors into our perception.

Hate is not so much the opposite of love, as the

separation of the outer self from the natural power of Divine Love and the inner senses that operate within it.

Hate as an emotion highlights our separation through individuation from Consciousness. It is the Fear* of losing personal identity, of returning to the fold, of being One again with Consciousness.

Beware the natural power of Attraction when it comes to hate – for if you hate, you will attract hate.

- **Hope**: The feeling of hope is associated with optimism, a combination of the emotions of Anticipation* and Joy*.

  A review of Anticipation* shows that this emotion can involve either Excitement or Anxiety in the steering of its energies. Hope can therefore take two contrasting routes.

  The first route is when the emphasis of our thoughts, feelings and emotions center on the lack of our desired manifestation or the negativity of the current situation. It is then that our Anticipation* involves the confounding energies of Anxiety in any Expectation.

  The other route involves maintaining a focus on the desired positive change in the situation. Focusing on the Desire invokes feelings of Excitement in our Anticipation*. Such grounding feelings and emotions marry readily with Joy* to produce an Expectation far more capable of creating the outcome we "hope" for.

- **Impatience:** Impatience is a feeling that signals to your conscious-mind that you are not allowing the energies that coalesce to form your desired reality to flow freely within "natural time" *(See Chapter 18, Ten Principles for Conscious Living)*.

  This feeling relates to the emotion of Trust* – of your Self and your creative abilities.

  Impatience is a symptom of your ego-self's attempt to force a desired probable event outside of its natural timing.

- **Impulse**: Neither a feeling nor an emotion, an impulse is a direct energy communication, an *instructional* prompting, from your Essence self that gets your outer self to act before the intervention of complicating thoughts or feelings.

  Impulses are lifelong communications directing your actions. They constitute a form of language used by your inner self, your outer self's guardian, to act with immediacy.

  We mistrust impulses because of established core beliefs that misinterpret the nature of the subconscious, and misunderstand our natural drive for survival.

  Despite the fact that our belief systems tell us to mistrust them, *impulses are not harmful to us*. Instead of ignoring or repressing impulses, trust that following them without too much analysis by the conscious-mind will be of benefit to you.

  Committing a violation has nothing to do with *natural* impulses. Such acts are contrary to the natural power (or law) of Divine Love, that directs all actions. Acts of violation of a natural principle or a societal law are often blamed on "an impulse" when in actuality they are instigated by mischievous, malevolent, or pathological patterns of thought.

- **Irritation**: A feeling often confused with Anger*, irritation can accrue an energy potential as elevated as the emotion of Anger, however, it is an energy configuration very different to that of Anger. The difference is that irritation empowers you, whereas Anger disempowers you.

  Even though they feel very much alike, one way of separating them is to notice whether you have paused in your actions to consider your choice options. This would be a sign that you are irritated rather than angry.

  Irritation usually stops you in your tracks and makes

you consider the situation and your choices for action. Anger is the emotion that has you believe, without consideration, that there are few choices if any available to you.

You *always* have choices in any situation, considering them is empowering as you are consciously in charge of your choices and subsequent actions. Anger disempowers you as it narrows or takes away completely conscious choice, replacing it with a reaction.

Anger, at best, pushes you into a choice that is not genuinely in line with your desires or intent; irritation engages your imagination. Irritation sees to it that the circumstances do not dictate how you should act and that you maintain a choice on how to proceed.

- **Joy***: Joy is a scientifically recognized primary emotion. It begins as a feeling that can escalate its intensity to emotion status. The feeling signals that in this moment you are validating and appreciating yourself.

  The emotion communicates that you are exercising a Trust* in yourself, an acknowledgement that you are expressing yourself freely in your choices and in accordance with Divine Love.

  Abraham states that while the basis of life is freedom, joy is the true "objective" of life.

  Joy is the feeling and emotion that informs you that you are freely expressing your personality in alignment with your intent and purpose.

- **Love**: Scientifically, love is recognized to be a feeling that is a combination of the emotions of Joy* and Trust*.

  From the metaphysical standpoint, love is neither a feeling nor an emotion, it is, like Fear*, a "state" of being. This state, is derived from how much your entire "emotional climate" is in alignment with Divine Love.

  "Human love" is our attempt to interpret the qualities of Divine Love.

Divine Love is an expansive "state" that encompasses, and can be expressed by, many feelings and emotions. *"In essence, it is a total knowing, Acceptance and Appreciation of what is,"* appears to be the most reasonable and succinct interpretation of Divine Love.

See, *Say That Again (9)* and *Chapters 4 and 17.*

- **Pain**: Pain is of particular interest to science as it assumes that the brain somehow generates physically expressed pain. In actuality, pain, whether physical, emotional, or psychological, is a non-physically based *feeling* which your inner self generates.

  Physical pain is a direct communication to your conscious-mind from your inner self in cooperation with the body-consciousness that immediate action is required.

  An enduring physical pain, along with emotional and psychological pain, communicates that your beliefs are in need of review and adjustment.

  Pain, as with any feeling, passes through your *perception*. It is your perception that identifies whether the feeling is positive or negative in nature; which is why physical pain can be experienced as both positive (pleasurable) or negative (unpleasant).

- **Rage**: Rage is an emotional-signal that arises out of the highly charged emotions of Anger*. When your choice of action appears to have narrowed to only one or two options the feeling of rage attempts to alert you to this in order for you to break your thinking patterns before acting rashly.

- **Remorse**: A feeling that is thought to be a combination of Sadness* and Disgust*. It is a feeling that stems from "natural guilt," thereby invoking the emotions of Sadness* and Disgust* at one's actions.

  The communication of these combined emotions is that it is imperative that you take time to look within yourself and deal with beliefs that have become so inappropriate as to be pathological or life threatening.

- **Sadness*/Sorrow**: Science recognizes sadness as a primary emotion.

    Sadness is actually the *emotional-signal,* which may, or may not lead to the emotion of *sorrow.*

    Sadness usually signals the loss of a preferred creation from your perception of reality. This could be a cherished object, an abandoned idea or concept, a beloved animal or plant, or of course, a fellow human being.

    When the loss appears to have obvious permanence, as in physical death, the signal of sadness may evoke the emotion of sorrow. We can think of sorrow as the emotion that steps in to prolong the feeling of sadness.

    Our mental blurring of the differing energies of the signal of sadness with the emotion of sorrow leads to a confused understanding of their information content.

    Sadness is a signal to your conscious-mind that you perceive a limitation of your choices. When you are just dealing with the emotional-signal of sadness – yes, you are recognizing the loss of something – however, the underlying communication is suggesting that if you employ the emotion of sorrow, you may enter into some type of *denial* of yourself and your creative abilities. This may relate to actions you have taken, to your future choice of actions, or to your freedom to act.

    The signal of sadness may incorporate the communication that you perceive your choices to be limited. Remember that Anger* and Anxiety are emotional states which also carry a message that you are subconsciously perceiving a limitation of your choices. Sadness contains this subconscious information, but when sorrow comes into the reckoning a greater subtlety of meaning emerges – largely missed by most of us.

When the energy of the emotion of sorrow enters the picture, Elias (Mary Ennis) suggests that part of the emotion's message comes from your Essence self – it is *feeling sad (!)* for your outer self. Your Essence is sad that you are not using the sorrowful experience to learn more about your co-creative abilities.

In the case of the death of a loved one, your Essence is sad that you do not understand that physical death is not the end to that person's existence, or their influence upon your creations.

Your Essence/inner self sends the signal of sadness to your conscious-mind as recognition that the loved one was of value to you in the co-creation of your reality.

It is a signal designed to bring your Mind into a state of *appreciation* – an expression of Divine Love – of the value of the other's contribution to your life. Sadness is thereby a feeling that has you recognize and appreciate that in *cooperation* with this other person or creature you were able to co-create mutually beneficial experiences.

The fact that the other person or creature chooses to no longer *directly* participate in your physical reality, appears to put a limit on your further choices in life. It is a realization that actually offers you more choices, more empowerment, and more clarity in relation to yourself.

- **Stress:** Stress occurs when you fail to recognize emotional-signals sent from your inner self, which inform you of the lack of *naturalness* in your actions. Emotional-signals, unrecognized, are apt to build in number and intensity in your subconscious. Failure to acknowledge their existence, and address the emotional energies that are associated with them, creates a highly debilitating effect upon your psychological and physiological structures.

Extreme stress, either in a particular moment, or acquired over a period, can eventually result in a nervous breakdown.

- **Surprise***: Surprise is a scientifically recognized primary emotion – the opposite of Anticipation*. In actuality, it is a *feeling*, which sweeps over you to inform you that the created event was not within your normal parameters of Expectation. You can think of it as a reminder to you that your expectations do not have to constrain your creative abilities.

- **Trust***: This is a scientifically recognized emotion. Trust though, according to channeled information, is not actually an emotion; it is a state of being resulting from an affinity with Divine Love. Attuning to Divine Love incorporates *feelings* of trust within you for your Self and your perception of reality.

  Expressing trust is an expression of your personal Freedom (the basis of life) to allow the natural flow of energy to move unencumbered along your chosen path of intent. In doing so, you are trusting that the probabilities relating to your Desire have been set in motion and their manifestation does not necessarily require any further injection of energy, such as that provided by an emotion. You trust in the natural flow of universal energy to manifest your Desire in "natural time."

  The Elias messages focus upon trusting your Self because, "You shall not betray yourself!"

  Yes, it is particularly difficult to trust your Self when you are under constant pressure from others to trust in them. Making things more difficult still is an ego-self that trusts only the information brought to it by your outer senses, and the knowledge it has contorted to fit within its belief systems.

  Know that when others proclaim that you should trust in the universe, this will indeed help you to some degree as it *is* the universe – Consciousness – that provides the ultimate state of Trust through Divine Love.

As you are a "portion" of Consciousness, trust is therefore implicit to the nature of your Self.

- **Vulnerable**: The feeling of vulnerability signals your conscious-mind that you are open to receive energy and information. We label this feeling as "negative" as we associate being open to receive as being open to attack, or without adequate protection. We assign this *belief* to the feeling, thus generating the energy potential of the emotion of Fear*.

    This habitual action conceals the feeling's good intent to inform you that in the present moment you are receptive to any form of feedback about your creations. See *Chapter 18, Ten Principles for Conscious Living*, for a definitive explanation of this feeling that is hugely important to your spiritual development.

- **Want:** A want is a feeling that your ego-self generates when information gathered by the outer senses filters through your belief systems. Because of the nature of belief systems, a Desire (generated by your inner self and your inner senses) can be misinterpreted as a want and vice versa.

- **Worry**: This is a feeling that combines Anxiety with Anticipation* – an Expectation of a negative creation. It's worth remembering Abraham's definition of worry if you find yourself doing it, "Worrying is using your imagination to create that which you do not want."

    Of course worrying, through anxiety, can lead to a fearful emotion. The message of the emotion is that you are perpetuating a lack of Trust* in your Self, and your ability to create that which you Desire. You are channeling your energies toward a negative outcome via a negative Expectation.

    Focus your attention upon an *excited* Anticipation of a

preferred outcome in order to quell worrying thoughts.

• **Worthiness**: To feel "unworthy" is to deny who you are. It is a feeling that is in complete contradiction to the natural flow of Source energy, and energies such as feelings and emotions, coursing through your Self.

These energies strive to have you express your uniqueness, your intent, your creativity, and your purpose. Feeling unworthy drives your Essence self to tears!

This is because your Essence self knows that as an expression of Consciousness your right to exist requires no justification. There is no measure of worthiness or validity for *your* consciousness within Consciousness as it is a part of It. To question your worth is to question the worth of Consciousness.

Your very existence implies that you have both value and worth.

ENDNOTES AND REFERENCES

Preface

1   Roberts J. *Seth Speaks: The Eternal Validity of the Soul.*
Englewood Cliffs, NJ: Prentice-Hall Inc.; 1972. p. ix.
Reprinted with permission of New World Library, Novato,
CA. (www.newworldlibrary.com).

Introduction

2   Many of the core publications of books dictated by Seth are
available at major bookstores. Go to
www.newworldview.com for suggestions on sequential
reading. A comprehensive list of Seth books and Seth-
related books is available at www.sethcenter.com.

3   TED – Technology Entertainment and Design – is a
conferencing network owned by the non-profit Sapling
Foundation, formed to disseminate "ideas worth
spreading." See www.ted.com

4   The term "outer self" is used when referring to the
collection of psychological elements that contribute to the
"physical you" – that is, the ego/ego-self, conscious-mind,
and your personality. You can think of your "body-
consciousness" as a layer of your Self that bridges the non-
physical and physical selves. "Focus personality" is an
equivalent term used by Jane Roberts in her Aspect
Psychology work for outer self.

5   "Probable realities" is a concept explored more fully in *Book
III: Live Your Purpose.*

6   Interestingly, "channel" also refers to a path for an electrical
current or *signal* in electronics. This definition isn't too far
away from describing the actions of a person channeling
metaphysical information.

7   Go to www.thepeacefulplanet.com for more information on

"Gaia" channeled through Pepper Lewis.

8   See, Helfrich P. The channeling phenomenon: A multidimensional assessment. *Journal of Integral Theory and Practice.* 2009;4(3): p. 141-161.

9   Sadly, Jerry Hicks withdrew his immediate attention on the physical realm on November 18, 2011. I dare say that his Essence self will be keeping a compassionate eye on our development. I have no doubt that he will eventually be seen as a pioneer in the broader understanding and evolution of human consciousness. For more information on Abraham go to www.abraham-hicks.com and www.lawofattractioninteraction.com. (830) 755 2299.

10   Seth defines "action" as the process by which the inner vitality of Consciousness "continually attempts to express itself in endless formations." (See, Roberts J. *The Early Sessions: Book 4 of the Seth Material.* Manhasset: New Awareness Network Inc.; 1998. p. 92.) Creation is an ever-present process that neither simply began with a Big Bang, nor ended after seven days.

11   James W. *The Varieties of Religious Experience: A Study in Human Nature.* New York: Mentor Edition; 1902/1958. p. 298.

12   Goswami A, Reed RE, & Goswami, M. *The Self-Aware Universe: How Consciousness Creates the Material World.* New York: Tarcher/Putnam; 1993. p. 215.

13   Panpsychism is either the view that all parts of matter involve mind, or the more holistic view that the whole Universe is an organism that possesses a mind. It does not say everything is alive; rather everything is *sentient* and that there are either many separate minds or one single mind uniting everything that is.

Amit Goswami, echoing the mystics of his native India, asserts that Consciousness, not matter, is the ground of all existence. He holds that the universe is self-aware and that

[C]onsciousness creates the physical world. Calling this theory "monistic idealism," he claims it is not only "the basis of all religions worldwide" but also the correct philosophy for modern science.

14   See, Wilber K, Patten T, Leonard A & Morelli M. *Integral Life Practice: A 21st Century Blueprint for Physical Health, Emotional Balance, Mental Clarity and Spiritual Awakening.* Boston & London: Integral Books; 2008.

15   This is not a prediction. This is Seth's loose positioning in linear time of when our shift in consciousness will be nearing completion. His knowledge of energy configurations associated with the myriad probabilities available to us, and his ability to view these probabilities within the *"spacious present"* allowed him to offer 2075 as a probable date for the end of the *Shift.*

16   For a compilation of Elias material pertaining to the *shift in consciousness,* see Tate D. *The Shift: A Time of Change.* Victoria, B.C.: Canada Trafford Publishing; 2003.

17   Roberts J. *The Afterdeath Journal of an American Philosopher: The World View of William James.* Englewood Cliffs, NJ: Prentice-Hall, Inc.; 1978. p. 113.

Chapter 1

18   Hicks E & J. Abraham, through Esther Hicks. Audio recording of a workshop at San Antonio, TX; April 21, 2001. © Jerry and Esther Hicks, Abraham-Hicks.com.

19   The term "channeling" refers to the process of information transference from the non-physical plane to our physical one. For a concise guide to the phenomenon see Hastings A. *With the Tongues of Men and Angels: A Study of Channeling.* Orlando, FL.: Holt, Rinehart, and Winston; 1991. For a definitive exploration of the channeling phenomenon and its many forms, see Klimo J. *Channeling: Investigations on Receiving Information from Paranormal Sources.* Berkeley, CA:

North Atlantic Books; 1998.

20 "This is why your Universe is expanding, and contrary to your belief system, the Universe will not shrink." Melanie – channeled by Tilde Cameron & Tina Fiorda. See, *A Book of Insight: Wisdom from the Other Side*. British Columbia, Canada: Stone Circle Publishing; 2008 p. 27. www.abook ofinsight.com.

21 Abraham (Esther Hicks) states, "the *basis* of life is freedom."

22 Roberts J. *The Nature of the Psyche: Its Human Expression*. Englewood Cliffs, NJ: Prentice-Hall, Inc.; 1979. p. 143.

23 Maturana HR & Varela FJ. *Autopoiesis and Cognition: The Realization of the Living*. Dordrecht, Holland: D. Reidel Publishing Co.; 1980.

24 The metaphysical literature describes a "victim mentality" as an insidious sense of powerlessness, which stems from beliefs that systematically undermine self-worth. A perceived powerlessness thwarts any desire to change.

25 Elias (Mary Ennis), for example, uses *Regional Areas*. The character *H-A* channeled by Tony Neate refers to a number of *Planes of Existence* that are another interpretation of the Areas within Consciousness concept. See, www.channel ling-online.com

26 When considering the properties of the physical universe and "the principle of locality," Einstein's Special Relativity Theory appears highly accurate. "Non-locality," the influence of one object on another distant object – verified by Bell's Theorem – runs contrary to relativity theory. Quantum theorists attempt to explain this anomalous phenomenon by suggesting other dimensions to the universe. David Bohm, for example, put forward the idea of an "implicate" and "explicate order" to describe the universe – a notion that suggests a non-physical as well as physical dimension to the universe.

27 Seth describes units of consciousness as "the smallest

psychological unit of individual consciousness which finds physical fulfillment in the formation of matter." (See Roberts J. *The Early Sessions: Book 2 of The Seth Material*. Manhasset, NY: New Awareness Network Inc.; 1997. p. 71.) He first refers to "electromagnetic energy units" in *The Early Sessions: Book 9 of The Seth Material*. Manhasset, NY: New Awareness Network Inc., p.416.

28 Theoretical physics postulates the possibility of faster-than-light non-physical "particles" named Tachyons.

29 Roberts J. *A Seth Book: The Unknown Reality: Vol.1*. New York: Prentice Hall; 1977. p. 72.

30 For an excellent comparison of Seth's ideas with those of physics and quantum physics see, Friedman N. *Bridging Science and Spirit: Common Elements In David Bohm's Physics, The Perennial Philosophy and Seth*. St. Louis: Living Lake Books; 1990.

31 The recent announcement (July 2012) from the CERN organization in Geneva of the discovery of the Higgs boson, or "God particle," may be our first "sighting" of Seth's "electromagnetic energy units." The true God particle, if you will – a Consciousness Unit, is unlikely to ever be detected as the frequency of its vibrational signature does not come anywhere within the confines of physical electromagnetic frequencies or those of the hypothetical quantum field or so-called Higgs field.

Chapter 2

32 Gestalt is a German term with no English equivalent. It is used to refer to *unified wholes* that cannot be fully understood by examining the parts that constitute the whole. This premise is foundational to the Gestalt Psychology movement.

33 Roberts J. *The Early Sessions: Book 3 of The Seth Material*. Manhasset, NY: New Awareness Network Inc.; 1998. p. 333.

34   For a compilation of mainstream scientific research that is beginning to fathom the nature of this domain, see McTaggart L. *The Field*. London: HarperCollinsPublishers Ltd.; 2001.

35   Lipton B. *The Biology of Belief*. Santa Rosa, CA: Mountain of Love/Elite Books; 2005. p. 26-7.

36   For more information, see Pert C. *Molecules of Emotion: The Science Behind Mind-Body Medicine*. London: Simon & Schuster; 1999; Oschman JL. *Energy Medicine: The Scientific Basis*. London: Harcourt Publishers Ltd.; 2000; Church D. *The Genie in Your Genes*. Santa Rosa, CA: Elite Books; 2007; and Lipton BH & Bhaerman S. *Spontaneous Evolution*. London: Hay House UK; 2011.

37   Seth first mentions the term "tissue capsules" in *The Early Sessions: Book 1 of The Seth Material*. Manhasset, NY: New Awareness Network Inc.; 1997. p. 312.

38   We explore *time, simultaneous time,* and Seth's oft-used expression, the *"spacious present,"* in *Book III* of *It's About You!*

39   You will find the term "conscious-mind" hyphenated for most of the book. This is to distinguish it as a facet of the overall structure of your mind. See *Chapter 6* for further explanation.

40   Seth coined the expression "feeling-tone" in Roberts J. *The Nature of Personal Reality: A Seth Book*. Englewood Cliffs, NJ: Prentice-Hall Inc.; 1974. p. 24/5.

41   EFT, devised by Gary Craig, is the most popular of self-help methods that fall under the umbrella discipline of Energy Psychology (EP). See, www.energypsych.org for further information on Energy Psychology and go to www.eftuniverse.com and www.garythink.com for more on EFT.

Chapter 3

42   Eddington A. *The Nature of the Physical World*. London: Dent;

1928. p. 68.

43   Roberts J. *The Early Sessions: Book 3 of The Seth Material.* Manhasset, NY: New Awareness Network Inc.; 1998. p. 42

44   In light of Seth's inner universe law of Energy Transformation, we can surmise that the empirical law of physics pertaining to energy is actually a scientific *belief* – a *"relative truth"*(explained in *Chapter 11*) – rather than an absolute law or *absolute truth*. It is this belief – that underpins the notion that the Universe is of finite energy resources. This notion in turn encourages our collective belief that every physical thing is in competition because of finite resources.

45   Payne JL. *Omni Reveals the Four Principles of Creation.* Forres, Scotland: Findhorn Press; 2001. p. 23.

46   Roberts J. *The Early Sessions: Book 2 of The Seth Material.* Manhasset, NY: New Awareness Network Inc.; 1997. p. 71

47   Our conscious-minds are unable to perceive that time is relative as we rely so heavily on our outer physical senses – which *take time (!)* to interpret the environment and the expression of an experience. When we awaken our conscious-minds to our inner senses, we will be better able to sense and perceive what Seth refers to as the *spacious present.*

Seth makes continual reference to the *spacious present* throughout his works, particularly in an attempt to illustrate how the present moment is the only point of action, the *"nowpoint,"* or *"point of power."* Eckhart Tolle provides an excellent alternative explanation of this notion of the spacious present in his seminal work *The Power of Now: A Guide to Spiritual Enlightenment.* Novato, CA: New World Library; 1999.

48   Schizophrenia: "It literally means *splitting in the mind* and was chosen by Bleuler (in 1910) because the disorder seemed to reflect a cleavage or dissociation between the functions of

feeling or emotion on one hand and those of thinking or cognition on the other." (Reber A. *Dictionary of Psychology*. London: Penguin Books; 1985.)

49   For a fascinating elaboration on the ego's protracted split from its inner guidance, see Taylor S. *The Fall: The Insanity of The Ego in Human History and The Dawning of A New Era*. Winchester: O Books; 2005.

50   Perception is a faculty of the ego-self elaborated upon in *Book II: Free Your Self*. For the purposes of this book, you can take the "filter" to be your ego-self's belief systems that your perception includes in the process of creation.

51   Remember that we are always a "part" or an individualized expression of Consciousness. The recent rise in people able to channel can be seen as an attempt by Consciousness to inform our short-sighted ego-selves that it is time to look inward in the pursuit of knowledge and "truth."

52   See the "inner senses" at http://www.eliasforum.org /digests.html

53   See *When the Impossible Happens: Adventures in Non-Ordinary Realities* by Stanislav Grof, M.D., Ph.D., Sounds True, Inc., 2006.

54   Experimentation involving the feeding of spiders with flies laced with drugs such as LSD, mescaline and cannabis show that web production becomes markedly impaired; evidence perhaps of a disturbance in the creature's ability to access its conceptual inner senses. Interestingly, caffeine appears to have the most destructive influence on web design – webmasters take note! See, Witt PN & Rovner JS. (Eds.) *Spider Communication: Mechanisms and Ecological Significance*. Princeton University Press; 1982.

55   For more information, see The Dolphin Communication Project run by Dr. Kathleen Dudzinski. www.dolphincom- municationproject.org

56   Dahl LM. *Ten Thousand Whispers: A Guide to Conscious*

Creation. Eugene, OR: The Woodbridge Group; 1995. p. 24.

Chapter 4

57 "The power of Magnetism" is an alternative expression used by several channeled guides.

58 Roberts J. *The Early Sessions: Book 4 of The Seth Material*. Manhasset, NY: New Awareness Network Inc.; 1998. p. 331.

59 Roberts J. *The Nature of Personal Reality: A Seth Book*. Englewood Cliffs, NJ: Prentice-Hall Inc. 1974. p. 53.

60 Abraham (Esther Hicks) states, "... the result of life is growth." It is likely Abraham uses the word "growth" as an easier term for people to relate to than the expression "Value Fulfillment" (Divine Love) promoted by Seth. Seth does though make it clear that "growth" is our own superficial interpretation of this fundamental "law" of the inner universe.

61 The meaning of the term "evolution" can be misconstrued to include the maxim of "survival of the fittest" – here it simply means, "... a development to a more complex form."

62 Roberts J. *The Nature of the Psyche: Its Human Expression*. Englewood Cliffs, NJ: Prentice-Hall, Inc.; 1979. p. 216.

63 We elaborate on the difference between "wants" and "desires" in *Book II: Free Your Self*.

64 For *the* most spectacular example of this principle of spontaneous physical change occurring through the embodiment of Divine Love, see Anita Moorjani's account of her experiences in relation to cancer and her near death experience in *Dying to be Me*.

65 Roberts J. *The Early Sessions: Book 2 of The Seth Material*. Manhasset, NY: New Awareness Network Inc.; 1997. p. 242.

66 Payne JL. As Omni in, *Omni Reveals the Four Principles of Creation*. Forres, Scotland: Findhorn Press; 2001. p. 20.

67 *Book III: Live Your Purpose* expands upon the concept of reincarnation.

68 Here's a secret of my own. The Law of Attraction (LOA) isn't a secret at all, it's simply one of the two *Natural Powers* (Divine Love being the other) that we have "lost" from our conscious awareness for a long time – along with the other *natural principles* that underpin our physical laws. It is indeed important that we become consciously aware again of the natural power of Attraction. However, it would be naïve to assume that a superficial knowledge of this natural power, in isolation, is all that's require to overcome life's challenges and become a master of conscious creation.

69 Payne JL. *Omni Reveals the Four Principles of Creation*. Forres, Scotland: Findhorn Press; 2001. p. 20.

70 Hicks E & J. *A New Beginning II*. San Antonio: Abraham-Hicks Publications; 1996. p. 103. © Jerry and Esther Hicks, Abraham-Hicks.com.

71 Confusion arises when we compare the Law of Attraction (described as like attracting like) with *magnetism* – as most of us understand it from elementary schooling. We are taught that opposite poles of a magnet attract, whereas "like" poles repel each other. The natural power of Attraction simply reflects the principle in magnetism that a "permanent magnet" produces an invisible force, pulling to it certain materials and repelling others. We can regard material attracted to the magnet as having electromagnetic properties that "resonate" with those of the magnetic force.

72 We look into the concept of "probable realities" in *Book III: Live Your Purpose*.

73 For more on Bashar and Darryl Anka go to http://www.bashar.org. The quotation: Anka D. (as Bashar), available at http://www.bashar.org/Transcripts/the-shift.html (Accessed September 1, 2007.)

74 Rose, channeled by Joanne Helfrich, suggests that to kill in order to relieve suffering is not in contradiction to the vital code of non-violation. In other words, *to kill within the*

principle of compassion – an expression of Divine Love – is not a violation.

Chapter 5

75   Roberts J. *The Unknown Reality: Volume II. A Seth Book.* New York: Prentice Hall Press; 1979. p. 608.

76   Omni (John L. Payne) supports distinctive groups or families within the human expression of Consciousness, although his interpretation generalizes to seven types (paralleling the visible color spectrum more closely) rather than nine.

77   Seth did not elaborate further on the genera of human intent other than brief descriptions of the characteristics of his "families of consciousness." His lengthiest explanation centered on the "Sumari" family as this was an intentional drive shared by him, Jane Roberts, and her husband Robert Butts. Robert Butts states in his notes at the end of session 734 in *The Unknown Reality: Volume II,* by Jane Roberts, that he regretted not questioning Seth further on the "families of consciousness" subject, particularly the "roles" they play.

78   For more on Rose, go to http://www.essence-of-rose.com

79   Roberts J. *The Unknown Reality: Volume II. A Seth Book.* New York: Prentice Hall Press; 1979. p. 562.

80   Ennis M. (1996). As Elias, session 67. Available from: http://www.eliasforum.org/transcripts. © Mary Ennis.

81   Ennis M. (1995). Ibid, session 59.

82   Ennis M. (1997). Ibid, session 185.

83   The list of the genera of human intent in *Appendix III* gives the colors assigned by Elias.

Chapter 6

84   We might view the recurrent patterns formed by fractal geometry as a loose reflection of this creation process. A fractal is a rough geometric shape that contains within itself

fragments that are an ever-diminishing replication of its whole. This diminishing scale of replication is termed *"self-similarity."* (Perhaps this expression would work better with a capital S!) Whilst generated from a mathematical construct, nature's geometric patterns frequently approximate to that of fractals.

85 Science is now beginning to understand that the egg cell's membrane has a choice in what sperm to accept into itself; it is not simply a case of which sperm is the strongest and therefore more able to get to the egg and penetrate the outer membrane. This original understanding derives from beliefs surrounding the distorted interpretations of evolutionary theory relating to "survival of the fittest" and "everything is in competition in order to survive."

86 Philosophers Friedrich Nietzsche and Ludwig Wittgenstein both make the point that language has one major limitation. That is, we confine our thinking to the language we are used to using—a language that reflects only the ideas and thoughts of the culture that uses it. This leads to a vocabulary limited to describing concepts of thought already explored and *approved* by societal mores. This makes it difficult to explore new dimensions of thought when there are no words to describe a concept that is new to our language. If we don't have the language to explain our thinking, we tend not to go there. (Seth often remarks that we simply do not have the language, *as yet,* for him to fully convey that which he is attempting to describe.)

87 As the renowned evolution biologist and futurist Elisabet Sahtouris Ph.D. remarks in an article entitled *A Scientist's Thoughts about Redefining our Concept of God* (see www.paraview.com/features/scientists_thoughts.htm), when referring to her conversation with the late Willis W. Harman Ph.D. in the co-authored *Biology Revisioned*:

"All nature is thus conscious in my worldview, and all of it has access to non-timespace; all of it is an aspect of God. The acorn knows the oak tree it will become."

88 Seth states in *The Nature of the Psyche: Its Human Expression* that the psyche is impossible to define in words. It's a non-physical expression of energy (it's clearly not a 'thing' – a physical expression of energy) that, although it has form, that form can take on countless definitions depending on *how* you attempt to define it and *who* is attempting it!

However, it is just about possible to describe how it affects you. You have a portion of the psyche within your Self – your Mind. This portion of it is your own inviolate personal "subjective area" within **the** Subjective Area within Consciousness. It is a "place" where your non-physical self resides, which you have yet to explore in a conscious fashion.

As it is within the Subjective Area within Consciousness there are no boundaries such as space and time; and as it's a part of Consciousness Itself – it creates you as you create it! It is an ever-changing place of experimentation. One contribution you make to the psyche's expansion through experience is a deeper understanding of the concept of time – which you provide by being in the physical realm where time is a psychological dimension under the scrutiny of Consciousness.

89 Roberts J. *The Early Sessions: Book 4 of The Seth Material.* Manhasset, NY: New Awareness Network Inc.; 1998. p. 227.

90 Cohen A. *Your Best Friend and Your Worst Enemy.* E-mail inclusion from *EnlightenNext Presents Andrew Cohen's Quote of the Week.* March 23, 2011.

91 Roberts J. *The Early Sessions: Book 3 of The Seth Material.* Manhasset, NY: New Awareness Network Inc.; 1998. p. 282.

92 Roberts J. Ibid. p.283.

Chapter 7

93 The inspiration for this metaphor of your subconscious area comes from Jane Roberts' Aspect Psychology works and her "vision" of a library of the psyche containing tomes of perennial wisdom meant for translation. See Roberts J. *Psychic Politics: An Aspect Psychology Book.* Englewood Cliffs, NJ: Prentice-Hall, Inc.; 1976. p. 18-19.

94 You can review the *Figure 1* diagram for a visual reference to what Jung is saying here. Jung places the ego within the sphere of the "inner self" – which isn't too far off the mark from the metaphysical perspective. Your ego's "small c" consciousness can be regarded as still "within" the consciousness of your Essence, within the inner self if you like, as your inner self is a "part" of your Essence. Remember that in non-physical reality, the home of your psyche, divisions and boundaries don't count for much. The other small spheres inside the Essence of *Figure 1* are there as representations of other personalities (from other lifetimes for example) that continue their existence within your eternal Essence – as time doesn't count for much either where your Essence is concerned.

95 From Friedrich von Hayek's term for an area within our minds (subconscious) that contains tacit knowledge of highly complex aspects of the nature of our reality – often in very abstract representative forms. This concept may be indicative of von Hayek's intuitive attempts to understand some of the complexities of the conceptual inner senses described in *Chapter 3*. According to von Hayek, this extremely basic knowledge of the nature of our reality is so abstract and complex that our conscious-minds are unable to access it and understand it – yet.

Chapter 8

96 For a description of the various human energy fields

proposed by philosophers and scientists alike, see Dale C. *The Subtle Body: An Encyclopedia of Your Energetic Anatomy.* Boulder, CO: Sounds True, Inc.; 2009.

97 For more information on the remarkable properties of our electrical body, see Becker RO & Selden G. *The Body Electric: Electromagnetism and the Foundation of Life.* New York: HarperCollins; 1998.

98 Dr. Hiroshi Motoyama (scientist and Shinto priest) and Dr. Valerie Hunt, professor of kinesiology at UCLA, are leading pioneers in the study of the electromagnetic systems of the body. Hunt discovered that radiation emanates from various sites within the body that are typically associated with the chakras. See, Ozaniec N. *Chakras for Beginners.* London: Hodder & Stoughton Educational; 1999.

99 Electrophysiology studies the electrical properties of cells, tissues and organs of the body. Advanced Kirlian photography makes "viewing" your body's electrical discharge, your "aura," possible. See Alden T. (2001). *Science Investigates the Human Aura.* Online report available at http://www.technosophy.com/humanaura.htm (Accessed March 27, 2008.)

100 Anastassiou CA, Perin R, Markram H & Koch C. (2010). *Ephaptic coupling of cortical neurons.* Article in Nature Neuroscience Advance Online Publication. Published online January 16, 2011; doi:10.1038/nn.2727

101 For a definitive explanation of thoughts within the electric field see, Roberts J. *The Early Sessions: Book 3 of The Seth Material.* Manhasset, NY: New Awareness Network Inc.; 1998. pp. 219-225.

102 Reviewed as a natural principle in *Chapter 3.*

103 Merrick R. *Interference: The Grand Scientific Musical Theory.* Fairview, TX: Self-Published; 2009. ISBN: 978-0-615-20599-1.

104 Walker EH. *The Physics of Consciousness: The Quantum Mind and the Meaning of Life.* New York: Basic Books; 2000.

105 Merrick R. *Harmonically Guided Evolution: The Universal Pattern of Life.* Article in Caduceus, Issue 79, Summer, 2010. p. 15.

106 Hicks E & J. *Manifest Your Desires: 365 Ways to Make Your Dreams a Reality.* Carlsbad, CA: Hay House, Inc.; 2008. #43.

107 Hicks E & J. Abraham. Audio recording of a workshop in San Antonio, TX. April 21, 2001. © Jerry and Esther Hicks, Abraham-Hicks.com.

108 Adapted from a suggestion made by Seth in, Roberts J. *The Nature of Personal Reality: A Seth Book.* Englewood Cliffs, NJ: Prentice-Hall, Inc.; 1974. p. 153-4; and suggestions on practicing purity of thought found in the works of Abraham – © Jerry and Esther Hicks, Abraham-Hicks.com.

109 Abraham advises that for concentrated purity of thought (that is, uninterrupted by contrary thoughts or feelings such as fear) to have an optimum effect on the physical system, it should be maintained for sixty-eight seconds. Don't worry if you run a few seconds over!

Chapter 9

110 The Chakras are non-physical energy centers that relate to spiritual, mental, emotional, and physical aspects of our being. Aligning with the spinal column, from the base of the spine to the crown of the head, there are seven in number. (Elias states that an eighth bodily "energy center" between the Heart and Throat is forming as part of the human evolutionary process – elaborated upon in *Book II*.)

111 Both Seth and Elias categorically state that the pineal gland is a primary physical structure involved in bridging the non-physical and physical fields of reality. The French seventeenth century philosopher René Descartes famously studied the pineal gland; declaring it to be the "principle seat of the soul, and *the place in which all our thoughts are formed.*" (*My emphasis.*) (29 January 1640, AT III:19-20,

CSMK 143) See Stanford Encyclopedia of Philosophy, http://plato.stanford.edu/entries/pineal-gland

112 Judith A. *Eastern Body Western Mind*. New York: Celestial Arts, Random House Inc.; 2004.

Chapter 10

113 Stibal V. *Theta HealingTM*. Carlsbad, CA: Hay House, Inc.; 2010. p. 67.

114 This system of beliefs relates to our individuation from Consciousness. Humanity is favored with a *conscious* awareness of Self made possible through the ego-self's capacity for Self-reflection. Because the ego-self believes that it is the totality of the Self, reflection upon how it came into being has produced a belief that it is separate from everything else, even any Source Entity that may be responsible for its creation. This belief generates the "primal fear" of aloneness within the seemingly hostile reality of the physical dimension.

In actuality, there is no separation through individuation. The ego's erroneous belief that it is separate from everything else and therefore, through logic, must be in competition with everyone and everything else for the finite energy resources of the physical plane, holds considerable sway over a wide variety of our actions.

115 Burrow JW. (Ed.) *The Origin of Species by Means of Natural Selection or the Preservation of Favoured Races in the Struggle for Life*. Charles Darwin. London: Penguin Books; 1968.

116 Roberts J. *The Afterdeath Journal of an American Philosopher: The World View of William James*. Englewood Cliffs, NJ: Prentice-Hall, Inc.; 1978. p. 90.

117 Allport GW & Odbert HS. Attitudes. In Murchison CM. (Ed.), *Handbook of Social Psychology*. Clark University Press; 1935.

Chapter 11

118 The natural power of Attraction, lately interpreted as the "Law of Attraction," has its foot set more on the rung of the natural principles in terms of "truth" than does the natural power of Divine Love. It, like the natural principles, relates more to the "how" of physical creation than Divine Love, which is closer to the "why" of physical reality.

119 Interestingly, we can consider the construct of "time" as our psyche's translation of the truth that *Energy* is always in motion, constantly transforming itself – always disassembling and assembling itself into *con*ceivable and *per*ceivable patterns. In order for us to perceive this truth of *Energy Transformation* (see the natural principles in *Chapter 3*) being played out in our physical dimension, we have constructed the spectacles of linear time.

120 For a discourse on the variety of ways of knowing see, Clarke C. *Ways of Knowing: Science and Mysticism Today.* Exeter: Imprint Academic; 2005.

Chapter 12

121 Ennis M. (1995). As Elias, session 45. Available from: http://www.eliasforum.org/transcripts. © Mary Ennis.

122 The primary male sex hormone (also produced by females, who are more sensitive to it) that affects sexual drive.

123 The *Ten things about beliefs you won't believe* section is a fusion of information on beliefs attributable to many channeled literature sources, not least, The Seth Material (Jane Roberts); Elias Transcripts (Mary Ennis); Abraham-Hicks archives (Esther and Jerry Hicks); Bashar through Darryl Anka; and Omni through John L Payne.

124 Ennis M. (2003). As Elias, session 1398. Available from: http://www.eliasforum.org/transcripts. © Mary Ennis.

Chapter 13

125 From Lloyd Fell's *Mind and Love: The Human Experience.* Biosong: Lulu.com.; 2010. p. 132.

126 We often refer to such feelings as a "premonition" or evidence of "precognition." We explore these notions further in *Book II* of *It's About You!*

127 Separating elements in order to define more clearly (reductionism) is our collective psyche's (mis)translation of the primary drive of Consciousness to individuate. This urge to separate drives certain scientific endeavors to distraction in their quest for the indivisible.

128 For those of us with a preference for the Crown chakra information-processing route, interpretations vary from automatic translation into an emotion, to an instinctive translation into a thought process.

Chapter 14

129 Ekman P. (Ed.) *Emotional Awareness: Overcoming the Obstacles to Psychological Balance and Compassion.* New York: Times Books; 2008. p. 13.

130 Miller GA. The magic number seven, plus or minus two: Some limits on our capacity for processing information. *Psychological Review.* 1956; 63:81-97.

131 We currently believe this analysis to mean comparisons with past events. Seth informs us that our beliefs restrict this analysis, which can include similar events from other dimensions of our existence (for example, other lifetimes) as well as future probable events from our current lifetime's future! More on this in *Book II*.

132 Interestingly, we tend to lose capacity in our short-term memory with age. Perhaps by way of compensation, many of us improve our ability to recognize and process feelings with age – a sign of a less paranoid ego?

Chapter 15

133 Ekman, P. (Ed.) *Emotional Awareness: Overcoming the Obstacles to Psychological Balance and Compassion.* New York: Times Books; 2008. p. 33.

134 Lakoff G & Johnson M. *Metaphors We Live By.* Chicago: University of Chicago Press; 1980.

135 Fell L. *Mind and Love: The Human Experience.* Biosong: Lulu.com.; 2010. p. 93.

136 See, *New Scientist,* Vol. 130 (1991), p. 49.

137 Sheldrake R. *A New Science of Life: The Hypothesis of Formative Causation.* London: Icon Books Ltd.; 2009.

138 Roberts J. *The Early Sessions: Book 3 of The Seth Material.* Manhasset, NY: New Awareness Network Inc.; 1998. p. 220.

Chapter 16

139 Roberts J. *The Nature of Personal Reality: A Seth Book.* Englewood Cliffs, NJ: Prentice-Hall Inc.; 1974. p. 153.

140 Ennis M. (1998). As Elias, session 331. Available from: http://www.eliasforum.org/transcripts. © Mary Ennis.

141 Roberts J. *The Early Sessions: Book 2 of The Seth Material.* Manhasset, NY: New Awareness Network Inc.; 1997. p. 276.

142 Roberts J. *The Early Sessions: Book 3 of The Seth Material.* Manhasset, NY: New Awareness Network Inc.; 1998. p. 270.

143 Hicks E & J. *Manifest Your Desires: 365 Ways to Make Your Dreams a Reality.* Carlsbad, CA: Hay House, Inc.; 2008. #79.

Chapter 17

144 Ennis M. (1998). As Elias, session 275. Available from: http://www.eliasforum.org/transcripts. © Mary Ennis.

145 Ennis M. (2002). Ibid, session 997.

146 Moorjani A. *Dying to be Me: My Journey from Cancer, to Near Death to True Healing.* Carlsbad, CA: Hay House, Inc.; 2012. p. 137.

147 Payne JL. *Omni Reveals the Four Principles of Creation.* Forres,

Scotland: Findhorn Press; 2001. p. 23.

148 See, Roberts J. *The Nature of the Psyche: Its Human Expression.* Englewood Cliffs, NJ: Prentice-Hall Inc.; 1979. p. 65-69.

149 Roberts J. Ibid. p. 92.

150 Extract from Abraham-Hicks AB_CD 20, #20 "Self Appreciation." © Jerry and Esther Hicks, Abraham-Hicks.com.

151 Moorjani A. Ibid. p. 138.

152 Payne JL. Ibid. p. 70.

153 Payne JL. Ibid. p. 96.

154 Roberts J. Ibid. p. 72.

Chapter 18

155 Ennis M. (1996). As Elias, session 66. Available from: http://www.eliasforum.org/transcripts. © Mary Ennis.

156 Moorjani A. *Dying to be Me: My Journey from Cancer, to Near Death to True Healing.* Carlsbad, CA: Hay House, Inc.; 2012. p. 108.

157 For more on Kris go to http://www.krischronicles.com.

158 Ennis M. (1997). Ibid, session 253.

159 Helfrich J. *The Way of Spirit.* In press. 2012.

160 Extract from Gilbert P. *The Compassionate Mind.* London: Constable & Robinson Ltd.; 2010. p. xiii. By kind permission of Constable & Robinson Ltd.

Epilogue

161 Payne JL. *Omni Reveals the Four Principles of Creation.* Forres, Scotland: Findhorn Press; 2001. p. 70.

BIBLIOGRAPHY

Preface

Roberts J. *Seth Speaks: The Eternal Validity of the Soul.* Englewood Cliffs, NJ: Prentice-Hall Inc.; 1972. p. ix. Reprinted with permission of New World Library, Novato, CA. (www.newworldlibrary.com).

Introduction

Goswami A, Reed RE, & Goswami, M. *The Self-Aware Universe: How Consciousness Creates the Material World.* New York: Tarcher/Putnam; 1993. p. 215.

James W. *The Varieties of Religious Experience: A Study in Human Nature.* New York: Mentor Edition; 1902/1958. p. 298.

LeShan L. *A New Science of the Paranormal: The Promise of Psychical Research.* Wheaton, IL: Quest Books; 2009.

Roberts J. *The Afterdeath Journal of an American Philosopher: The World View of William James.* Englewood Cliffs, NJ: Prentice-Hall, Inc.; 1978. p. 113.

Chapter 1

Hicks E & J. Abraham, through Esther Hicks. Audio recording of a workshop at San Antonio, TX; April 21, 2001. © Jerry and Esther Hicks, Abraham-Hicks.com.

Maturana HR & Varela FJ. *Autopoiesis and Cognition: The Realization of the Living.* Dordrecht, Holland: D. Reidel Publishing Co.; 1980.

Roberts J. *A Seth Book: The Unknown Reality: Vol.1.* New York: Prentice Hall; 1977. p. 72.

Roberts J. *The Nature of the Psyche: Its Human Expression.* Englewood Cliffs, NJ: Prentice-Hall, Inc.; 1979. p. 143.

Chapter 2

Lipton B. *The Biology of Belief.* Santa Rosa, CA: Mountain of Love/Elite Books; 2005. p. 26-7.

Roberts J. *The Early Sessions: Book 3 of the Seth Material.* Manhasset, NY: New Awareness Network Inc.; 1998. p. 333.

Roberts J. *The Nature of Personal Reality: A Seth Book.* Englewood Cliffs, NJ: Prentice-Hall Inc.; 1974. p. 24.

Chapter 3

Dahl LM. *Ten Thousand Whispers: A Guide to Conscious Creation.* Eugene, OR: The Woodbridge Group; 1995. p. 24.

Eddington A. *The Nature of the Physical World.* London: Dent; 1928. p. 68.

Grof S. M.D., Ph.D. *When the Impossible Happens: Adventures in Non-Ordinary Realities.* Sounds True, Inc., 2006.

Payne JL. *Omni Reveals the Four Principles of Creation.* Forres, Scotland: Findhorn Press; 2001.

Roberts J. *The Early Sessions: Book 2 of The Seth Material.* Manhasset, NY: New Awareness Network Inc.; 1997. p. 14.

Roberts J. Ibid. p. 71.

Roberts J. *The Seth Material.* New York: Bantam Books. 1970.

Chapter 4

Byrne R. *The Secret.* New York: Simon & Schuster Ltd.; 2006.

Bruce A. *Beyond the Secret.* New York: The Disinformation Company Ltd.; 2007.

Collins English Dictionary. Definition of the term "nature" (1). Glasgow: HarperCollins; 2003.

Hicks E & J. *A New Beginning II.* San Antonio: Abraham-Hicks Publications; 1996. p. 103. © Jerry and Esther Hicks, Abraham-Hicks.com.

Payne JL. As Omni in, *Omni Reveals the Four Principles of Creation.* Forres, Scotland: Findhorn Press; 2001. p. 20.

Payne JL. Ibid. p. 20.

Roberts J. *The Nature of Personal Reality: A Seth Book.* Englewood Cliffs, NJ: Prentice-Hall Inc. 1974. p. 53.

Roberts J. *The Nature of the Psyche: Its Human Expression.* Englewood Cliffs, NJ: Prentice-Hall, Inc.; 1979. p. 216.

Roberts J. *The Early Sessions: Book 2 of The Seth Material.* Manhasset, NY: New Awareness Network Inc.; 1997. p. 242.

Roberts J. *The Early Sessions: Book 4 of The Seth Material.* Manhasset, NY: New Awareness Network Inc.; 1998. p. 331.

Chapter 5

Ennis M. (1996). As Elias, session 67. Available from: http://www.eliasforum.org/transcripts.© Mary Ennis.

Ennis M. (1995). Ibid, session 59.

Ennis M. (1997). Ibid, session 185.

Roberts J. *The Unknown Reality: Volume II. A Seth Book.* New York: Prentice Hall Press; 1979. p. 562.

Chapter 6

Cohen A. *Your Best Friend and Your Worst Enemy.* E-mail inclusion from *EnlightenNext Presents Andrew Cohen's Quote of the Week.* March 23, 2011.

Pinker S. *The Blank Slate: The Modern Denial of Human Nature.* New York: Penguin Books; 2002.

Roberts J. *The Early Sessions: Book 4 of The Seth Material.* Manhasset, NY: New Awareness Network Inc.; 1998. p. 227.

Roberts J. *The Early Sessions: Book 3 of The Seth Material.* Manhasset, NY: New Awareness Network Inc.; 1998b. p. 282.

Chapter 8

Anastassiou CA, Perin R, Markram H & Koch C. (2010). *Ephaptic coupling of cortical neurons.* Article in Nature Neuroscience Advance Online Publication. Published online January 16, 2011; doi:10.1038/nn.2727

Hicks E & J. *Manifest Your Desires: 365 Ways to Make Your Dreams a Reality.* Carlsbad, CA: Hay House, Inc.; 2008. #43.

Hicks E & J. Abraham. Audio recording of a workshop in San Antonio, TX. April 21, 2001. © Jerry and Esther Hicks, Abraham-Hicks.com.

Merrick R. *Interference: The Grand Scientific Musical Theory.* Fairview, TX: Self-Published; 2009. ISBN: 978-0-615-20599-1.

Merrick R. *Harmonically Guided Evolution: The Universal Pattern of Life.* Article in Caduceus, Issue 79, Summer, 2010. p. 15.

Walker EH. *The Physics of Consciousness: The Quantum Mind and the Meaning of Life.* New York: Basic Books; 2000.

Chapter 9

Judith A. *Eastern Body Western Mind.* New York: Celestial Arts, Random House Inc.; 2004.

Chapter 10

Allport GW & Odbert HS. Attitudes. In Murchison CM. (Ed.), *Handbook of Social Psychology.* Clark University Press; 1935.

Burrow JW. (Ed.) *The Origin of Species by Means of Natural Selection or the Preservation of Favoured Races in the Struggle for Life.* Charles Darwin. London: Penguin Books; 1968.

Malthus TR. *An Essay on the Principle of Population.* London: J. Johnson; 1798.

Roberts J. *The Afterdeath Journal of an American Philosopher: The World View of William James.* Englewood Cliffs, NJ: Prentice-Hall, Inc.; 1978. p. 90.

Stibal V. *Theta Healing*™. London: Hay House UK Ltd.; 2010. p. 67.

Chapter 12

Ennis M. (1995). As Elias, session 45. Available from: http://www.eliasforum.org/transcripts. © Mary Ennis.

Ennis M. (2003). Ibid, session 1398.

Chapter 13

Fell L. *Mind and Love: The Human Experience.* Biosong: Lulu.com.; 2010. p. 132.

Hicks E & J. *Ask and It Is Given: Learning to Manifest Your Desires.* Carlsbad, CA: Hay House, Inc.; 2004. p. 114.

Chapter 14

Ekman P. (Ed.) *Emotional Awareness: Overcoming the Obstacles to Psychological Balance and Compassion.* New York: Times Books; 2008. p. 13.

Miller GA. The magic number seven, plus or minus two: Some limits on our capacity for processing information. *Psychological Review.* 1956; 63:81-97.

Chapter 15

Darwin C. *The Expression of the Emotions in Man and Animals.* (Ekman P. Ed., 1999). London: Fontana Press; 1872.

Ekman, P. (Ed.) *Emotional Awareness: Overcoming the Obstacles to Psychological Balance and Compassion.* New York: Times Books; 2008. p. 33.

Fell L. *Mind and Love: The Human Experience.* Biosong: Lulu.com.; 2010. p. 93.

Lakoff G & Johnson M. *Metaphors We Live By.* Chicago: University of Chicago Press; 1980.

Roberts J. *The Early Sessions: Book 3 of The Seth Material.* Manhasset, NY: New Awareness Network Inc.; 1998. p. 220.

Sheldrake R. *A New Science of Life: The Hypothesis of Formative Causation.* London: Icon Books Ltd.; 2009.

Chapter 16

Ennis M. (1998). As Elias, session 331. Available from: http://www.eliasforum.org/transcripts. © Mary Ennis.

Hicks E & J. *Manifest Your Desires: 365 Ways to Make Your Dreams a Reality.* Carlsbad, CA: Hay House, Inc.; 2008. #79.

Roberts J. *The Nature of Personal Reality: A Seth Book.* Englewood Cliffs, NJ: Prentice-Hall Inc.; 1974. p. 153.

Roberts J. *The Early Sessions: Book 2 of The Seth Material.* Manhasset, NY: New Awareness Network Inc.; 1997. p. 276.

Roberts J. *The Early Sessions: Book 3 of The Seth Material.* Manhasset, NY: New Awareness Network Inc.; 1998. p. 270.

Chapter 17

Ennis M. (1998). As Elias, session 275. Available from: http://www.eliasforum.org/transcripts. © Mary Ennis.

Ennis M. (2002). Ibid, session 997.

Fromm, E. *The Art of Loving.* New York: HarperCollins Publishers Inc.; 1956.

Moorjani A. *Dying to be Me: My Journey from Cancer, to Near Death to True Healing.* Carlsbad, CA: Hay House, Inc.; 2012. p. 137.

Moorjani A. Ibid, p. 138.

Payne JL. *Omni Reveals the Four Principles of Creation.* Forres, Scotland: Findhorn Press; 2001. p. 23.

Payne JL. Ibid, p. 70.

Payne JL. Ibid, p. 96.

Roberts J. *The Nature of the Psyche: Its Human Expression.* Englewood Cliffs, NJ: Prentice-Hall, Inc.; 1979. p. 92.

Roberts J. Ibid, p. 72.

Chapter 18

Ennis M. (1996). As Elias, session 66. Available from: http://www.eliasforum.org/transcripts. © Mary Ennis.

Ennis M. (1997). Ibid, session 253.

Gilbert P. *The Compassionate Mind.* London: Constable & Robinson Ltd.; 2010. p. xiii.

Helfrich J. *The Way of Spirit.* In press. 2012.

Moorjani A. *Dying to be Me: My Journey from Cancer, to Near Death to True Healing.* Carlsbad, CA: Hay House, Inc.; 2012. p. 108.

Payne JL. *Omni Reveals the Four Principles of Creation.* Forres,

Scotland: Findhorn Press; 2001. p. 23.

Epilogue

Ennis M. (1997). As Elias, session 165. Available from: http://www.eliasforum.org/transcripts. © Mary Ennis.

Payne JL. *Omni Reveals the Four Principles of Creation.* Forres, Scotland: Findhorn Press; 2001. p. 70.

Endnotes

Alden T. *Science Investigates the Human Aura.* 2001. Online report available at http://www.technosophy.com/humanaura.htm (Accessed October 15, 2011).

Becker RO & Selden G. *The Body Electric: Electromagnetism and the Foundation of Life.* New York: HarperCollins; 1998.

Cameron T & Fiorda T. *A Book of Insight: Wisdom from the Other Side.* British Columbia: Stone Circle Publishing; 2008. p. 27. www.abookofinsight.com.

Church D. *The Genie in Your Genes.* Santa Rosa, CA: Elite Books; 2007.

Clarke C. *Ways of Knowing: Science and Mysticism Today.* Exeter: Imprint Academic; 2005.

Descartes R. (29 January 1640, AT III:19-20, CSMK 143) See Stanford Encyclopedia of Philosophy. http://plato.stanfo rd.edu/entries/pineal-gland (Accessed September 15, 2010).

Dale C. *The Subtle Body: An Encyclopedia of Your Energetic Anatomy.* Boulder, CO: Sounds True, Inc.; 2009.

Friedman N. *Bridging Science and Spirit: Common Elements In David Bohm's Physics, The Perennial Philosophy and Seth.* St.Louis: Living Lake Books; 1990.

Hastings A. *With the Tongues of Men and Angels: A Study of Channeling.* Orlando, FL.: Holt, Rinehart, and Winston; 1991.

Helfrich P. The channeling phenomenon: A multidimensional assessment. *Journal of Integral Theory and Practice.* 2009;4(3): p. 141-161.

Klimo J. *Channeling: Investigations on Receiving Information from Paranormal Sources*. Berkeley, CA: North Atlantic Books; 1998.

Lipton BH & Bhaerman S. *Spontaneous Evolution*. London: Hay House UK Ltd.; 2011.

McTaggart L. *The Field*. London: HarperCollinsPublishers Ltd.; 2001.

Moorjani A. *Dying to be Me: My Journey from Cancer, to Near Death to True Healing*. Carlsbad, CA: Hay House, Inc.; 2012.

Reber A. *Dictionary of Psychology*. London: Penguin Books; 1985.

Roberts J. *The Nature of Personal Reality: A Seth Book*. Englewood Cliffs, NJ: Prentice-Hall, Inc.; 1974. p. 153-4.

Roberts J. *Psychic Politics: An Aspect Psychology Book*. Englewood Cliffs, NJ: Prentice-Hall, Inc.; 1976. p. 18-19.

Roberts J. *The Nature of the Psyche: Its Human Expression*. Englewood Cliffs, NJ: Prentice-Hall Inc.; 1979. p. 65-69.

Roberts J. *Dreams, "Evolution" and Value Fulfillment, Volumes I & II*. New York: Prentice Hall Press; 1986.

Roberts J. *The Early Sessions: Book 1 of the Seth Material*. Manhasset, NY: New Awareness Network Inc.; 1997.

Roberts J. *The Early Sessions: Book 4 of the Seth Material*. Manhasset, NY: New Awareness Network Inc.; 1998. p. 92.

Oschman JL. *Energy Medicine: The Scientific Basis*. London: Harcourt Publishers Ltd.; 2000.

Ozaniec N. *Chakras for Beginners*. London: Hodder & Stoughton Educational; 1999.

Pert C. *Molecules of Emotion: The Science Behind Mind-Body Medicine*. London: Simon & Schuster; 1999.

Tate D. *The Shift: A Time of Change*. Victoria, B.C.: Canada Trafford Publishing; 2003.

Taylor S. *The Fall: The Insanity of The Ego in Human History and The Dawning of A New Era*. Winchester: O-Books; 2005.

Tolle E. *The Power of Now: A Guide to Spiritual Enlightenment*. Novato, CA: New World Library; 1999.

Wilber K, Patten T, Leonard A & Morelli M. *Integral Life Practice:*

A 21st Century Blueprint for Physical Health, Emotional Balance, Mental Clarity and Spiritual Awakening. Boston & London: Integral Books; 2008.

Willis WW & Sahtouris E. *Biology Revisioned.* Berkeley, CA: North Atlantic Books; 1998.

Witt PN & Rovner JS. (Eds.) *Spider Communication: Mechanisms and Ecological Significance.* Princeton University Press; 1982.

GLOSSARY OF TERMS

Many philosophers are aware that in order for us to understand better the other dimensions of reality that play a crucial part in our existence, a new lexicon is required. A new language must be developed with a vocabulary that encompasses terms that describe concepts and phenomenon that as yet only metaphors can give a hint as to their nature. This Glossary begins this development; it consists of terms we need to come to terms with! Italicized terms within definitions indicate that they are themselves contained within the Glossary.

2075 – This is the approximate date suggested by Seth for the completion of our collective *shift in consciousness*.

Action – Action is a property of existence. It is "basically electrical" in nature and a by-product and part of all realities. It arises from the vitality of *Consciousness* and is therefore a property of *Divine Love*. We interpret action as "movement" in the physical plane. Science is yet to explore the concept of electrical action beyond its obvious physical manifestations.

All That Is – A metaphysical term that often appears in the literature that approximates to the religious concept "God." It means to convey an absolute guiding influence steering all manifestations in all dimensions of existence. See *Consciousness*.

Akashic Records – A term from Hindu philosophy describing the "Mind of God" – a metaphorical "library" which contains the records of all of God's actions and experiences in all its dimensions of existence. You might conceptualize it as the vastly extending rooms, buildings and grounds of your subconscious library within the *Subconscious Area within Consciousness*. Metaphysical literature suggests that this store of knowledge is accessible through *Astral Projection* or other *altered states of consciousness.*

Altered states of consciousness – These are mental experiences that relate to accessing subconscious information and knowledge from various *Areas within Consciousness*, particularly the *Subjective Area* and the *Transitional Area*. *Channeling, Hypnosis, Astral Projection,* and *dreaming* are examples of altered states.

Areas within Consciousness – The term used by the author to distinguish between the various dimensions in which *Consciousness* expresses Itself. They are comparable with Seth's *"Frameworks of Consciousness"* or Elias's "Regional Areas." See Chapter 1 and Say That Again (5).

Artificial guilt – Artificial guilt stems from the transgression of laws and ethical codes constructed as part of a particular *belief system.* For example, feeling guilty about performing a sexual act because you believe it to be sinful can produce artificial guilt. See Chapter 4 and *natural guilt.*

Aspect Psychology – A theoretical model of the *psyche* devised by Jane Roberts to aid our understanding of the psychological concepts put forward by the channeled entity called Seth.

Astral Body – Also referred to as the *"Subtle Body,"* a non-physical body "form" that loosely resembles the physical form in order to combat disorientation. It allows you to "travel" within other dimensions of Consciousness. Your *Dream Body* is a form of Astral Body.

Astral Projection – Astral Projection is an altered state of consciousness that utilizes your *Astral Body.*

Beliefs – A belief is a *thought* or collection of synonymous thoughts that incorporates an energy potential capable of influencing your actions.

Belief Systems – The various and many beliefs organized by individuals and groups into core topics that dominate our thinking. These systems are organic in nature, constantly overlapping and interacting with each other.

Bisexuality – *Sexuality* and gender are features of our physical expression. Our Essence selves are, from our physical point of view, bisexual, in that they encompass both energy expressions. Expressing the characteristics of the male and female genders in the physical environment is part of the learning process for your *Essence self.*

Body-consciousness – Your body-consciousness is an electromagnetic "layer" to your physical self that works within the *subconscious area* of your *Mind*. It maintains all of the processing systems of your *outer self*. It not only manages your physical body's functions along with your electrical body's functions; but also initiates the transfer of information from the *electric field* (*Subjective Area within Consciousness*) to the physical field (*Objective Area within Consciousness*).

Chakra – A spinning vortex of energy that processes *Source energy* as it moves from the *Subjective Area within Consciousness* into and through the physical body. Metaphysical literature confirms the mapping by Eastern traditions of **some** of these "Energy Centers" – seven such vortices aligning with the spinal column. There are others linked to the physical form. Elias describes the formation of an eighth chakra, between the Throat and Heart that will augment energy transfer during and after the *Shift*. See Chapter 9.

Channeling – One of a variety of *altered states of consciousness* used to access knowledge from the *Subjective Area within Consciousness*. See the Introduction.

Channeled guides – A term used to refer to the numerous Entities, Essences, "probable selves" and personalities that communicate with the physical realm through *channeling*.

Collective unconscious – A term coined by Carl Gustav Jung to suggest that our *Mind* contains not just mental activity personal to us, but also impersonal mental activity inherited from the collective mind of humanity. See Chapter 7.

Consciousness/consciousness – Consciousness, with a capital

"C," modifies the definition of the concept traditionally referred to as God. Consciousness with a small "c" means to convey an individuated expression of Consciousness, as in *"human consciousness."* Refer to the Introduction and Say That Again (1).

Consciousness Units, CUs – The smallest individuated "portions" of *Consciousness*. See Chapter 1 and Say That Again (6).

Conscious-mind – The hyphenated term used by the author to differentiate the chosen mind made conscious by the ego from the collection of minds within the *Mind* available to it in the *Subconscious Area*. The hyphen allows for the word "mind" to be used as a collective noun. See Say That Again (14) and *Mind*.

Coordinate Points – These are mentioned in The *Seth Material* as points where *Source energy* from the *Subjective Area within Consciousness* "enters" the physical plane. Theoretically, these coordinate points facilitate the conversion of *Electromagnetic Energy Units* into physical matter via *Quantum Fields*. We can think of *Chakras* as personal coordinate points.

Dis-ease – A term coined by Seth to infer that illness is a condition created by your *inner self* in cooperation with your *body-consciousness* to indicate that the natural (ease of) flow of energy through your physiology has become impeded.

Desire – A desire emanates from your inner self's guidance on your expression of *intent*. It originates as a pure feeling uncorrupted by your *belief systems*. See *Want*.

Divine Love – The term given to the all-pervasive force that describes the vitality of Consciousness. *"Value Fulfillment"* is the term preferred by Seth. See Chapter 4, Say That Again (9), and Chapter 17.

Dream-Art Science – This is a term coined by Seth to describe a future practice that integrates both inner and *outer senses* as well as the ego-self's intellectual faculties in our pursuit of knowledge. He suggests three exemplars of this practice:

Dream-art scientist – a scientist with a less specified, broader range of study that includes dream explorations

True mental physicist – a physicist that primarily uses his mind rather than instruments to identify with the "functions" of the universe

Complete physician – a healer specializing in bringing to light a person's *intent* and *purpose*, and reinforcing their spiritual strength.

Dream Body – a form of *Astral Body*. According to Seth, there are three forms of Dream Bodies.

Dreaming – An *altered state of consciousness*.

Duplicity – A belief system (see Chapter 12) that has grown from our thoughts on the nature of duality or "dualism" and the differences expressed in the physical realm. Difference and contrast occur in the physical realm in order that we can make choices on what we prefer to create. Duplicity involves then making a judgment on the choices made – right/wrong, good/bad – etcetera. This judgmental aspect leads to conflict, both within our minds, and in the physical environment. Its strength within our *belief systems* stems from a lack of trust in our outer selves and our ability to make beneficial choices. Duplicity is explored in Book II of *It's About You!*

Ego/Ego-self – The ego or ego-self is a psychological structure within the *outer self* for interpreting what you perceive in the physical field. The ego-self incorporates self-reflection in the process of choosing a *reality* from the myriad *probable realities* available to it in the *Subjective Area within Consciousness*. See Chapter 6 and Say That Again (13).

Electric field – The electric field is a term used to encompass a variety of electromagnetic energy fields based in the dimension of existence "closest" to the physical dimension. See Chapter 8.

Electromagnetic Energy Units, EEs – Units of energy, formed from CUs (see *Consciousness Units*), within the *electric field* that are "slowing" their *vibrational frequency* in preparation for entry into the physical dimension's electromagnetic spectrum. See Chapter 1 and Say That Again (6).

Emotional climate – A metaphor to describe the overall state of your personality's *mood*. See, *Tonal frequency*.

Emotional-signal – The special kind of feeling that signals the onset of an emotion. See Chapter 13 and *Feelings*.

Emotions – Emotions are independent configurations of *energy* that exist within the *Subjective Area within Consciousness* and express their energy in the physical realm through the actions of certain animals. In humans they also convey a communication to the *conscious-mind* regarding impediments within the psychological structure (invariably *beliefs*) that affect the natural flow of *Source energy* through the body. See Chapter 15 and Say That Again (18).

Energy – We can conceive of Energy (with a capital "E") as being the substance of *Consciousness*. This Energy (*Source Energy*) needs to "slow" its *vibrational frequency* if it is to enter the physical dimension to be expressed as matter. *Consciousness Units* and *Electromagnetic Energy Units* perform this task. The energy (small "e") of the physical plane, as described by Einstein in his famous equation $E = mc^2$, represents Source Energy slowed to within the electromagnetic spectrum of light.

Entity – Seth's preferred term for *Essence*.

Entity/Essence names – Several metaphysical guides suggest that the *Identity* of our Entity or Essence self has a name that can be ascertained through meditation or entering an altered state of consciousness. Seth would call Jane and Rob Butts by their Entity names – Rubert and Joseph respectively.

Energy centers – The term used by Elias to describe points of *Source Energy* transfer in relation to the human body. See *Chakra*.

Essence – The most popular term used in metaphysical literature for the overall structure of the Self and its functions. See Chapter 2.

Essence self – The term used by the author to refer to the non-physical aspects of the Self.

Evolution – Evolution refers to the constant state of change that exists in all dimensions of *Consciousness*. This change is driven by the desire of Consciousness to know Itself through experience. In order to do this, individuated portions of Itself (*CUs*) cooperate in forming more complex structures capable of creating experiences for themselves, thus adding to the overall experiences of Consciousness.

Expectation – An expectation is a compelling combination of various emotional energies. Desires become expectations as they attract to themselves these emotional energies. The exactness by which a desire becomes manifest through expectation depends upon the degree of conscious control exercised over the emotions involved. See Chapter 16 and Appendix IV.

Families of Consciousness – A metaphorical expression first appearing in the *Seth Material* to aid understanding of the varying expressions of *intent* within *human consciousness*. See *Genera of the intent of human consciousness*.

Families of intent – A phrase that refers to the *genera of the intent of human consciousness*.

Fear – Like *Love*, fear expresses itself through all forms of information transfer. It can come as *impulses* to act, or express itself through an *emotional-signal* leading to an *emotion*. This spectrum of expression indicates that fear is actually a state of being rather than a feeling or emotion. See Chapter 18 and Appendix IV.

Feelings – Feelings are independent electromagnetic energy forms – **distinct from emotions** – that alert the *conscious-mind* to information or knowledge about to transfer **directly** from the *inner self*. The transfer may seem instantaneous, or when the feeling is of the *emotional-signal* variety (which precedes emotional energy about to transfer), a momentary delay occurs for purposes of conscious acknowledgement. We are yet to understand the significance of this delay or exploit its purpose. See Chapter 13 and Say That Again (17).

Feeling-tone – A term coined by Seth that refers to the *vibrational frequency* of all expressions of Consciousness, including your Self. See Chapter 2 and Chapter 13.

Focus Personality – The expression used by Jane Roberts in her *Aspect Psychology* work to describe the psychological structures of an individual attuned to the physical world. See *Outer self*.

Frameworks of Consciousness – Seth's term for the numerous levels, layers or dimensions of *Consciousness*. See *Areas within Consciousness*.

Future – Probable energy configurations yet to manifest in the physical realm.

Garden of Beliefs – The Garden of Beliefs is a metaphor introduced by the author to describe the subconscious "place" within your *Mind* where *thoughts, beliefs* and *emotions* combine to produce your *emotional climate* or *tonal frequency.*

Genera of the intent of human consciousness – According to a number of *channeled guides*, the expression of *intent* through *human consciousness* conforms to nine basic descriptive groups. These "psychic groupings" translate as specific activities (roles) and character traits adopted by an individual's *personality*. The most suitable generic terms for these genera of human intent are:

Teachers, Spiritualists, Innovators, Reformers, Exchangers, Artists, Healers, Imagers, and Nurturers. See Chapter 5 and Appendix III.

Gestalt – A German word to describe something we cannot understand completely by examining its parts. The combination of parts produces a unified whole, which has a "quality," a new identity, which is lost if we separate the parts out from one another.

Hate – Hate is not the opposite of *love*. The opposite of love is *fear*. Hate is a state devoid of love, brought about through an intense fear of separation. It is the fear of losing personal identity, of returning to the fold, of being "One again" with Consciousness. See Appendix IV.

Human consciousness – A complex, evolving expression of *Consciousness*.

Human love – An interpretation of the qualities of *Divine Love*. See Chapter 17.

Hypnosis – An altered state of consciousness and method to induce such a state. See *Altered states of consciousness*.

Identity – The unique "aware-ized" quality of any individualized expression of Consciousness. An Identity (note the capital "I") exists for the smallest indivisible unit of Consciousness – a Consciousness Unit (CU) – and for any cooperative creation formed from them. You, for example, are a complex identity *gestalt* formed from *CUs*. Your Self's overall Identity resides within your *Essence self*. This Identity has a *tone of intent*, a *vibrational signature* unique to your overall *Self*. Your *personality* constructs a *tonal frequency* which your *ego-self* imagines to be representative of its own identity (note the small "i"), unaware of the narrowness of this assumption. See Chapter 2.

Imagination – Your imagination is the mental playground of your ideas, *thoughts* and visualizations that formulate your *wants* and *desires*.

Impulses – Impulses are **direct** *instructional* prompts emanating from your *Essence self* for you to direct your physical actions in a certain way. They are specifically designed to bypass thought processing.

Individuation – The process by which *Consciousness* comes to know Itself. Not to be confused with the Jungian term describing the process that integrates the varying aspects of the *Mind* into a cohesive whole, thus attaining "self-realization." See Chapter 1 and Say That Again (4).

Inner self – Your inner self acts as an emissary to your *Essence*. It is that part of your *Essence self* that focuses upon looking after and assisting your *outer self* as it explores and experiences the physical world. See Chapter 2.

Inner senses – A set of senses that your *inner self* uses to obtain information from the *Subjective Area within Consciousness* pertinent to your overall Self and your outer self's expression in the physical domain. See Chapter 3.

Intellect – A mental faculty that your *ego-self* uses to discriminate between information it perceives as important to the Self and that which is unimportant. *Belief systems* often inhibit this faculty.

Intent – Intent is a directional force **within and part** of *Consciousness* powering learning and growth for It and *all* Its individuated forms of expression. See Chapter 1 and Say That Again (3).

Intention – An intention is not particularly concerned with your *intent*. It is more to do with your ego-self's concerns as to its immediate needs and wants.

Karma – From Hinduism and Buddhism, we can loosely describe karma as negative actions arising from "the *evolution* of all afflictive or disturbing *emotions*." Resolving these actions may involve more than one lifetime, or reincarnation. See *Reincarnation*.

Law of Attraction/LOA – The popular term used in the Mind/Body/Spirit fraternity that relates to the *natural power* of Attraction. A feature in the teachings of Abraham. See Chapter 4 and *Natural Powers*.

"laws of the inner universe" – Seth's expression, along with "natural laws," for the *natural principles*. See Chapter 3

Love – Love expresses itself in a vast number of ways. This is because it is constantly seeking expression, as it is the vitality of *Consciousness*, the lifeblood of existence. It can be an *impulse* to act, or express itself through an *emotional-signal* leading to an *emotion*. This spectrum of expression indicates that love is actually a state of being rather than a one particular translation of its being like *human love*. See *Divine Love* and *human love*, Chapter 17 and Appendix IV.

Mass event – Realities created "en masse" involving a large number of individuals. "Negative" mass events, such as disasters and epidemics, convey messages from the collective *psyche* to the collective consciousness of humanity on the nature of our collective *belief systems*.

Metaphysics – Metaphysics has meant many different things. Its meaning in relation to the term's use by the author is that it is an attempt to describe the nature of our existence and the realities we perceive as a whole.

Mind – A collective noun that describes a number of psychological constructs, not least a variety of minds within the Mind, each with their own characteristics and abilities. Your Mind is the portion of the *psyche*, situated within your *Essence*, most closely involved with your *inner self* in maintaining your physical existence. See Chapter 6 and Say That Again (14).

Mood – Your mood is a measure of the collective *tone* of the *emotional-signals* stored within your *Garden of Beliefs*. See *emotional climate*.

Natural Aggression – Natural aggression stems from natural *impulses* to do with the expression of *intent* through creative actions. Nature displays *natural aggression* through acts such as a flower bursting from its bud, a butterfly emerging from its cocoon, and any birth process where new life comes into the physical realm. Blocking the impulses of natural aggression can lead to inappropriate acts of *Violation*.

Natural Approach – A term that describes an emerging postmodern *worldview*, which integrates traditional spiritual practices for accessing knowledge from the *Subjective Area* *within Consciousness*, with the scientific rationale of the modern worldview that seeks to map and clarify the *Objective Area within Consciousness* through reason and logic.

Natural Grace – A term used by Seth to describe a state of joyful acquiescence to the natural power of *Divine Love*. All expressions of *Consciousness* come into existence reflecting this grace of being. Our egos' *belief systems* cause us to resist its influence, which our inner selves constantly attempt to remedy. Natural Grace cannot be taken from you and you can never "fall from Grace."

Natural guilt – Natural guilt results from transgressing the primary ethic implied by *Divine Love* of non-violation. The feeling of natural guilt is essentially a direct message from your *inner self* informing your *conscious-mind* that such a transgression has occurred. Heed the message by ceasing to act in this way – *for your own good,* as well as that of any other party that may be involved. See *Artificial guilt* and Chapter 4.

Natural hypnosis – A term used by Seth to describe the constantly occurring psychological process by which our conscious-minds acquiesce to suggestion. This is why a concentrated focus attained in a period of formal *hypnosis* suggesting a desired set of thoughts can be of benefit; the benefit's duration being reliant upon the strength of any countermanding beliefs held. (Think of planting the thoughts in your *garden of beliefs* in the hope that they don't become strangled by the growth of established beliefs.) Seth points out that as our beliefs are integral to the ego's structure; it is inevitable that natural hypnosis continually underpins your beliefs, as during the day it is your *ego* that is the constant source of suggestion. You can thus think of your *reality* as the result of your ego's hypnotizing spell.

Natural laws – An expression used by Seth to refer to his *"laws of the inner universe."* *"Natural principles"* is the author's preferred expression for these precepts that underpin physical existence. See *natural principles* and Chapter 3.

Natural powers – A term used by the author to distinguish between the two primal *natural principles* or "laws" highlighted by several metaphysical guides that influence the creation of our reality – *Divine Love* and *Attraction*. See Chapter 4 and Say That Again (9) and (10).

Natural principles – a set of principles by which *Consciousness* operates when expressing Itself through the medium of physicality. See Chapter 3 and Say That Again (7).

Natural time – Natural time refers to natural rhythms and cycles involved in the expression of *Consciousness* in the physical realm. We are easily able to discern these rhythms displayed in the natural world – seasonal cycles and physiological cycles, for example. Natural time accords with the progression of an *action* in respect of a myriad set of related probable actions occurring in the *Subjective Area within Consciousness* where linear *time* is of little consequence to that progression. In other words, the "timing" of an event in the physical domain involves many non-physical calculations. We squeeze our energies into linear time-confined channels rather than allow them to flow naturally through us in their own natural time. See the **Ten Principles for Conscious Living** at the end of Chapter 18.

Objective Area within Consciousness – The physical dimension of existence. See *Areas within Consciousness*.

Outer self – A term used by the author to refer to the three central psychological structures that constitute the part of the *Self* that is concerned with its expression in the physical dimension. The *ego/ego-self, conscious-mind* and *personality*. See Say That Again (12).

Outer senses – The five physical senses of sight, hearing, smell, taste and touch.

Past – Energy configurations that have passed through an expression in the physical domain.

Perception – Your perception is the vital instrument through which you create your *reality*. It incorporates and employs the sum total of all of the energies and functions that constitute your *Self*. These are the non-physically and physically oriented structures of your consciousness, along with the creational keys of your *dreams, thoughts, beliefs, feelings, emotions* and *impulses* your *Mind* entertains. In essence, your perception is how you view and interact with your Self, the physical world, and others that share the physical experience. It forms your awareness of the *Objective Area within Consciousness*, your *worldview*.

Personality – Your personality is an electrically encoded counterpart to your *ego-self*. From a linear time perspective, it "begins" life along with your ego. It has a constantly (both in physical time and outside of it) changing and evolving nature. Its "form" is electrical in quality, residing within the electrical dimension of *action*. Your personality maintains a unique *tonal frequency*. See Chapter 6 and Say That Again (14).

Personal intent – Personal intent is the potential you hold to fulfill your own spiritual ambitions within the pool of probabilities chosen for your current lifetime.

Physical realm/plane/dimension or reality – Conventional terms used to describe the *Objective Area within Consciousness*. Seth refers to this area as "Framework 1."

Practicing Idealist – Someone who seeks to make the world a lovelier place through expressing his or her ideals in the physical world. In doing so, they are fully cognizant of the vital ethical code of non-violation and aware that the end can never be justified by the means. See *Violation*.

Present – The moment point of now.

Principles – A principle is not a law in the way we conventionally understand the term. As Omni (John L. Payne) declares, "A principle tells of the nature of things, an action or a flowing of energy, more of a state of being." Therefore, principles do not govern you, *Consciousness* does not decide that you must adhere to them; they are **universal** principles that describe the nature of the universe and how things work.

Probable realities – This term relates to the pool of probable events that you have not brought into the physical domain for exploration. They do exist, however, in the *Subjective Area within Consciousness*, where your *Essence self* can explore them. Your *inner senses* allow your *outer self* the opportunity to access these probabilities.

Psyche – The psyche is probably **the** standout term that requires a radical rethink in defining. Seth says that it is impossible to define in words we currently use. The psyche is a non-physical expression of energy that, although it has form, that form can take on countless definitions depending on *how* you attempt to define it and *who* is attempting it! Seth does make it clear that one non-physical psychological form it should not be equated with in any definition is the *Mind*.

You have a **portion** of the psyche within your *Self* – which is your *Mind*. This portion of the psyche is your own inviolate personal "subjective area" within **the** *Subjective Area within Consciousness*. It is a "place" where your non-physical self resides.

As it is within the Subjective Area there are no boundaries such as space and *time*; and as it is a part of *Consciousness* Itself – the psyche creates you as you create it! It is an ever-changing "place" of experimentation.

Psycho-electric pattern – Seth used this term to describe the rudimentary configuration of energy that exists in the *electric field* prior to entering the human psychological system, where it is transformed into a thought.

Purpose – Your purpose is your own unique goal that you plan to attain in this lifetime whilst observing the *natural power* of *Divine Love*. It is a set of actions; a directional path of *intent* you desire to pursue for the expansion, growth and evolution of your own consciousness.

Quantum Fields – Quantum Theory postulates that Quantum Fields exist to explain the nature of subatomic particles and their actions. Metaphysical literature suggests such fields exist as an interfacing "area" between the *Objective Area* and the *Subjective Area within Consciousness*.

Rational Approach – The approach to acquiring knowledge that relies upon cognitive (thinking) processes. The approach champions the reason and logic of the *conscious-mind* above the inner intuitional abilities of the *Self*, or indeed, the *Natural Approach*.

Reality – There is not just one reality. Your *perception* of the physical world is *a* reality personal to your *Self*. There are therefore, at least as many realities as there are people. In actuality, there are as many realities as *Consciousness* has expressions of Itself. Mind-boggling as this appears, realities group together in dimensions of existence in accordance with their principles of expression. *Dreams*, for example are very real in dream-reality, appearing to be "not so real" in physical reality because they do not conform to the laws or principles of physics. There are "types" of reality – primary and secondary realities – that conform to certain truths – see *Truth*.

Reincarnation – Reincarnation, or "multiple lifetimes" is a topic that runs through most channeled literature. Your *Essence self* manifests an individualized portion of itself (*outer self*) frequently in the physical dimension. Each manifestation builds a new *personality* that returns to your *Essence* on physical death – expanding and evolving its consciousness. Traditional ideas on "*karma*" in relation to reincarnation are a distortion of its relevance to our Selves brought about by beliefs about "*time*" and "cause and effect."

Self, self – Self with a capital "S" signifies the entirety of the construct of your Self; a small "s" refers to a part of the Self.

Self-reflection – Self-reflection is an ability that marks an evolutionary stage of an expression of *Consciousness* in the physical realm. All physical objects, from sub-atomic particles to the elements that make up huge physical objects have a rudimentary self-awareness. This is because they are made of "aware-ized" energy that emanates from Consciousness. The freedom to "self-express" is an evolutionary step enjoyed by life forms; self-reflection is a further evolutionary step for physical matter as the life form now incorporates a psychological element – a *Mind* that facilitates this *action*. The ability to self-reflect allows for **conscious self-awareness**. See Chapter 1.

Seth Material – The collection of material authored by the "energy personality" known as Seth, and Jane Roberts – transcribed and edited by Rob Butts. Yale University's Sterling Memorial Library now houses the Seth Material.

Sexuality – According to Elias (Mary Ennis), sexuality and *emotions* are **the** two primary drives in the expression of *human consciousness* in the physical realm – See Chapters 12 and 17.

Shift – The most popular abbreviated term used in the Mind/Body/Spirit movement for the *shift in consciousness* – the evolutionary changes occurring in *human consciousness* during the late 20th Century and first half of the 21st Century. The term "shift" first appears in the Elias transcripts.

Shift in consciousness – See *Shift*.

Simultaneous time – An alternative metaphor to Seth's "spacious present" to explain the nine basic dimensions (derived from possible combinations of Past, Present and Future) involved in any "moment point" or "now."

Source, Source Energy – Source is the term used in conjunction with *All That Is* by Abraham (Esther Hicks) and several other channeled guides to refer to *Consciousness*. Source Energy is reference to the transformation of the Energy of Consciousness into physical expression.

Spacious present – A term used by Seth meant to encapsulate how Consciousness expresses Itself outside, as well as inside, the concept of time.

Spirituality – Spirituality is to do with our concern for our non-physical self's needs rather than our physical self's needs. Our egos have become unaware of our primacy as spiritual (non-physical) beings and that the physical realm is simply our spiritual Self's current focus of amusement. See Chapter 12.

Subconscious – The subconscious is an *Area within Consciousness*. *Your* subconscious is an area within your *Mind* that can provide you access to this Area within Consciousness. It is a way station or bridge between the Subjective and Objective Areas, a "place" where your *inner self* is able to communicate and interact with your *outer self*. Your *body-consciousness*, a feature within your subconscious area, controls your autonomic nervous system. See Chapters 2 and 7.

Subconscious Area within Consciousness – See *Subconscious*.

Subjective Area within Consciousness – The non-physical dimensions – see *Areas within Consciousness*.

Subtle body – A term widely used in metaphysics and Eastern philosophical traditions that equates with *Astral Body*. According to Seth, we have several "subtle bodies" or "dream bodies" for maneuvering our awareness in the *Subjective Area within Consciousness*.

Survival – Our interpretation of the quality or drive of Consciousness that maintains Its existence.

Thought – Thought is a mechanism used by your conscious-mind to translate and interpret information gathered by both your inner and outer senses. **A thought**, in its **purest** form, is a "psycho-electric pattern" that begins its existence in the *electric field*. This energy pattern then transforms into what you recognize as a thought when exposed to the psycho-logical and physical systems that form your *outer self*. See Chapter 8 and Say That Again (15).

Time – Time is a psychological construct that enables us to perceive the progression of *action* in the physical dimension.

Tissue Capsule – A term coined by Seth referring to the energy containment "skin" that encapsulates the energies that constitute your *Essence self*. See Chapter 3 and Figures 1 and 2.

Tonal frequency – Tonal frequency is an expression describing the combined frequencies of the thoughts, beliefs and emotional energies maintained by your *personality*. Because, psychologically, your *ego-self* closely mirrors your *personality*, it regards this combination of frequencies as representative of your outer self's *identity*. See *Identity*.

Tone – Tone is a *vibrational frequency* emitted by an expression of Consciousness. See "relative truths" in Chapter 11.

Transition – A term used in channeled literature to refer to the process we call "death." Transition is a process by which your personality transfers itself to Essence for continued existence. It is a process that usually begins well in advance of the physical body's chronological death in preparation for entry into the *Transitional Area within Consciousness*.

Transitional Area within Consciousness – An *Area within Consciousness* where your *Self* creates certain psychological structures in order that your *outer self* can operate within the physical realm. It is to this Area that your *ego-self* and *personality* come as they re-orientate and acclimatize to existence after the physical body has died. See Say That Again (5).

Truth – A truth you hold is a *belief* in which you have invested a lot of energy. There is only one absolute Truth – *Consciousness* and Its existence. All other truths are relative to it. See Chapter 11 and Say That Again (16).

Unconscious – A condition that occurs when the brain has stopped attending to the outer physical senses – as in a coma.

Value fulfillment – The term used by Seth to describe the primary *natural principle* driving physical existence. See *Divine Love*.

Vibrational frequency – A term synonymous with *vibrational* *signature.*

Vibrational signature – A vibrational signature is the primal *tone* of the *Identity* of an individuated expression of *Consciousness*. Your vibrational signature is the primal tone of your overall Self's Identity. This tonal quality of your existence transcends and includes the *tonal frequency* of your current lifetime's *personality*.

Violation – A violation is a deliberate act to end, harm or undermine the physical or psychological freedom of another expression of *Consciousness* in the physical realm. See Chapter 4 and *natural guilt*.

Want – A "want" may be the ego's interpretation of a desire (see *Desire*) for a particular experience; or more often than not, is a constructed need for an experience formulated by the *ego-self* in relation to certain beliefs on what is desirable.

Way of Spirit – An expression used by Rose (Joanne Helfrich) to describe an individual's path of *intent* and *purpose*.

Worldview – A worldview is the entire collection of an individual's or a society's beliefs and values held about the world and how we interact with it. You can regard worldviews as the frameworks on which we build our realities. Your own worldview is a unique interpretation of *reality*, a dynamic phenomenon that interacts and combines with other worldviews. See the Introduction, Say That Again (2) and *Perception*.

INDEX

2075
as approximate end date of
current shift in
consciousness, 32, 372

A
Abraham, 23, 24, 57, 60, 82,
159, 163, 178, 215–219, 235,
242, 247, 253, 261, 263, 264,
275, 277, 288, 290, 324, 335,
340, 343, 345, 350, 357, 381,
388
Action
act upon themselves, 256
action of repression, 257
electric field of action, 162,
241, 256, 257
action of non-acceptance, 259
self-generating, 256
Acceptance
acts of, 275
as a feeling, 322
defining a belief, 178
in relation to Divine Love,
265–268, 287, 294, 336
is about, 290
key to acceptance, 287
of a child, 271
of actions, 258
of all that is, 291
of our self, 195
of beliefs nullifies their

power, 202
of what is, 81, 270
Affection
continued acts of, 272
deep affection, 271/2
in relation to Divine Love,
272
in relation to Nurturers, 97,
319
Affirmations, 34
Aligning with, 95, 313, 318
All That Is – see
Consciousness
Allowance, 268
genuine expression of love,
273
in relation to Divine Love,
265, 270
of your Self, 303
Altered states, 14, 48, 199, 373
Amygdala, 238
Anger, 173, 191, 211, 216, 223,
228, 233, 234 – see *Appendix
IV,* 322, 330, 334, 335, 336,
337
in relation to anxiety, 251,
324
Anka, Darryl, 190, 223, 326
reality as a reflection, 86
Anxiety, 155, 216, 237, 247–
252, 259, 279, 296, 324, 325,
326, 327, 330, 333, 337, 340

using EFT with – see
Appendix II
Appreciation, 75, 80, 89, 92,
213, 235, 268, 270–272, 291,
293, 294, 303, 314, 318, 324,
336
as a quality of Divine Love,
265, 294
in relation to forgiveness,
329, 330
in relation to sadness, 338
of self, 275–277, 294
Areas within Consciousness,
46, 48, 133, 186, 305, 373, 379
objective area, 47–49, 55, 56,
63, 78, 115, 186, 238, 283, 374,
384, 385, 387, 389
subjective area, 47–54, 56–58,
67, 69, 100, 103, 119, 163, 186,
237, 238, 283, 288, 373–377,
381, 382, 384, 386, 387, 389
Aristotle, 162
Artificial guilt, 91, 323, 331,
373 – see Natural guilt
Artists, 74 - see Genera of
human intent
Astral Body, 73, 373, 389
Attitudes, 184, 202, 204, 271,
316
Attraction, 159, 265, 272, 273
climate of, 159, 243
Law of, 24, 80, 85, 159, 290, 381
Natural Power of, 24, 80,
84–87, 152, 159, 162, 187, 217,

260, 267, 272, 289, 297, 305,
333, 384
Aura, 159
auric field, 151
human, 151
Autonomic nervous system,
138, 238, 389
"autopoiesis", 43
"aware-ized", 40, 50, 51, 380,
388

B
Base information processing
route – see Chakra, base
Bashar, 86, 190, 223, 326
"basic laws of the inner
universe", 64
Becher, Johann J., 185
Beck, Aaron T., 160
Behavior, 18, 32, 75, 86, 92,
145, 167, 177, 285, 290, 321
complaining, 293
habitual, 20, 105, 228, 230,
231
in relation to beliefs, 34, 178,
190, 202
in relation to intent, 19, 20,
93, 94, 95, 105, 113, 146
reactive behaviors, 215, 228,
234
spontaneous, 67, 319
"being-ness", 69, 72–75, 93
Beliefs
in relation to perceiving,

176–184
in relation to thoughts, 150–164
in relation to truths, 186–191
ten things about your beliefs, 201
Belief Systems, 193–200
Belonging to (a genus or family of human intent), 94, 95, 98, 99, 101, 102, 105, 113, 145, 167, 312
Bio-electromagnetic energy centers, 166
Biologist, 43, 54, 206, 241
Bisexual
bisexuality, 374
in relation to identity of Essence, 273, 274
Black hole, 285, 286
"blank slate", 119, 120, 124
Body-consciousness, 138, 152–155, 161, 162, 164, 175, 177, 178, 206, 208, 209, 218, 219, 225, 228, 229, 249, 324, 336, 374, 375, 389
Body language – see Language
Bohm, David, 241
Boredom, 246
Brain, 14, 25, 127, 128, 130, 167, 208, 336
and neural cells, 152
cerebral cortex, 153
effect of oxytocin on, 279, 280
in relation to ephaptic

coupling, 153
function, 25, 30
in relation to consciousness, 27
in relation to emotions, 238, 242
in relation to mind, 127
in relation to thought, 157, 158, 208
unconscious, 136, 390
Bruce, Alexandra, 85
Buddha, 176
Buddhism, 171, 381
Buddhist, 160, 210, 221
Butterfly, 73, 83, 322, 382
Butts, Robert, 94, 377, 388
Byrne, Rhonda, 24

C
Cameron, Tilde, 24
Campus – see Subconscious
Capsule – see Tissue capsule
Caterpillar, 83
"causal field", 55, 56
Cause and effect, 47, 76, 240, 387
Cells, 54, 55, 57, 83, 143, 152, 153, 164, 168
cancerous, 83
cellular, 41, 54, 162, 164, 168
effect of emotions on, 239, 262
neural, 152
Chakra, 151, 166, 174, 374, 375

Base chakra, 170, 171, 209

Crown chakra, 167, 171, 175, 195

Solar plexus chakra, 166–173, 175, 196, 206, 209, 212, 214

Throat chakra, 168, 208, 209, 325

Channel, 14, 21, 22, 23, 181, 206, 242, 296, 317, 328

channeling, 23, 24, 33, 71, 105, 340, 374

channeled entity, character, 23, 284, 301

channeled guides, sources, 15, 22, 23, 32, 46, 60, 71, 80, 92, 94, 95, 104, 105, 186, 206, 210, 213, 235, 253, 259, 275, 290, 299, 300, 301, 312, 374, 379, 388

channeled information, material, 12, 16, 21, 22, 23, 66, 322, 339

channeled knowledge, 22, 24

channeled literature, teachings, 14, 16, 36, 38, 57, 62, 80, 85, 89, 96, 98, 103, 104, 118, 120, 136, 139, 186, 187, 205, 210, 221, 238, 252, 270, 283, 387, 390

Chemical, 218, 238, 241, 279

electro-chemical, 55, 152, 168

elements, 40

enzymes, 168

in relation to emotions, 257

signals, 152

Choice, 194, 200, 205, 212, 230, 265, 273, 277, 291, 376

conscious choice, 122

in relation to anger, 233, 234, 323, 330, 334, 335, 336

in relation to anxiety, fear, 250, 251, 324

in relation to beliefs, 190, 192, 204

in relation to emotions, 237, 252, 320

in relation to intent, 101–104, 114

in relation to joy, 335

in relation to sadness, 337, 338

in relation to the ego, 121, 122, 126

of action, 114, 192

of minds, 161

"Chunks" of information, 224, 227

Clairvoyant, 22, 78

Clapton, Eric, 74

Climate of attraction – see Attraction

Clinical hypnosis – see Hypnosis

Cognitive therapy, 160

cognitive behavior therapy (CBT), 160

cognitive psychology, 223

Cohen, Andrew, 125

Coincidence, 69, 104, 105
Collective Mind – see Mind
"collective unconscious", 135,
  145, 146, 374
Collins English Dictionary, 88
Color
as a relative truth, 187, 188
in relation to chakras, 166, 174
in relation to Essence, 60
  in relation to the genera of
  human intent, 100, 102–104,
  108–110, 112, 313
Compassion, 72, 73, 115, 163,
  291, 292, 294, 316, 324, 329,
  330
  as a quality of Divine Love,
  265, 268, 275
Competition, 45
  and Darwin, 181–183
Complete physician, 376
Computer analogy, 122, 129,
  130, 132, 133
Conceptual inner senses – see
  Inner senses
"conceptual sense", 69
Conscious-mind – see Mind
Consciousness, 17, 18, 25–30,
  32, 36, 40–42, 45–51, 53–59,
  64–79, 81–90, 93–115, 122,
  136, 142, 146, 151, 169, 170,
  174, 186–190, 194, 195, 205,
  208, 222, 238, 239, 255, 256,
  264, 265, 267, 269, 274, 275,
  279, 283, 295, 298, 303, 313,
  339, 341, 373
  a force that patterns energy, 29,
  66
  altered states of – see Altered
  states
  areas – see Areas within
  Consciousness
  as All That Is, 26, 28, 372
  as awareness of self, 40, 42,
  264, 267
  as God, 17, 27, 39, 44, 55
  as Source, 28
  as Source Energy, 44, 48, 66
  as Truth, 186–190, 270, 314
  breath of, 50
  capital 'C', small 'c', 25–29,
  187, 374
  "Consciousness Units (CUs)",
  49–51, 54–57, 100, 142, 375,
  377
  equivalence to Energy, 66, 377
  evolution of, 36, 39, 42, 46, 122,
  267–269, 299, 388
  expressions of, 18, 28, 36, 41,
  65, 81, 82, 89, 93, 144, 159,
  186– 188, 199, 222, 235, 267,
  291, 297, 312, 318, 341, 379,
  383
  "families of consciousness", 94,
  105, 312, 317
  "frameworks of", 379
  getting to know Itself, 40, 41,
  151, 265, 269
  individuation of, 41–43, 47,

118, 144, 145, 195, 265, 275, 283, 291, 302, 333
in relation to Attraction, 84–87
in relation to beliefs, 190, 192, 255
in relation to Divine Love, 65, 66, 81–84, 265, 267, 276, 291, 375
in relation to emotions, 256, 262, 267
in relation to extinction, 41, 42
in relation to fear, 281, 283, 328
in relation to human consciousness, 30, 33, 35, 39, 42, 93–115, 145, 150, 156, 195, 255, 264, 265, 271, 274, 283, 295, 375, 382
in relation to inner senses, 68–79
in relation to intent, 28, 36, 39, 283
in relation to Mind, 142
in relation to natural principles, 64–68, 290, 314
in relation to perception, 385
in relation to personality, 129, 132
in relation to the ego, 122, 123, 145, 267
in relation to time, 67
in relation to the will to love, 267, 269
in relation to violation, 88–90
of Self, 132

of the body – see Body-consciousness
shift in – see Shift
survival of, 208, 285, 328, 332
vitality of, 48, 270, 275, 372
Contrast, 56, 82, 169, 179, 200, 212, 265, 269, 270, 274, 282, 287, 288, 291, 376
Cooperation, 41, 55, 57, 65, 68, 92, 338
Core systems of beliefs, 194–201
Craig, Gary, 311
Creation, 26, 28–30, 39, 49, 51, 53, 63, 65, 70, 77, 80, 82, 84, 85, 96, 102, 111, 150, 156, 158, 176, 187, 190, 205, 216, 268, 270, 284, 291, 293, 294, 323, 324, 327, 329, 332, 337, 338, 340
co-creations, 271, 330, 338
conscious creation, 68, 77, 78, 81, 150, 230
creative abilities, skills, 176, 268, 303, 329
effects of beliefs on, 190, 191, 194, 201, 204, 213
effects of emotions on, 196, 210, 243, 255, 256, 283
fundamental principle of, 268
in relation to fear, 281, 282, 287
of the universe, 200

of your reality, 20, 77, 80, 85, 89, 114, 152, 159, 176, 189, 192, 201, 268, 321
natural principle of, 64, 65, 68, 82, 89, 290, 294, 295, 315, 329
un-preferable creations, 265, 270
Crown information processing route – see Chakra, crown

D
Dahl, Lynda, 78
Dalai Lama, 171, 220
Darwin, Charles, 157, 181–183, 239
Death, 41, 44, 67, 82, 89, 90, 130, 268, 337, 338, 387
in relation to transitional area, 48, 49, 390
moment of physical death, 132
survival of, 132
Depression, 160, 235, 325, 326
Descartes, René, 238
Desire, 19, 40, 42, 82, 114, 150, 158, 211, 215, 216, 259–262, 267, 270, 273, 278, 282, 285, 288, 291, 295, 296, 325, 326, 327, 331–333, 335, 339, 340, 375, 378, 380, 391
Diaphragm, 170
Discounting yourself, 72, 221, 236, 330

Divine Love, 28, 39, 65–68, 80–90, 131, 171, 209, 236, 244, 264–280, 282, 284, 287–294, 303, 317, 322, 324, 325, 328, 331, 333–336, 338, 339, 340, 372, 375, 380, 382–384, 386, 390
"always a protection", 280
as a relative truth, 186–191
"value fulfillment", 80, 303, 375, 390
Doppelgänger, 132
Dreams, 20, 35, 47, 48, 127, 130, 131, 147, 152, 156, 262, 385, 387
lucid dreaming, 73
Dolphin communication, 75
Doubt, 237, 250, 251, 324, 326, 328
Duality, 145, 200, 212, 288, 376
Duplicity, 212, 213, 271, 273, 287, 288, 290, 304, 322, 376
as a core system of beliefs, 200, 201
Durability, 51, 67, 68, 82, 157, 179, 332

E
Ecological awareness, 88, 276
Eddington, Sir Arthur, 63
Eden, Donna, 311
EFT (Emotional Freedom Techniques), 20, 21, 62, 72, 262

basic "shortcut" version of – see *Appendix II*, 307

Ego, ego-self, 13, 35, 40, 42, 43, 49, 53, 56, 58, 69, 82, 93, 114, 115, 118–133, 136, 138–146, 155, 156, 161, 163, 176–179, 183, 191–193, 195, 197, 207, 224–233, 239, 240, 242, 248–250, 253, 257–262, 267, 268, 275, 279, 283, 285–287, 293, 296, 297, 299–301, 323, 324, 328, 333, 339, 340, 376, 380, 381, 383, 389–391

as part of the outer self, 120, 121, 384

ego's folly, 139

ego's identity, 179

ego's purpose, 123

inner ego, 57 (see inner self)

in relation to action, 258

in relation to anxiety, 248–250

in relation to emotions, 256–259, 262

in relation to evolution, 267, 268

in relation to inner senses, 70, 73, 76

in relation to intellect, 123, 124, 225, 375, 381

in relation to Mind, conscious-mind, 126–128, 161, 223, 228, 229, 375

in relation to information processing, 168

in relation to the inner self, 155, 156

in relation to the personality, 130–133, 179, 385

in relation to the subconscious, 138–142, 229

manipulating the personality, 124, 125, 131, 161

our worst enemy, 125

suppressing our will to love, 285

Einstein, Albert, 48, 74, 147, 241, 377

Ekman, Paul, 209, 210, 220, 221, 235

Electric Field, 53, 151–154, 156, 159, 162, 166, 170, 174, 177–180, 207, 237, 242, 243, 255–257, 262, 265, 374, 376, 377, 386, 389

"Electric Universe", 53

Electrical body, 151, 152, 154, 166, 374

Electromagnetic

energy body, 151, 374

energy forms, 85–87, 207, 211, 238, 378

energy patterning properties, 74

field, 151, 159, 241, 376

frequency of the personality, 201

identity of thoughts, 162

spectrum, 27, 50, 66, 188, 377

systems, 218, 280

Electromagnetic Energy Units (EEs), 49–52, 54, 142, 174, 375, 376, 377

Elias, 23, 32, 72, 90, 95, 98, 100–102, 112, 144, 161, 166, 171, 188, 193, 194, 196, 197, 200, 211, 212, 236, 247, 253, 265, 266, 270, 281, 287, 303, 312, 313, 325, 332, 338, 339, 373, 374, 377, 388

E-motion, 50, 242

Emotions, 233–263 – also see *Appendix IV*

as core system of beliefs, 196

a vitality of the universe, 196, 262

emotional climate, 162, 219, 242, 243, 264, 286, 335, 377, 379

"emotional set-point", 159, 219

emotional-signal, 209–225, 229, 233–236, 242–244, 246–250, 253, 272, 281, 282, 299 and see *Appendix IV*

"emotioning", 206

independent electric actions, 242

in relation to beliefs denied, rejected and repressed, 256–259

latent emotions, 221

not a reaction, 236, 237

not limited to humans, 237

Empathy, 69, 72, 92

Empathic inner senses – see Inner senses

Endocrine system, 238, 321

Energy, 377

as a relative truth, 187, 189

balls, 154–156

body, 151

boundaries, 73

cannot be retained, 256, 257

centers, 162, 377 – see Chakra

electro-chemical energy patterns, 168

emotional, 20, 21, 62, 122, 141, 157, 169, 171, 179–181, 206, 207, 226–228, 230, 234, 245, 246, 249, 257, 265, 272

"energy transformation", 64, 66, 67, 83, 159

exchanges, 169

in relation to Attraction, 85–87

in relation to beliefs, 178, 188–191, 195, 201–204

in relation to Consciousness, 26, 27, 29, 30, 38, 43, 44, 48, 51, 54–56, 262

in relation to Divine Love, 265, 279

in relation to Essence, 57, 73

in relation to fear, 282–288

in relation to feelings and emotions, 161, 168, 170, 196,

198, 201, 206, 207, 210–213, 218, 231, 233–235, 237–243, 252, 255–257, 259, 289, 320–341
in relation to intent, 94
in relation to moods, 230
in relation to physical reality, 78, 83, 151, 213
in relation to thoughts, 158, 159, 201
management, 220, 221
manipulation of, 74
path of transformation, 66
processing, 166–175, 208
psych-electric patterns of, 166
resource, 34, 210, 218, 234, 249, 283
signatures, 155, 214, 215, 252
Units of, EEs, 49, 50–52, 54, 142
"you give off", 86
Energy Psychology, 262, 311
Enneagram system, 104–106
enneatype, 105, 106
"wing", 105
Ennis, Mary, 23, 32, 72, 90, 95, 112, 161, 193, 312, 338, 388
Ephaptic coupling, 153
Epigenetics, 54, 168, 239
Essence, 70, 121, 135, 145, 167, 169, 170, 174, 214, 215, 221, 238, 244, 255, 273, 297, 314, 315, 322, 377, 378, 381

Entity, 57
Essence body, 55
Essence self, 57, 73, 84, 88, 92, 93, 105, 118, 123, 183, 195, 198, 207, 210, 213, 229, 269, 281, 288, 303, 312, 329, 335, 338, 341, 378, 380, 386, 387, 390
feeling the identity of, 60
formation of, 55–59
Higher self, 57
in relation to bisexuality, 273
in relation to containing "capsule", 73
in relation to Mind, 127, 133, 382
in relation to personality, 130–132
in relation to physical expression, 94–101, 112–114, 118–120
in relation to the ego, 121–125, 177
"personality essence", 14
vibrational equilibrium of, 236
vibrational signature of, 60–62, 214
Entity – see Essence
Evolution, 22, 28, 39–43, 46, 77, 81, 82, 84, 95, 96, 102, 111, 118, 122, 125, 150, 185, 239, 257, 267–269, 278, 299, 312, 321, 378, 386, 388
Theory of, 157, 181–183

Exchangers – see Genera of
human intent
Exercises, 61, 106, 164, 172
Existence, 19, 31, 38–40, 45,
47–49, 55, 56, 64–68, 76, 78,
121, 127, 128, 130, 131, 133,
139, 144, 147, 167, 197, 204,
237, 252, 264, 294, 300, 313,
314, 341
in relation to action, 129
in relation to death, 90, 132,
268, 338
in relation to Divine Love,
81, 82, 84, 87–90, 265, 266,
270
in relation to the ego, 177
in relation to fear, 264,
283–285, 328, 332
in relation to emotions,
239–241
in relation to thought, 153,
156, 157, 164
in relation to truth, 186
Planes of, 46, 151
Expectations, 259–262
"explicate order", 241
Extinction, 41, 42

F
Families – see Genera of
human intent
Fate, 19, 99
Fear, 281–298
immobilizing, 281

two forms of expression, 281
Feelings, 206–217
ebb and flow, 218–223
feelings consume energy, 218
"feeling good", 164, 215
gut feeling, 170
separating feelings from
emotions, 234
– see *Appendix IV*, 320
Feinstein, David, 311
Fell, Lloyd, 240
Feng Shui, 213
"field of action" – see Action
"fight or flight", 207, 210, 281
Financial
abundance, 33
freedom, 278
institutions, 300, 316
systems, 34
Fiorda, Tina, 24
fMRI, 25
Fourth Way, 105
"frameworks", 46
Freedom of expression, 41–43,
114, 122
Freud, Sigmund, 18, 45, 119,
135, 136, 138, 139, 285
Fromm, Eric, 279
Future, 379

G
Gaia, 23, 89
Gall bladder, 170
Garden of Beliefs, 18, 31, 138,

140, 179, 180, 184, 193, 194,
196, 201–203, 213, 217, 221,
225, 228, 230, 231, 238, 239,
242, 246–248, 250, 256, 257,
260, 264, 282, 289, 301, 302,
379
Gasparetto, Luiz Antonio, 74
Gender, 111, 146, 196, 197, 273,
374
Gene pool, 84, 183
Genera of human intent,
93–115, 379
"families of consciousness",
94, 95, 105, 111, 312
"psychic grouping", 94, 98,
379
"psychical grouping", 95
"psychical races", 95
Artists, 97, 99, 314, 317, 318,
379
Exchangers, 97, 316, 317
Healers, 97, 98, 317
Imagers, 97, 318
Innovators, 97, 315
Nurturers, 97, 112, 146, 319
Reformers, 97, 315, 317
Spiritualists, 97, 314, 317
Teachers, 97, 99, 112, 313,
317, 318
– also see *Appendix III*
Gestalt, 53, 54, 120, 124, 142,
145, 147
psychic gestalt, 56, 58, 59
God – see Consciousness

God particle, 188
Goswami, Amit, 29
Grandbois, Serge, 95, 284
Grand Unified Theory, 188
Gratitude
in relation to Divine Love,
275, 293
as attractor of abundance,
294
Gravity, 90
as a relative truth, 188
Growth
in relation to action, 129
in relation to beliefs, 184, 195
in relation to Consciousness,
40, 55
in relation to Divine Love,
81, 82, 84
in relation to intent, 19, 22,
39, 95, 96, 102, 312
Guardian newspaper, 130
Guilt, 331
"artificial", 91, 323, 373
natural and unnatural, 90,
222, 323, 331, 383
Gurdjieff, Georgei Ivanovitch,
105
Gut feeling – see Feelings

H
Habitual behavior – see
Behavior
Hamlet, 163
Happiness, 81, 84, 237, 295,

331
Unhappiness, 286
Hawking, Stephen, 130
Healers – see Genera of human intent
Helfrich, Joanne, 95, 98, 288, 303, 313, 316
Hicks, Esther, 23, 24, 82, 159, 163, 178, 215, 242, 275, 288, 324
Higher self – see Essence
Human
  aura – see Aura
  consciousness – see Consciousness
Hume, David, 228
Huxley, T.H., 36
Hypnosis, 48, 373, 380
  clinical, 139
  natural, 383
Hypothalamus, 169, 279

I
Iceberg analogy, 142
"id", 139
"idea constructions", 64
Identity
  in relation to Consciousness, 50, 51
  in relation to human consciousness, 54–60
Imagers – see Genera of human intent
Imagination, 27, 31, 223, 247,

253, 254, 262, 332, 335, 340, 380
"implicate order", 241
Impulses, 74, 158, 167, 209, 322, 334, 378, 380, 385
  direct instructional prompts, 207, 210, 215
  "spark before the flame"
Individuation, 40–43, 65–68, 103, 118, 122, 125, 187, 195, 275, 283, 302, 333, 380
  in relation to Divine Love, 265
  in relation to Jungian theory, 144–146
Industrial revolution, 182
Information processing, 158, 198, 229
  routes/centers, 166–175, 188
Inner self – see Self
Inner senses, 15, 18, 48, 57, 58, 63 –79, 83, 92, 93, 114, 136, 144, 163, 164, 166, 199, 212, 231, 242–244, 294, 333, 340, 381, 386
  conceptual, 72, 74, 75, 93, 146, 167, 169, 315
  empathic, 72, 73, 75, 93, 169–171, 173, 292, 315, 325
  time-based, 75, 76, 93, 105, 296, 316
"inner vibrational touch", 69
Innovators – see Genera of human intent

Inspiration, 69, 74, 199, 208, 320

Integral Theory, 191

Intellect, 122–126, 132, 141, 142, 155, 167, 172, 173, 195, 224, 248, 381

Intent, 19, 31, 38–51, 54, 120, 150, 185, 381

in relation to Consciousness, 28, 36, 39, 43, 65, 189, 283

in relation to human consciousness, 26, 55, 93–115, 127, 130, 312–319, 379

in relation to Jungian theory, 145, 146

intention, 19, 61, 381

personal intent, 17, 19, 32, 38–40, 60, 93–115, 121, 126, 143, 158, 167, 204, 210, 211, 222, 244, 261, 277, 278, 282, 283, 289, 291, 293, 295, 303, 375, 385, 386

Interference Theory, 157

Intuition, 69, 171, 173, 199, 209, 320

"intuitive knowing", 214

Islam, 105

J

James, William, 26, 29, 35, 182, 205

Jeans, Sir James, 29

Johnson, Mark, 240

Judgmental, 200, 212, 213, 230, 265, 271, 287, 288, 290, 291, 304, 319, 322, 376

Judith, Anodea, 173, 174

Jung, Carl, 35, 105, 135, 136, 279, 374

Jungian theory parallels on the Self, 144–146

K

Killing, 89

Koestler, Arthur, 35

Kris, 95, 284

L

Lakoff, George, 240

Language, 13, 119, 120, 152, 155, 170, 235, 240, 241, 266, 334, 372

body language, 244

Law of Attraction (LOA), 24, 80, 85, 87, 159, 290, 381

Law of gravity, 90, 188

Laws of Physics, 18, 47, 62, 63

Lavoisier, Antoine, 185

Lazaris, 4

LeShan, Lawrence, 24

Lewis, Pepper, 23

Librarian – see Subconscious

Library – see Subconscious

Lieutenant Commander Data, 137

Life forms, 40, 41, 84, 122, 233, 388

Light
electromagnetic spectrum of, 27, 50, 66, 377
emitted by a star, 60
velocity of, 50
visible spectrum, 112
Limbic system, 238
Linnaean Society, 183
Lipton, Dr Bruce, 168
Liver, 170
Locke, John, 119
Long-term memory, 223, 224
Love – *see also* Divine Love
between individuals, 273
human love, 81, 171, 187, 188, 264, 265, 270–275, 285, 335, 380, 382
motherly love, 272, 274, 279
will to love, 267–269, 271–273, 275, 276, 285

M

Magnet, 85, 100, 267, 272, 273
"magnates", 100
magnetic balls, 247
magnetic field, 85
Malthus, T.R., 182
Mass events, 33, 300, 382
Maturana, Humberto, 43, 206, 279
Maxwell, James Clerk, 241
Meditation, 48, 61, 77, 78, 230, 294, 377
meditational practices, 139, 160
Medium – see Stage medium
"mental enzymes", 167, 169
Merrick, Richard, 157
Metaphor, 240–242
Metaphysics, 21–30, 35, 36, 382
Micro-expressions, 244
Mind
as a multi-faceted collective feature of the psyche, 13, 18, 27, 48, 58, 76, 86, 93, 111, 120, 121, 126–128, 133, 142, 143, 156, 157, 161, 174, 178, 189, 207, 223, 242, 251, 338, 379, 382, 386, 388
as the immediately conscious facet of the overall Mind – "conscious-mind", 13, 18, 23, 25, 26, 29, 33, 34, 38, 55, 56, 58, 60, 63, 69, 70, 73, 74, 81, 82, 90, 93, 96, 105, 107, 109, 119, 127, 132, 133, 140, 141, 152–163, 166–172, 176–178, 193, 196, 199, 200, 206–209, 211, 212, 215, 217–233, 235–237, 242–244, 246–253, 258, 261, 271, 299, 300, 321, 323–325, 327, 330, 331, 333, 334, 336–338, 340, 375, 383, 387, 389
in relation to fear, 281, 284
in relation to the subconscious, 135–138, 256, 389
"Mind of God", 372

"supra-conscious-mind", 146
the Mind's purpose, 127
universal mind, 29
Mind/Body/Spirit movement, 23, 85, 381, 388
Mindfulness, 139, 160
Modern worldview – see Worldview
Molecular biology, 162
"molecules of emotion", 239
Moment point, 67, 86, 385, 388
Money, 277, 278, 300
Mood, 215, 216, 219–221, 264, 377, 382
Moorjani, Anita, 266, 276, 277, 282
"morphogenetic fields", 241
Mother Teresa, 171
Myers, F.W.H., 35

N
Natural guilt – see Guilt
Natural Powers, 80–92, 158, 289, 384
of Attraction, 84–87
of Divine Love, 81–84
Natural Principles, 41, 47, 63–68, 74, 77–79, 83, 85, 87, 89, 91, 92, 114, 118, 158, 187, 264, 269, 289, 291, 314, 317, 384
Natural selection, 182, 183
Natural time – see Time
Nature, 41, 88, 89, 97, 315, 322, 382
Near death experience (NDE), 266
Negative thoughts – see Thought
Nervous breakdown, 249, 250
Nervous system, 71, 127, 152, 238, 242, 321, 389
Neurology, 152
New Age, 158, 278
New Scientist, 241
Newtonian physics, 48
Nurturers – see Genera of human intent

O
Obfuscating, 172
Objective Area – see Areas within Consciousness
"Odic force", 151
Omni, 57, 64, 68, 89, 253, 267, 269, 277, 278, 300
"organs of supersensory perception", 15
Orientations, 197
Outer self – see Self
Out of body experiences (OBEs), 73
Oversoul – see Essence
Oxygen, 185
Oxytocin, 279, 280

P
Pain, 209, 217, 285, 291, 292,

295, 336

Pancreas, 170

Panpsychism, 29

Past, 75, 76, 177, 258, 384, 388

Past life recall, 76

Patience, 75, 97, 295, 319
impatience, 296, 333
in relation to natural time, 296

Pauli, Wolfgang, 36

Payne, John L., 24, 64, 68, 89, 253, 267, 277, 385

Perception, 20, 30, 47, 70, 72, 75, 76, 78, 112, 122, 123, 128, 174, 183, 190, 194, 197, 201–205, 242, 243, 336, 385, 387
as a core system of beliefs, 198

Personal intent – see Intent

Personality, 17, 18, 39, 42, 49, 58, 85, 87, 92, 94–101, 104–106, 114, 122, 129–133, 138, 140, 159–162, 167, 168, 171, 174, 190, 206, 228, 247, 253, 277, 302, 335, 385
as a "climate of attraction", 159
as a "field of action", 124, 129, 162
as the gardener of thoughts and beliefs, 179, 193, 194, 225–232, 249
birth of, 118–120, 131

focus personality, 379
in relation to death, 132, 133, 387, 390
in relation to Divine Love, 267, 292
in relation to emotions, 206, 207, 210, 231, 237, 239, 242, 243, 258, 286
in relation to mood, 219, 220, 264, 377
in relation to the ego, 121, 123–126, 131–133, 136
in relation to the genera of human intent, 95, 96, 98, 99, 101, 110, 113, 235, 312–319
in relation to Jungian theory, 144–146
in relation to suicide, 269
in relation to thoughts, 160–162
manipulation of by the ego, 123–125
purpose of, 131
tonal frequency, 179, 180, 201, 207, 258, 380, 390
types, 95, 105

"personality essence" – see Essence

"personal unconscious", 135

Pert, Dr Candace, 239

Phlogiston, 185

Picasso, Pablo, 74, 100

Pineal gland, 167, 208, 238

Pinker, Steven, 119

Pituitary gland, 169, 279

"planes of existence", 46

Plutchik, Robert, 277, 278, 321

Postmodern worldview – see
Worldview

Power of Attraction – see
Natural Powers

"practicing idealist", 17, 385

Precognition, 76

"pre-conscious", 136

Probabilities, 19, 36, 48, 113,
114, 142, 247, 282, 286, 316,
339, 385
"probable realities", 20, 70,
85–87, 157, 269, 296, 376, 386
probable self, 76

Psyche, 26, 27, 30, 33, 36, 39,
41, 44, 56, 58, 101, 103, 105,
106, 111, 120, 124, 127, 129,
133, 135, 139, 141, 144, 146,
147, 178, 182, 212, 229, 260,
261, 315, 317, 373, 382, 386
in relation to beliefs, 190,
203, 205, 255
in relation to dreams, 152
in relation to emotions, 256
in relation to thoughts, 160,
229
psychic gestalt, 56, 58, 59
psychic grouping, psychical
grouping, psychical races –
see Genera of human intent
"psychoelectric pattern" – see
Thought

Psychological climate, 73

Psychology, 95, 120, 135, 139,
160, 272
Analytical, 144, 145
Aspect, 373, 379
"basic organic psychology",
168
Buddhist, 221
Cognitive, 223
Energy, 262, 311

Purpose, 19, 31, 32, 35, 38–40,
44, 54, 60, 92, 99, 100, 113,
115, 124, 125, 127, 143, 185,
191, 234, 235, 238, 244, 259,
261, 277, 278, 287, 289, 291,
293, 295, 301–303, 313,
324–326, 330–332, 335, 341,
376, 386

Q
Quantum
Fields, 47, 51, 66, 240, 375,
387
Mechanics, 157, 240
Physics, 29, 36
Theory, 35, 47, 241, 387

R
"rainbow bridge", 174

Rape, 91, 331

Reality, 12, 14, 16–18, 20, 22,
31, 36, 38, 40, 42–46, 48, 53,
54, 56, 62–64, 68, 69, 71, 73,
75, 77, 78, 80–82, 84–89, 92,

93, 100–102, 112, 114, 123,
125, 127–129, 131, 150–153,
156, 158, 159, 161, 167, 174,
176, 183, 185, 190–192, 194,
196, 198, 201, 203–205, 207,
219, 232, 237, 240, 243, 247,
252, 253, 256, 266, 270, 278,
283, 287, 292–297, 301, 302,
321, 329, 333, 337–339, 372,
376, 383–385, 387, 391
 as a mirror/reflection, 86, 217
 as a relative truth, 186, 187,
 189, 190
Reductionism, 53, 111
Reincarnation, 84, 381, 387
"regional areas", 46
Reformers – see Genera of
 human intent
Relationships, 174, 271–273
 as a core system of beliefs,
 197
Religion, 28, 36, 44, 45, 170,
 199, 289
Repression
 the action of, 257
Roberts, Jane, 14, 23, 64, 69, 94,
 181, 373, 379, 388
Rose, 95, 98, 288, 303, 313, 316,
 318, 391

S
Sadness, 191, 234, 236, 325,
 336–338
Safeguards, 76, 77

Safe universe, 28, 44, 45, 163
Say That Again – see *Appendix
 I*, 305
Schizophrenia, 70
Science, 44, 45, 49, 129, 151,
 162, 238, 240, 241, 372
 as a core system of beliefs,
 188, 199
 biological science, 279
 dream-art science, 375
 in relation to Consciousness,
 29
 in relation to emotions, 321
 on love, 277
 psychological science, 136
 religion of, 36
 "spiritual science", 36
 "sciousness", 26, 27
Self, 13, 18, 19, 23–25, 32, 33,
 35, 42, 46, 49, 53–60, 65, 75,
 78, 83, 86, 88, 91, 92, 110, 114,
 118, 122, 124–133, 135,
 141–144, 150, 162, 170, 179,
 195, 198, 206, 213, 221, 230,
 236, 243, 244, 256, 267, 275,
 276, 278, 280, 284, 287, 288,
 290–298, 302, 303, 318, 325,
 328–330, 333, 339, 340, 341,
 378–381, 384–387, 389–391
 computer-self, 132
 denial of, 236
 ego-self – see Ego
 electromagnetic self, 162
 Essence self – see Essence

evolution of, 39, 43, 125
graphical representation of,
142, 143
inner self, 57, 58, 62, 69–71,
74, 77, 87, 88, 90, 93, 99, 100,
105, 120, 121, 125, 127, 128,
130–133, 135, 138, 139, 141,
144, 152–154, 161, 166, 167,
170, 174, 176, 191, 192, 197,
206–212, 218–220, 222, 228,
229, 233, 236–238, 243, 244,
252, 261, 288, 292, 294, 295,
297, 299, 320, 325, 328, 331,
334, 336, 338, 340, 375, 378,
381–383, 389
inner self's dilemma,
154–156
in relation to intent, 96,
98–101
Jungian comparisons to,
144–146
outer self, 58, 69, 71, 78, 90,
94, 105, 119–121, 123, 124,
127, 128, 131, 133, 135, 138,
150, 152–154, 157, 166, 170,
190, 193, 195, 204, 207, 209,
213, 216, 226, 228, 230,
235–237, 242, 243, 252, 259,
273, 286, 288, 289, 295, 298,
303, 320, 322, 326, 330, 331,
333, 334, 338, 374, 376, 381,
384, 386, 387, 389, 390
self-actualizing, 55
self-awareness, 41, 42, 51, 90,

103, 122, 233, 264, 267, 269,
279, 388
self-development, 15, 101,
233
self-discipline, 21
self-doubt, 237, 328
self-examination, 285, 286
self-expression, 17, 42, 81, 82,
202, 204, 206, 388
self-generating, 256
self-healing, 16, 20, 317
selfishness, 277
self-knowledge, 17, 118, 288
self-love, 16, 275–277, 324
self-reflection, 42, 233, 264,
267, 269, 288, 376, 387, 388
self-worth, 44, 277
"selfish genes", 45
Sequence of mental machinations, 254
Sensations, 169, 209, 229, 231
Sensing, 212, 215, 326, 328, 331
as a core system of beliefs,
198
Separation from Source, 195
Seth, 15, 17, 23, 32, 43, 46, 49,
51, 53, 57, 60, 64, 65, 67, 69,
72, 73, 80, 83, 91, 94, 95, 100,
105, 118, 120, 127, 129, 130,
132, 136, 141, 144, 153, 156,
158, 162, 168, 178, 187, 213,
239, 241, 253, 256, 259, 262,
269, 274, 280, 301, 312, 317,
322, 372, 373, 375–377, 379,

381, 383, 385, 386, 388–390
The Seth Material, 15, 24, 64, 65, 68, 69, 89, 158, 301, 375, 378, 388
Sexual
act, 91, 197, 274, 331
expression, 91, 267
orientation, 197
preference, 197, 273
Sexuality, 91, 196, 267, 272, 274, 374, 388
as a core system of beliefs, 196–198
in relation to human love, 271–273, 285
Sheldrake, Rupert, 241
Shift (in consciousness), 30–36, 39, 42, 43, 70, 71, 77, 82, 92, 114, 192, 233, 262, 268, 269, 300, 317, 372, 374, 388
Short-term memory, 224, 229
Sixth sense, 69
Skinner, B.F., 119
"slow down", 174, 245
vibrational signature/frequency, 51
Small intestinal tract, 170
Socrates, 14, 197
Solar plexus information processing route – see Chakra, solar plexus
Soul – see Essence
Source – see Consciousness
Source Energy – see

Consciousness
"spacious present", 67, 75, 76, 86, 112, 113, 120, 252, 269, 295, 299, 388
"spark before the flame" – see Impulses
Spencer, Herbert, 182
Spider, 74, 169
Spiritualists – see Genera of human intent
Spirituality, 199, 200, 298, 389
as a core system of beliefs, 194, 271
Spontaneity, 67, 75, 113, 295, 296
Stage medium, 22
Stahl, Georg E., 185
Star Trek, 138
Steiner, Rudolph, 15, 35, 36
Stomach, 170
Subconscious, 56, 62, 76, 99, 105, 114, 130, 136, 139, 140, 146, 155, 177, 220, 229, 230, 235, 243, 248, 253, 258, 263, 267, 271, 273, 284, 292, 334, 389
Area, 48, 49, 58, 75, 122, 135, 145, 177–179, 219, 228, 229, 295, 372, 374, 375, 389
campus, 59, 136, 138
garden, 190, 201, 217, 219, 226, 231, 236, 256, 379
kitchen, 261
information, 69, 70, 328, 337,

373
librarian, 137, 138, 141
library, 14, 118, 136, 140, 152,
154, 155, 157, 164, 176, 193,
208, 218, 223, 224, 232, 239,
248, 249, 253, 257, 372
The subconscious, 58, 138,
146
Your subconscious, 58, 73, 93,
130, 135, 136, 138, 146, 152,
153, 255–257, 338, 389
Subjective Area – see Areas
within Consciousness
Subtle Body, 73, 373, 389
Subtle forces, 152, 241
Suffragette movement, 35
Sufi mysticism, 105
Suicide, 269
Sumari, 94
Suppression, 36, 172, 284, 314
Surviving physical death, 132
"survival of the fittest", 45,
182, 183

T
Tabula rasa, 119
Teachers – see Genera of
human intent
TED, 16
Teilhard de Chardin, Pierre, 35
Telepathy, 168
telepathic, 78, 315
Ten things about beliefs,
201–204

Ten things about the nine
families of human intent,
110–114
Testosterone, 197
Thalamus, 169
Theory of Relativity, 195
The Secret, 24, 85
Beyond The Secret, 85
The Work, 105
Thought, 150–165
as a mechanism, 163
as a "psychoelectric
pattern", 153, 154, 157
habits of, 34, 159, 160
independent nature of, 156
negative thoughts, 160, 162,
221, 223, 247
quality of, 159, 171
thought-based, 167, 169, 173
"thoughts create reality", 158
Throat information processing
route – see Chakra, throat
Thymus, 169
Thyroid, 169
Time, 389
concept of, 56, 67, 72, 389
dimension of, 81, 188
elasticizing property of, 56
in relation to cancerous cells,
83
in relation to emotions, 245,
246, 253
in relation to the electric
dimension/field, 131, 156

in relation to spontaneity, 295

in relation to the subconscious, 223, 228

in relation to thoughts and beliefs, 156, 157, 162, 253

in respect of durability, 82, 83, 157, 179

linear time, 47, 75, 76, 82, 112, 118, 119, 133, 240, 252, 299, 385

natural time, 75, 279, 294, 296, 314, 333, 339, 384

simultaneous time, 112, 120, 388

time-outs, 230

Time-based inner senses – see Inner senses

Tissue capsule, 55, 73, 390

"tissue capsules", 73

Tolle, Eckhart, 23

Tone, 390

as a relative truth, 187

"feeling-tone" – see Vibrational

in relation to emotional-signals, 211, 212, 219, 382

in relation to Essence, 60, 61, 102

in relation to human intent, 103, 111, 112, 313, 380

of being, 54, 61

negative in, 191, 210

vibrational tone – see Vibrational

Traditional worldview – see Worldview

Transition, 390

in relation to death, 89, 90

in relation to the Shift, 36, 77, 92

Transitional Area, 49, 269, 282, 373, 390

Trust, 22, 35, 71, 114, 139, 141, 168, 170, 172, 192, 222, 228, 230, 261, 277, 278, 289, 295–297, 300, 304, 326, 333–335, 339

lack of, 200, 212, 247, 278, 281, 282, 326, 329, 340, 376

state of, 278, 279, 282, 340

Truth, 30, 31, 36, 45, 104, 112, 162, 167, 179, 183–192, 202, 265, 266, 313, 387, 390

as a core system of beliefs, 195

degrees of, 187

in relation to beliefs, 186, 190, 202, 229, 251, 286

in relation to Divine Love, 265, 266, 270, 291

one absolute Truth, 186, 187, 189, 270, 314

relative truth, 188, 189

the Truth, 187, 188

truth seekers, 16, 36

Twain, Mark, 186

Types – see Personality types

U

Uniqueness, 61, 275, 341

V

"value fulfillment" – see
Divine Love

Values, 30, 31, 64, 184, 316, 325, 391

Varela, Francisco, 43

Vibrational
boundaries, 103, 104
constant, 187
equilibrium, 236
"feeling-tone", 60, 170, 213–215, 221, 229, 379
frequency, 51, 66, 83, 112, 142, 377, 379, 390
signature, 50, 51, 60–62, 72, 85, 93, 102, 113, 158, 162, 178, 181, 187, 191, 213–215, 318, 380, 390, 391
tone, 60–62, 102, 111, 112, 187, 242, 253, 313, 390

Victim mentality, 44, 297, 323, 325, 329

Vital ethical code, 80, 87, 88, 385

Violate, 87–89, 91, 222, 291, 331

von Reichenbach, Dr Karl
Ludwig, 151, 152

Vulnerable, 285, 296–298, 340

W

Walker, Evan Harris, 157

Wallace, Alfred Russel, 157, 181–183

Wants, 82, 215, 380, 381

Way of Spirit, 293, 303, 391

Weiss, Dr Brian, 6

"Wheel of Emotions", 321

Wilber, Ken, 31, 191

Will to love, 267–276, 285

"wing" – see Enneagram
system

Work journal, 35

Worldview, 15, 21, 22, 25, 30, 31, 33–35, 38, 39, 44–46, 88, 104, 119, 173, 192, 195, 198–200, 315, 382, 385, 391

Worrying, 218, 247, 340

BOOKS

O is a symbol of the world, of oneness and unity. In different cultures it also means the "eye," symbolizing knowledge and insight. We aim to publish books that are accessible, constructive and that challenge accepted opinion, both that of academia and the "moral majority."

Our books are available in all good English language bookstores worldwide. If you don't see the book on the shelves ask the bookstore to order it for you, quoting the ISBN number and title. Alternatively you can order online (all major online retail sites carry our titles) or contact the distributor in the relevant country, listed on the copyright page.

See our website www.o-books.net for a full list of over 500 titles, growing by 100 a year.

And tune in to myspiritradio.com for our book review radio show, hosted by June-Elleni Laine, where you can listen to the authors discussing their books.

mySpiritRadio